Western Tourism
Can Paradise be Reclaimed?

Clare A. Gunn

tourism dynamics

COGNIZANT COMMUNICATION CORPORATION
New York • Sydney • Tokyo
www.cognizantcommunication.com

Western Tourism
Can Paradise be Reclaimed?

Cognizant Communication Offices:

U.S.A. 3 Hartsdale Road, Elmsford, New York 10523-3701
Australia P.O. Box 352 Cammeray, NWS, 2062
Japan c/o OBS T's Bldg. 3F, 1-38-11 Matsubara, Setagaya-ku, Tokyo

Library of Congress Cataloging-in-Publication Data

Gunn, Clare A.
Western tourism : can paradise be reclaimed? / by Clare A. Gunn. — 1st ed.
p. cm. — (Tourism dynamics)
Includes bibliographical references (p.).
ISBN 1-882345-44-4 (pbk. : alk. paper)
1. Tourism — West (U.S.) — Planning. 2. Tourism — Environmental aspects — West (U.S.) 3. Economic development — West (U.S.) — Planning. 4. Economic development — Environmental aspects — West (U.S.) I. Title. II. Series.

G155.U6G86 2004
338.4'79178—dc22

2003026292

Printed in the United States of America

Printing: 1 2 3 4 5 6 7 8 9 10 Year: 1 2 3 4 5 6 7 8 9 10

DEDICATION

To my wife, Mary Alice, my sons
and grandchildren

Contents

List of Illustrations

Foreword

Every year hundreds of new books are published—many are good, a few are fine, and several outstanding volumes always appear. This volume is one of the truly GREAT books of our era, filled with enduring values that are important to the future of tourism. If read by grass-roots Americans as well as town councilors, entrepreneurs, planners, and politicians, the expressed philosophy could change the face of America and the way we vacation on our land.

Clare Gunn is internationally respected as an American pioneer in the field of landscape architecture, and the first to have earned a doctorate in this discipline. *Western Tourism. Can Paradise be Saved?* summarizes his 50 years of teaching, research, and consulting in three unique ways.

First, Dr. Gunn briefly recounts the 8575-mile autocamping trip of 1929 when elder brother Lauren, age 17, drove the family of four in their Model A Ford around the American West. Clare, then 12 years old, admits to such excitement and wonderment at the differing landscapes that in all probability that trip ultimately decided his career. The family vacation was the fulfillment of dreams held by very many Depression era citizens. Some were newcomers to this continent, having immigrated during the period from 1880 to 1924; others wanted to visit the families and friends who had "gone West" to settle as pioneers or seek riches in the Gold Rush; and for many more, including the Gunn family, the first cheap mass-produced car gave Americans their once-in-a-lifetime opportunity to actually see their country. To know their land was part of the patriotism of the people whom Tom Brokaw termed "the greatest generation."

Seventy years later, Dr. Gunn reexamines the four principal sectors of the earlier trip. In 2003 no freeway-frenzied teenager with a pedal-to-the-metal mentality would submit to driving amidst dust, mud, and detours on roads that were sometimes only two wagon tracks, and endure 29 flat tires as well as camping and cooking in a tent by the road. What this second section records are observations on important landmarks—and how they have changed over time as a consequence of the increased growth of tourism. In the 1930s, the average visitor stay at Grand Canyon was 5 days; Americans came and camped, hiked, and savored the Park. In the 2000s, the average visitor (at least one third of whom are foreign tourists) stays 3 hours—just long enough to take a quick photo, eat lunch, buy a souvenir (often Indian jewelry assembled from ready-made parts fabricated in Asia), and possibly see a short Native American dance performance. The impacts of sheer numbers, and changing lifestyles, are evident everywhere throughout the West.

Third, the great strength of the book lies in the summaries imbedded throughout the respective chapters. Some are case studies of best practices, many by former students and colleagues of Clare Gunn. Landscape architects have been remarkably successful in forming community-wide alliances, which with near-consensus among all stakeholders, could foster remediation and/or develop sustainable development plans. By contrast, Dr. Gunn also identifies critical issues that must be addressed now if "Paradise" is to be saved.

This volume establishes an important baseline for further research. It is to be hoped that in 10 years another scholar will revisit and review, to provide time-depth to the analyses presented here. Such further study is critical to the "saving of Paradise," particularly in light of the predicted mass tourism—possibly numbering in the millions of visitors—anticipated to stream from Asia to the American West in the next 10 years as a result of globalization. These newcomers introduce new ethnicities, new visitor interests, new dietary preferences, and new styles of travel and tourist behavior. The sheer numbers threaten environmental fragility as new entrepreneurs expand and extend existing tourist zones. Knowledge and vigilance are essential to the task, if the American West is to retain even its present identity.

The book is a literary gem, written in simple clear prose. It is indeed an honor to be invited to introduce the chef-d'oeuvre of the master of the craft who writes so knowingly, "No one can return to the past but many of the values obtained here by travelers in the past are planning and design challenges for the future."

Valene L. Smith
Professor of Anthropology
California State University, Chico
Chico, California

Preface

The purpose of this book is to provide planners, designers, and developers of tourism in America's West pertinent information on how past pitfalls and erosive development can be replaced by a brighter tourism future. Although tourism in this very significant region is a powerful economic generator, it now faces a crisis of many threats to its sustainability, most of which can be reversed. The opportunities for extending the spectacular foundations of tourism in the West are abundant but demand new plans and actions. Sufficient leadership and planning ability are now in place but need new concerted direction.

The content of this book is the result of an examination of a 70-year history of tourism in the West, ever since the autocamping explosion in the 1920s, and application of the best and most recent tourism planning principles and practices. When these principles and practices are applied, western tourism can reclaim past values that made it a travel icon in the first place. For the reader to understand the author's background for this work, the following comments are offered.

Serendipity has given me the good fortune of melding together a variety of separate disciplines and personal experiences in the field of tourism planning. With my genes came a love of land and landscape beauty and a bit of artistic talent. These qualities were then refined and amplified by university training and experience in the field of landscape architecture. Testimony to this was obtaining the first doctoral degree in this field in the country and being named "Fellow" of the American Society of Landscape Architects. Important for my career in tourism planning was gaining insight into "reading the landscape," also called "critical observation," used by anthropologists, geographers, and landscape architects. This nonquantitative research method proved valuable in assessing the historic, social, economic, and environmental qualities of existing development of the land.

A 21-year period of technical assistance to the developers of tourist and resort facilities in Michigan stimulated my concern over the significance of external as well as internal factors for business success. It was in this postwar period that I learned of the great importance of natural and cultural resources of a region for successful tourism. I became interested in the macro as well as micro scales of planning and development. My perspective of tourism was broadened greatly by years of research, teaching, and public service in six universities: University of Massachusetts, Michigan State University, Texas A&M University, University of Hawaii, University of Guelph (Ontario), and Clemson University. Experience in departments of park, recreation, landscape architecture, hotel management, and tourism broadened my view of the multidisciplinary nature of tourism and the critical need for greater integration of the many parts. Tourism planning consulting projects within the United States and Canada as well as overseas offered practical application of my planning concepts.

These experiences led to writing books, such as *Motel Planning and Business Management* (coauthor); *Vacationscape—Developing Tourist Areas*; *Tourism Planning—Basics, Concepts, Cases*; and chapters in several other books. Many of my conference presentations, workshop meetings, and journal articles focused on tourism planning fundamentals.

An equally important foundation for this book is a long-standing fascination with America's West, its fact and fiction. Its rich cultural history, its economic booms and busts, and its dramatic landscapes have been the source of legend, lore, prose, poetry, film, and music, creating an icon of travel paradise. Tourism here passed through several phases, from wealthy elite train travel, burgeoning autocamping, to a significant modern huge land user and major contributor to the western economy.

My professional as well as personal interest may have been sparked by my father's insatiable desire to travel in the 1920s in spite of our meager financial circumstances. In the summer of 1929 he was able to gear up for a 6-week autocamping tour of 8575 miles in a Model A Ford from Michigan throughout the West and return. Without realizing it at the time, we were part of that explosion of autocamping travel to the West in the 1920s stimulated by Henry Ford's mass production of Model Ts and As.

For many decades since, my travels there have added to my interest in tourism's great growth and also concern over its negative impacts. Because my philosophy has been that of fostering visions and actions to overcome obstacles, I decided to delve more deeply into an examination of tourism's growth issues in this region. This meant survey of literature, contacting knowledgeable resources, repeating travels, and reviewing the succinct log and snapshots of our family's autocamping travel in the West in 1929. My own recall (I was 12 years old at the time), reinforced by my parents' retelling, has allowed elaboration of this adventure. I sought answers to the question whether the image of paradise can be restored in face of massive tourism development.

Therefore, I have written this book.

For help extended to me on this book it is impossible to acknowledge all who have contributed over these many years. I wish to thank especially some who have supplied me with research materials, such as: Mike Ferris, USFS, Hood River, OR; David LeBeau, Library Services, Chevron, San Ramon, CA; Dr. Patricia Stokowski, professor, Department of Recreation, Park and Tourism Sciences, Texas A&M University, College Station, TX; Dr. Keith A. Sculle, Head, Research and Education, Illinois Historic Preservation Agency, Springfield, IL; Lee H. Whittlesey, Park Historical Archivist, Yellowstone National Park, WY; Thomas E. Combrink, Senior Research Analyst, Arizona Hospitality Research & Resource Center, Northern Arizona University, Flagstaff, AZ; Michele M. Hellickson, Superintendent, Petrified Forest National Park, AZ; Douglas R. McManis, The American Geographical Society, New York, NY; Dr. Peter J. Hugill, Department of History, Texas A&M University, College Station, TX; David Woodworth, Recreation Vehicle Industry Association, Philadelphia, PA; Nancy Andring, Secretary, Columbia River Gorge Commission, White Salmon, WA; Norman A. Bishop, Resource Interpreter, Yellowstone National Park, WY; Mrs. Beverley Engel, Administrator, Salvation Army Lytton Adult Rehabilitation Center, Healdsburg, CA; Tina O'Banion, Executive Director, Hood River County Chamber of Commerce, Hood River, OR; Tandy Young, President, Native American Travel Service, Scottsdale, AZ; Kristin DeNure Hunt, Troy, ID;

Fred O. Phillips, 'Ahakhav Tribal Preserve, AZ; Dennis Glick, Greater Yellowstone Coalition, WY; Jurgen A. Hess, Columbia River Gorge National Scenic Area; Dr. Peter Williams, Simon Fraser University, British Columbia; Dr. Kathleen Andereck, Arizona State University West; Prof. William A. Mann, University of Georgia; Theodore J. Wirth, Billings, MT; Ethan Carr, NPS, Denver, CO; Robert Cates, California Department of Parks and Recreation; Michael Kelly, tourism consultant, Toronto; and Michael Barbitta, Benziger Family Winery, Glen Ellen, CA.

I genuinely appreciate the encouragement and support from Dr. Valene Smith, Department of Anthropology, California State University, Chico. Her works have been an inspiration for many years. From professional designers Professor Michael D. Murphy, Landscape Architecture and Urban Planning, Texas A&M University, Professor Joanne Westphal, Landscape Architecture Program, Michigan State University, and John Ormsbee Simonds, FASLA, landscape architect, the text benefited from substantive comments. Special thanks must be given to Dr. John D. Hunt, an experienced tourism researcher, educator, and friend, whose input was valuable throughout the preparation of this manuscript. I owe much to my Mother, whose log of our 1929 autocamping trip was the foundation for documenting the early days of western automobile travel. To son, Richard, I am grateful for photographic assistance and to son, William, for his help in retracing portions of the original trip. And especially appreciated is the interest, support, and word processing performed by my wife, Mary Alice, of over six decades.

Introduction

Fortunately, the history of tourism in the West has been well documented.[1] Therefore, the purpose of this book is not to duplicate such a fine book but rather to identify changes over the last seven decades, good and bad, and what these mean for future planners and developers of tourism in this unusual region. The intent is not to damn tourism here as a scourge but to state several negative outcomes, most of which can be remedied. This book is not antidevelopment of tourism but rather it advocates the need for *better planning and development* in the future. The purpose is not to portray developers of tourism businesses in the West as environmental culprits but rather to stimulate better husbandry of natural and cultural resources, the very foundation for tourist businesses. The objective is to commend hotel and restaurant schools for their education and training of internal management and yet to fault universities and colleges for their lack of adequate multidisciplinary teaching and research of tourism in its full complexity, especially the topic of tourism planning.

The intent is not to condemn state and local promoters in the West for carrying out their mandates of marketing and advertising but instead to state a major void at these levels—no leadership or guidance for overall tourism planning and development. The purpose here is not to criticize transportation leaders and agencies for great strides in technical and engineering advances but to stimulate sharper focus on the environmental and social consequences of their actions. The intent is not to paint designers and planners as incompetent professionals but rather to praise those who have engaged in sustainable environmental projects and encourage greater involvement in the future, especially in the very important western region of the United States.

Rather, the purpose here is threefold, using western tourism history as background: *to alert tourism developers to the critical need for reversing present erosive trends and fostering environmental sustainability; to stimulate new communication, cooperation, and even collaboration among public and private developers; and to identify opportunities for greater involvement by landscape architects for future sustainable design.*

Ever since the explosion of autocamping travel in America in the 1920s, the West has been a favored destination for millions. Many communities that had every good reason for becoming ghost towns following the demise of forestry, fishing, and mining have recovered with a new tourism economy. Without question is the reality of tourism as a powerful economic engine in the West. Well documented is the fact that, compared to any other area of the nation, the western economy is more dependent upon tourism.[2] Ten of the key 13 western states are among the most tourism-dependent states in the US based on per capita receipts from tourism expenditures.

Although no one would advocate the return to travel conditions of the 1920s, there are lessons to be learned from past tourism in the West. Even though tourist facilities and generations of travelers have changed over these 70 some years, tourism designers and developers of today need not continue to follow the willy-nilly patterns and practices of the past. The unplanned and irresponsible use of the land for the monumental growth of tourism has taken its toll on resources, the very life blood of most tourism. Unavailable in the early days of tourism were concerns over tourism's burgeoning impact on the environment and the need for planning. Tourism development followed the same philosophy of past exploitation of timber, fish, and minerals—take all that can be taken from the land regardless of the consequences. Now the newer tourism terms such as ecotourism, nature tourism, culture tourism, and sustainability reflect a new awareness of the finite extent of the land and the critical need for design and planning the steamrolling land development for burgeoning tourism growth.

The book is organized so that the autocamping case of the 1920s is woven into the body of the text. This narrative is included not for nostalgic or sentimental reasons but rather to exemplify the attitudes, feelings, limitations, and other qualities exhibited by travel camping day after day in this spectacular region. Such an organizational mix allows the reader to compare the early characteristics of tourism with those of today. Although tourism has been and continues to be significant in many states of the geographical region referred to as the West, for reasons of brevity the book is narrowed to the major destinations that were popular in the 1920s as well as today—Arizona, California, Oregon, and Yellowstone. And the scope does not include major urban targets such as Denver, San Francisco, and Las Vegas, even though they are significant travel destinations.

Chapter 1, "Western Tourism: Boom and Strain," provides an historic sketch and its meaning for tourism planning in this region. The remarkable changes brought by mass mobility are described. The changing roles of government and local conflicts have had a significant impact on tourism development here. This chapter closes with the modern challenge of the planning and design of tourism toward the goal of environmental sustainability.

Chapters 2 through 9 alternate between descriptions of the 1929 Gunn autocamping trip and the seven decades of changes in tourism in four major destinations: northern Arizona, northern California, Oregon and the Columbia River, and Yellowstone. For example, Chapters 2, 4, 6, and 8 elaborate the autocamping trip whereas Chapters 3, 5, 7, and 9 identify lessons from 70 years of tourism development in these same destinations. Presented in this format, the reader can readily make comparisons between a case of the travel explosion of the 1920s and today's tourism development. Those who now live in these areas will be able to do a better job of tourism in the future by reflecting on their past.

Chapter 2, "1929 Western Tour: Part I," offers a personal narrative of the Gunn family autocamping preparations and the first leg of their 1929 western trip. Although this is just one case, it is likely representative of the many thousands of novice travelers who surged toward the West in the 1920s. This chapter begins with description of the motivations and automobile retrofitting for the journey westward from Michigan. It follows with a reconstructed narrative of the day-by-day activities along the first leg of the trip, to and through northern Arizona. This narrative reveals the special nature and hazards of travel then, perceptions of the travelway, strange attractions along the way, and rewards from such travel in that unusual period.

Chapter 3, "The Northern Arizona Destination," follows with a deeper examination of 70 years of travel and tourism change in the fascinating corridor in northern Arizona. Problems as well as opportunities of development toward more sustainable tourism are outlined. This corridor remains a major domestic and international travel destination but faces critical need for greater planning vision.

Chapter 4, "1929 Western Tour: Part II," returns to the Gunn family journey from Arizona to California and northward along the coast. Of special appeal are features such as the dramatic Pacific coast and mountain landscape, the small towns, and visiting long-lost friends. To us Michiganians this was an exotic paradise. Although some tourist development and promotion had begun, the land then was primarily in its raw, undeveloped, pre-Disney stage readily available from the crude roads and slow-moving travel. Travel services were minimal.

Chapter 5, "The Northern California Destination," is a description and appraisal of changes in tourism in the northern California area. This region is distinguished from southern California as proven by the several attempts to secede and create a state of its own. It is more verdant, rural, and conservative with its own special tourism history.

Chapter 6, "1929 Western Tour: Part III," narrates the special appeals of Oregon and sightseeing along the Columbia River, much more primitive than today. The original slow-paced scenic mountain drive has been replaced by high-speed Interstate travel. Even so, a great amount of planning and resource protection is now retaining much of its lure and enjoyment.

Chapter 7, "Oregon and Columbia River Destination," reveals much of its past history as well as new plans for overall sustainable tourism. Significant are new interpretive centers describing its past, especially the hardships and visual impressions of the Lewis and Clark Expedition of 1804–1806. The trend toward overuse is being met with new programs of sustainability.

The final leg of the 1929 autocamping journey is described in Chapter 8. This encompasses experiences in Yellowstone National Park, followed by the anxiety of the trip back to Michigan. Tourist values and relationship with the land were very important to us in this period before mass tourism.

Chapter 9, "Yellowstone National Park Destination," examines the struggle of the National Park Service to cope with mass tourism over seven decades. This discussion demonstrates how difficult it has been to maintain flexibility of policy in order to meet dramatically changing economic, social, and environmental issues. The future planning and management challenges are many.

Chapter 10, "Sustainability Challenges for Planners and Designers," provides specific actions needed by these professionals if tourism is to strive toward the most desirable goals. Especially critical is the role of landscape architects because, throughout this seven-decade period, they have exercised a strong environmental advocacy as well as creating sustainable project development for both the public and private sectors. They now have abundant opportunities and professional responsibilities for creating better western communities, new understanding of travel market segments, more sustainable tourism projects, stronger environmental protection, and new educational programs for better tourism planning and design.

Chapter 11, "Meanings for the Future," reveals conclusions from this examination of tourism in the West from the romantic paradise to the overwhelming environmen-

Symbolic of enduring natural and cultural resources of the West, the very foundation for tourism, is the spectacular Grand Canyon of the Colorado. However, if past negative impacts are to be overcome and the goal of sustainability is to be achieved in the future, new planning and aggressive leadership are required.

tal pressure and adaptation of recent tourism. Identified are those qualities that are worth emulating in the future in spite of the need for adaptation to change. No one can go back to the conditions of the 1920s but there are values that can and should be incorporated into new planning and design for tourism in this region. Included are: conclusions, assets, constraints, and opportunities. Guidelines are offered for restoring the West as a major tourism icon.

Endnotes

[1]A very comprehensive book on the history of tourism development in the West is *Devil's Bargain: Tourism in the Twentieth Century American West* (1998) by Hal K. Rothman. Lawrence: University Press of Kansas.

[2]U. S. Travel Data Center. (2000). *Travel expenditures in the designated U. S. Bureau of Census western region.* Washington, DC.

Chapter 1

Western Tourism: Boom and Strain

Was tourism of the West planned? Bits and pieces were but, as an overall system, it just happened. Just as the gold rush of 1845 caught the region by surprise, so did the tsunami-like wave of automobile tourists in the 1920s. National, state, and city parks began to be visited by tourists but were not overtly planned for them. The dominant policies for these sites were resource protection and minimum impact from outdoor recreation. Some excellent site planning in national parks was designed for the small number of visitors in those early years but soon became obsolete with new masses of tourists.

Areas began to respond to the huge volumes of new visitors. Property owners along roads in the 1920s began to capitalize on the new flows of tourists by letting them camp, offering groceries, and building campgrounds, gas stations, and cabins. Site and building design was of the property owner's invention. Rail lines generally were well sited but were planned primarily for commerce, not tourism. Promoters and advertisers soon saw the opportunities of hawking the travel attractions of the West but made no linkage with the planning of these attractions.

This pattern of land use was a logical growth of the free enterprise system for business. Public agencies interpreted their own mandates for planning of their lands and made no reference to private sector development for tourism. Not yet understood was the difference between tourism and other forms of economic development. Tourism was an umbrella concept that covered a multitude of plans and decisions by a great number of independent decision makers.

Tourism as a System

Over many decades, segments of tourism have received a great amount of attention. For example, management and operational information on lodging and food service, often called the "hospitality industry," can be found in current publications.[1] Other special topics are now treated in depth, such as for highway passenger transportation, marketing techniques and segmentation, park and recreation areas, and theme parks. Recently, new phases have appeared in print, including adventure tourism, ecotourism, literary tourism, alternative tourism, and cultural tourism.[2] There is even a book on the sociolinguistics of tourism.[3] For generations, personal travel anecdotes have provided fascinating and romantic reading.

Important as these many parts of tourism may be to the growth of western tourism, they are not tourism in its broad context. Tourism encompasses a huge agglomeration of actors, physical development, and programs that almost defy definition. And these activities had profound economic, social, and environmental implications in the West in the 1920s and in the seven decades that followed.

Tourism is a relatively recent concept when viewed in the context of history. One of the first writings to identify tourism as a functioning system was *Vacationscape.*[4] When the entire scope of development is viewed, all the functional parts could be grouped into a demand (market) side and a supply (development) side. The supply side is composed of all that is created for tourism functions and is made up of five components, each including hundreds of individual parts but highly interdependent: *transportation* that moves people to and from attraction destinations, *attractions* that offer activities for user participation, *services/facilities* for support of travel and attraction use, *information* that assists users in knowing and enjoying their travel, and *promotion*. Such a model helps in understanding the extent and complexity of tourism. The many separate parts of each component have their own place and environmental requirements but most important is their *interconnectivity*.

The concept of tourism as a system, especially when applied to the 1920s in the West, exposes important geographical, place, and sustainable dimensions. At no time before or after has tourism experienced such growth and impact. It is true that one form in the late 1800s, of visiting resorts in response to the new railroad-steamboat era, produced magnificent hotels for the wealthy elite. This *class* tourism had become important also with rail-carriage travel to the West at the turn of the century. But *mass* tourism did not appear until the advent and proliferation of the low-cost automobile. Sociologist Dulles stated: "What had once been largely restricted to the genteel members of society had become the property of the people as a whole."[5]

This interdependence within the system is not yet fully understood. For example, any change in transportation and access, as demonstrated by the terrorist debacle of September 11, 2001, will have a serious impact on volumes of visitors to attractions. Just as in an automobile, if one part of the system weakens or fails, such as a weak battery or a plugged gas filter, the entire system will fail to run smoothly or even may quit entirely. Thus it is with the tourism system—all components and parts within are dependent upon the successful functioning of all other parts. This simple truth is not well recognized or practiced by the myriad actors of tourism development.

The West as Foundation for the Tourism System

In the 1920s, this interdependence of the many parts of the tourism system was not part of the development agenda. The historic background of this special place as related to planning offers some enlightenment on why this was true.

No other nation had a Wild West. No other geographical place has performed such a profound role in history. The American West, a geopolitical accident, is now believed by anthropologists to be host to the first people of North America who traveled across the Beringian land bridge over 15,000 years ago.[6] Later it became host to another very significant group of travelers—autocampers of the 1920s. This special place contained unusual lures that continue today: once part of Spain, Mexico, and Russia; locale of first national parks of the world; site of first major western exploration by Lewis and Clark; landscape contrasts of ocean coast, mountains, ancient forests, and deserts; a human outburst of the gold rush; birthplace of movies; huge vineyards and massive agricultural production; first nuclear explosion; and the amazing works of the ancient Anasazi.

No other geographic area triggered such an explosion of mass travelers as the American West, where two major factors combined for the detonation: the icon of western paradise and mass production of the cheap automobile. For generations, the intoxicating lure of the West had penetrated the psyche of midwestern and eastern America. But, until the mass production of low-cost automobiles, this exceptional place was available only to the small minority of the moneyed elite, coming by train.

This special place, over the last seven decades, has experienced the ferocious bombardment from both in-migration and tourism, domestic and foreign. To accommodate these many new millions of people, equal to the population of many countries, a critical question centers on how well the land use was planned to withstand this invasion. An historical flashback reveals many lessons for today's tourism developers—how the advantages can be retained and pitfalls avoided.

As with the several economic booms in the West, tourism has become a major employer and producer of revenues. Entrepreneurship has blossomed into full bloom, creating new attractions, services, and shops, and forming a very large protourism constituency including businesses, chambers of commerce, and tourism promoters.

Their concentration on internal operation has been essential to their success. In the past when traveler volume was comparatively low and development was reasonably small, this business focus was sufficient. As both land development and traveler volumes have become so huge, lacking has been education, awareness, and publicity regarding stress on the land environment, the very foundation for most tourism in the West. Even the environmental protection constituency has missed a role in tourism, spending most of their talent and moneys on issues related to urban growth and extractive industries such as mining and timber.

A powerful and constant element throughout the history of the West has been and continues to be the single most important element: the land. It is finite in scope; there is no more. The dominant philosophy has been (and continues to be) take from the land's abundant resources, because they have been considered infinite. As one western writer has put it succinctly, "paradise has been worked to death."[7] Salmon have really disappeared from the waters, old-growth timber is nearly gone, burgeoning agriculture and ranching are desertifying the West, and old mines are poisoning the streams. In spite of cries from conservationists, protectionists, and ecologists, this philosophy of wanton land development continues to dominate the West. This book's summary of past history of tourism's growth reveals its adherence to this same philosophy. All these impacts and more are observable throughout the West. The question must be asked regarding how future growth of tourism can benefit from the knowledge of changes in the past as a foundation for guidelines to avoid its own destructiveness.

The West: From Formidable to Fantastic

The early West, with its frightening and inhospitable deserts, forests, mountains, Indians, and predators, was a horrible place, not desired by European settlers. If it were to be settled, it must be conquered and tamed. It was this battle for the West that challenged the frontiersmen. The axe, plow, rifle, and foolhardiness then became the tools for mastering this monster. Nature was not to be loved but to be destroyed, a concept contrary to embedded traditional Chinese and Japanese integration of people with nature.[8]

It wasn't until the 20th century that America began to believe that the forests and wild lands were beautiful and of practical value.[9] Not only were the resources of the West productive for agriculture and forestry but also for attracting visitors, who, in turn, brought new dollars to communities beginning to starve from dwindling mining of the past. Thus, within only a few decades, the image of the West completely reversed. From a hostile and forbidding land, it had become a romanticized paradise.

As the settlers had moved westward, the communities they formed reflected a lack of permanence. True, the pattern for their towns was generally copied from eastern cities but with one major exception: no central public space.[10] Only the bare dirt main street could have provided the setting for shootouts, popularized by John Wayne movies. This place pattern was a clue to the individualism of the times rather than cohesive social order. Speculation was rampant; sell and move on.

It wasn't until after the industrial revolution and the new wave of technology that the fears of the West were erased and it became virtually a geographic flatland for development anywhere—desert, mountain, forest. In the 1960s, anywhere and everywhere the eastern prototype of green grass, fountains, swimming pools, and curbed streets became an overlay dropped upon the landscape from on high. Mostly symbolic was this "back-to-nature" movement because it was less real than imaged.[11]

It is difficult to know the extent to which "nature faking" has influenced the American reversal of nature hating to nature loving.[12] In the early 1900s, writers such as John Burroughs, Ernest Thompson Seaton, Charles G. D. Roberts, and William J. Long had flooded the literary market with tales of humanized wild animals. All claimed their tales were founded in facts of their own observation but natural scientists questioned this as fakery. That animals somehow acquired human reasoning powers in their daily lives seemed preposterous. But these tales were very popular and convincing to adults as well as children. Later, Walt Disney's animated cinemas gave further credence to humanized animal thought and action. Paralleling these events was the mass marketing of cuddly soft and lovable dolls and toys depicting lions, tigers, bears, and even snakes. The imprint of safe and friendly wild animals, such as Teddy Bear, Smokey Bear, Bambi, Simba, and Dumbo, became firmly imbedded in the minds of children. It is no wonder that when families visit natural resource areas with wildlife they get as close as possible, not only to photograph but to feed and pet. The desire for close contact with wild animals is further reinforced by vivid advertising images in popular publications and videos. Managers of wildlife places have had to assume a new role of educating and policing visitors on the inherent danger of interfering with wild animal behavior.

In the 1920s, it was the age of the flapper girl, literary sex, and F. Scott Fitzgerald's novels of hangovers. Much has been written about the "roaring twenties," a period of social upheaval and economic prosperity. The postwar milieu seemed dominated by excesses. Author Donovan summarized this period:

> Flappers and flagpole sitters and human flies; bath tub gin and bobbed hair and the big bull market; racketeering and radio and Rotary clubs; mah-jongg and Miami Beach and marathon dancing; petting parties and Prohibition and psychoanalysis; compassionate marriage and crossword puzzles and cocktail parties—these are but a few of the phenomena that were spawned or that flowered in that incredible decade, the Roaring Twenties.[13]

An unprecedented growth in the American economy followed "the war to end all wars." Industrial expansion and personal incomes boomed. The American mindset of build it and sell it produced significant advances in science and technology. New electrical appliances within the home, coast-to-coast telephone, candy bars, and packaged foods came on the market. The New York Stock Exchange became so busy following President Coolidge's assurance of continued growth of the economic boom that the ticker could not keep up. New building technology spurred new skyscraper construction in major cities. It was in this halcyon time that the West became the favored travel destination. Visitors flocked to this fantasyland.

The Creation of an Icon

It was not only the newly available and cheap automobile, and certainly not the roads, that induced travel to the West. The seductive lure of the West had been built up over generations, long before the cheap automobile gave masses the opportunity to experience that fantasyland. Tales from returning travelers and especially the literary genre of the day must have had a great influence on potential travelers. Painters, writers, explorers, and returning travelers proliferated the image of the West as paradise.

According to research by landscape architect William Mann, landscape qualities triggered an array of mental pictures within the minds of early travelers: the picturesque, romantic, sublime, beautiful, pleasurable. Mann cites George Vancouver's reactions to the west coast when he visited from 1792 to 1794 as enchantingly beautiful, delightful, elegant, and engagingly diversified.[14] Entries by Merriweather Lewis on the Lewis and Clark explorations to the West are filled with elaborations of the landscape, paraphrased as vistas of delicious fruits, fragrant perfumes, and magnificent scenery that amuses the mind. Views of rocky cliffs and walls called to mind imagery of castles and man-made structures—sculptures, galleries, columns, pyramids, and towers. English explorer David Thompson, after visiting the lower stretches of the Columbia River, expounded on the hills that softened the "rude" scenery, a most admirable situation, romantic bold scenery, and, as Lewis, how the landscape appeared as castles and structures. The West was characterized as the "Garden of Eden," an amazing descriptor considering the extreme difficulties encountered by these explorers. As one reviews today's tourist promotional literature it is clear that landscape beauty has become an entrenched icon of the West.

Certainly Zane Grey, Max Brand, and Owen Wister, who systematized the popular Western novel, had much to do with creating an image of the West as a primitive and exciting place.[15] Steinbeck wrote, "It wasn't Indians that were important, nor adventures, nor even getting out here [the West] . . . it was westering and westering. Every man wanted something for himself, but the big beast that was all of them wanted only westering."[16] Bret Harte and Mark Twain had much to do with furthering the myths of the West. Painters such as Albert Bierstadt, George Catlin, Thomas Moran, and Thomas Nuttall embellished the scenic appeals of western places. For the first time, automobiles and roads provided realization of new freedoms and access to that wonderland known as the West. In all, the motorist's West stood for the same qualities associated with stagecoach days: independence, open space, simplicity, a more leisurely pace—all in direct contrast with the crowded, frenzied, congestive East.[17]

For populations in eastern United States a desire to visit the West had been incited also by the many writings of conservation and national park advocates, such as Gilbert H. Grosvenor, an early editor of *National Geographic Magazine.* He was among a party of 15 led by Stephen T. Mather (later the first director of the National Park Service) who visited the West in 1915 and in April 1916 produced a special issue, "The Land of the Best."[18] Every Congressman was given a copy, a major influence to establish the National Park Service (NPS) in 1916. Evidence of this publication's continuing focus is the July 1979 issue devoted entirely to "Our National Parks."

Another significant social factor in the 1920s was the shift from macho male dominance of camping to admission of women and families.[19] This change removed a critical travel stigma and fostered mass travel by camping rather than using inns and hotels. Families accepted the somewhat primitive form of living in order to gain the treasure of a western experience. Never before or since has as large a population travel camped. It was reported that in 1925 over 5 million cars, over half of all in the nation, were involved in travel camping.[20]

In the 1920s, the greatest travel lures for easterners to travel west were the spectacular and abundant natural resources of the West. Snapshots and anecdotes of returning travelers provided enticing images of exotic landscape and wildlife attractions. Santa Fe Railroad ads in the *National Geographic* included vivid sketches and photographs of the Grand Canyon and Petrified Forest. Nothing like these wonders were available for residents of the East and Midwest. Another appeal was actually seeing and perhaps wading in another ocean: the Pacific.

The near-supernatural landscape of Yellowstone was hard to believe. Quaking land near geysers and mud-pots, abundance of black bears, and dramatic waterfalls were powerful magnets. Certainly, the majesty of towering and rocky mountains, often reaching beyond 12,000 feet in elevation, outranked anything in the East, even the Appalachians.

Characteristic of the travelers of the late 1920s was their consistent destination objectives. Although some sought the cultural attractions of the Mormon Tabernacle in Salt Lake City, old Spanish missions, and Indian settlements, the overwhelming lures were the natural resource attractions, especially the national parks. The era of gigantic theme parks was yet to come. The National Park System was managing 33 national parks and monuments by 1929, mostly located in the West.[21] Best known by residents of the Midwest and East were probably Yellowstone, Grand Canyon, Yosemite,

Mt. Rainier, Rocky Mountain, Mesa Verde, and Zion. These encompassed natural features not found near the homes of would-be travelers from the East. In magazines and by word of mouth of earlier travelers, they had learned about the exotic attractions of the West such as geysers, hot springs, huge waterfalls, high mountains, Grand Canyon of the Colorado, granite peaks, Sierra Nevada mountains, giant sequoias, ancient volcanoes, flowered meadows, Rocky Mountain scenery, bear, moose, deer, and colorful canyon and mesa scenery.

Most of these attractions were, and continue to be, on public lands. Since the beginnings of the conservation movement and establishment of national parks in this country, the policy dichotomy of the NPS for public use and resource preservation has endured. Stephen T. Mather, the first director of NPS, encouraged visitor use as well as protective resource management.[22] Another major land manager of the West, the US Forest Service (FS), favored a policy of multiple use, including outdoor recreation, a major activity component for western tourists. It manages over 180 million acres of land, much of which is devoted to camping, picnicking, hiking, fishing, skiing, hunting, resorting, scenic viewing and photography, wildland adventure, and nature study.[23] Many other federal and state agencies manage vast acreages of western lands that are now overrun by tourists. Yet, few managers admit they are in the realm of tourism and have few policies and practices relating to tourism. Because the business sector of tourism today depends on the remaining beauty and grandeur of the West, it is time that its members become stronger advocates for environmental protection of these magnificent assets. Such a charge demands new commitment and understanding of how the entire tourism system functions.

The New Mass Mobility

Although the story of transportation development has been well chronicled elsewhere, relevance to the places of tourism needs further explanation.

By the 1920s trains had passed through phases of invention, feverish expansion, slaughter and regulation, engineering and technological improvement, and the pinch from new automobile travel. Many inventors and investors contributed to train development, such as George Mortimer Pullman, Webster Wagner (sleeping cars, parlor cars, dining cars), Eli H. Janney (automatic coupler), and George Westinghouse (air brakes).[24] The railroads gave us time zones, replacing the nationwide complicated and conflicting rules of setting clock times. Between 1897 and 1917 passenger travel in the US increased by over 600%.[25] But train travel was soon threatened by the automobile. By 1925, automobile visits to the Grand Canyon had begun to exceed train tourists.[26]

Automobiles did not burst onto the travel scene in an instant because at first they were too costly and mainly a socialite toy. The first designers catered primarily to the wealthy and often customized autos to meet their individual tastes. For example, a 1915 Daimler, built for an Indian prince, had drapes, electric lighting, and a special outside seat and footrest for a servant.[27] Elegance and opulence dominated automobile styling in the US as well. "The bigger the star, the bigger the car" illustrated the influence of Hollywood. Another phase was the novelty of racing cars, introducing the concept of "sports" cars as they are known today. The Stutz Bearcat was probably the most outstanding of these in the 1920s.

The thrill of adventuring and experiencing the exotic lands of the West in the 1920s were worth the many flat tires from stone bruises over these primitive roads. This new ability to travel, fostered by mass production of cheap automobiles, triggered the western explosion of seven decades ago.

Even though the automobile had been around awhile, it was the low-cost, mass-produced automobile, especially the Ford, that changed tourism and America forever. This new personalized vehicle gave the masses mobility and destination flexibility.

Never before or since has travel grown so rapidly, especially for the more modest income classes, as did the impact of mass automobile production and purchase in the late 1920s. Trains, steamboats, and jet air travel have had great influence on certain places over the years, but nothing has ever equaled this period of auto travel growth. No other force has ever had as great an egalitarian effect on American society. Woodrow Wilson is quoted as saying "nothing has spread socialist feeling in this country more than the use of the automobile."[28]

The automobile has been identified as a new form of architecture. Architectural researcher Folke Kihlsted states that for the first time it was a creation of mobile artistry, engineering, and architecture.[29] In 1920, Dietz Lumber Company produced a "house to drive in," a craft-built house mounted on a Model T Ford chassis. It is suggested that the entire prefabricated mobile home concept grew from these early experiments. Modern recreation vehicles (RVs) exemplify mobile shelters often fully equipped with plug-in features—water, electricity, waste removal.

The ubiquitous Ford Model T weighed only 1200 pounds so the 20-horsepower engine was powerful enough for even the most rugged roads. Spare parts were readily available over rural and urban America through mail-order houses. The simplicity of the Ford, its low cost, and the new freedom of personal direction and travel schedule captured the attention of the masses, and buy they did. With moving-belt assembly line manufacture, 2 million Fords at $350 each were produced in 1926.[30] Populations heretofore excluded from travel due to cost and social status now had access to destinations throughout the nation, a new opportunity for dream fulfillment of experiencing the West.

Ford's new Model A, brought out in 1928, was an adaptation of the more classic lines of its superior, the Lincoln.[31] It featured wire wheels and hard rubber steering wheel, replacing the simple wooden ones of the earlier 1920s. By the end of 1929, 1 million of these cars had been produced. And, for the first time, these new models were enclosed. Almost 90% of all American cars sold in 1929 were closed models whereas nearly the same percent were open touring cars 10 years earlier.[32] This innovative model sported many new features such as four-wheel brakes, shock absorbers, shatter-proof windshield, and a 40-horsepower engine (at 2200 rpm) with a 3 and 7/8-inch bore and 4 and 1/4-inch stroke.[33]

The Roads Weren't Ready

Slow to respond to this automobile invasion was the conversion of Indian, cattle, and wagon trails into roads for this onrush of automobiles. No one wanted to accept the responsibility of meeting the needs of these new swarms of travelers—states, federal government, private sector? A key political issue was local resentment of tourist use that did not help pay for road construction and maintenance. Crossing rivers presented a special problem, solved at first by ferries due to the high cost of bridges. But some critics, here and abroad, viewed this linkage as the last straw. A British observer had this comment: "The modern car ferry linking the growing network of motorways is a potent factor in the worldwide spread of man's lethal, oppressive, ubiquitous private chariot, the motor car."[34] Actually, the League of American Wheelmen, as their members sought exploration of the countryside, is responsible for starting a better roads movement.[35] Finally, a Federal Highway Act was passed in 1916 and modified in 1921. But even then, political rivalry between state and federal roles slowed progress.

As might be predicted, greatest road improvements first occurred in the Midwest and especially around Detroit, the birthplace of automobile manufacturing. Michigan cities were the centers of carriage, wagon, bicycle, and then automobile production. By 1927, 15 million Model T cars had been built by Ford and about 200 establishments located in 28 Michigan towns were engaged in automobile production.[36] Grade separations were in place by 1929 and land speculators were already extolling the virtues of paved roads: "One block of concrete pavement is worth a mile of promised improvement in real estate selling."[37] It wasn't until 1928 that the first nationwide specifications for road construction were established, although it took many more years for states to implement them.

Finding one's way on these early roads was not easy. Locals, who were often piqued by the tourist invasion, were not reliable sources of guidance. In the 1920s, some highway designation had begun and the first major highway map of the US was produced by Rand McNally in 1926.[38] This map clearly shows that road quality of the West lagged far behind that of the East.

Gradually, travel to and around the West improved. With federal assistance, a US-designated highway system began to provide a network of concrete roads from the East to the West and within key western states. Begun in 1956 as the National System

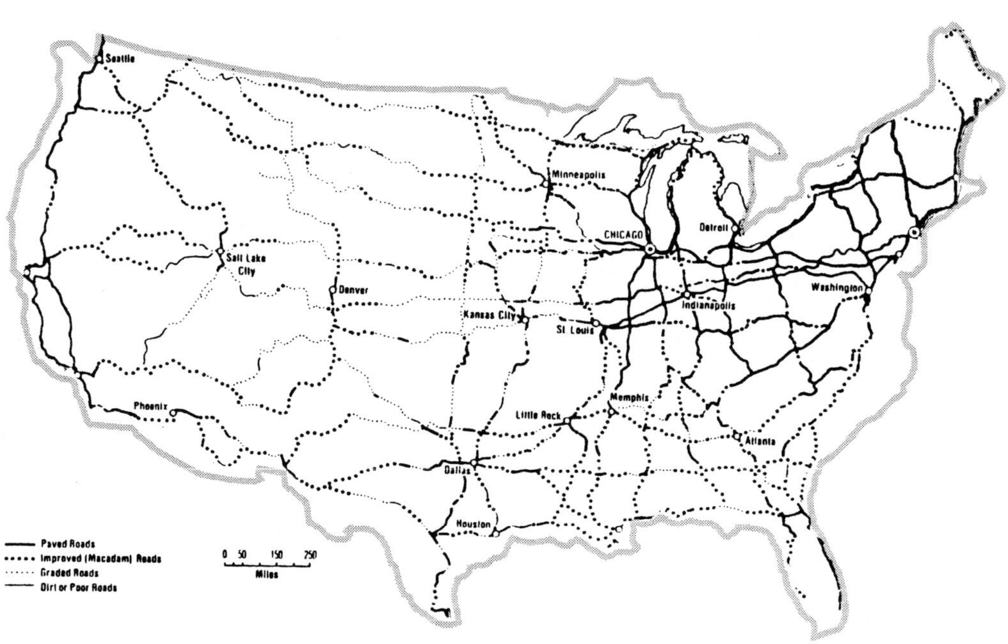

The 1926 road map of the United States clearly shows the difficulty for travelers from the East to reach the West over poor roads across plains and mountains. However, even then there were paved roads along the Pacific coast. (Source: Douglas R. McManis, American Geographical Society)

of Interstate and Defense Highways is today's Interstate highway system, the dominant thoroughfare for tourist travel throughout the country.

Greyhound, with its slogan "Leave the driving to us," became the dominant scheduled bus line, preceded by the Pioneer Yellow Bus Line, introduced in 1927.[39] But long-distance bus transit in America has always been plagued by a social stigma of low-class patronage. In spite of many management efforts to upgrade and provide the only travel means for rural areas and small towns, especially in the West, it has been difficult to maintain good levels of use. Both bus and rail travel dropped substantially with the tremendous growth of air and automobile movement.

Throughout these decades of escalating automobile use, a major force has been the private nonprofit American Automobile Association (AAA), begun in the early 1900s. It started as a lobby group for driver rights of better roads. The treasurer of the Long Island Automobile Club, F. G. Webb, is credited with being the father of AAA.[40] Over several decades, AAA has become a major force promoting better highways, developing detailed travel guides, selling automobile insurance, initiating motel inspection and rating, and carrying on safety programs.

A most memorable experience for travelers for many decades was the ubiquitous Burma Shave roadside signs. The slow cruising speed and narrow highway right-of-way gave travelers ample visual opportunity to grasp the humor of these sign sequences climaxed with the Burma Shave logo. Created in Minnesota, this new brushless shaving cream was first named Burma Vita, because an essential oil came from Burma and the cream was thought to add vigor to the user.[41] After an experiment with a series of crude signs on Route 65 to Albert Lea, the first mass-produced signs were made in 1926. From then on these humorous signs, spaced about 100 paces apart, became a memorable attraction along especially boring roadside landscapes. Examples abound: HARDLY A DRIVER/IS NOW ALIVE/WHO PASSED/ON HILLS/AT 75; WHEN YOU DRIVE/IF CAUTION CEASES/YOU ARE APT/TO REST/IN PIECES; and YOUR SHAVING BRUSH/HAS HAD ITS DAY/SO WHY NOT/SHAVE THE MODERN WAY/WITH BURMA SHAVE. Even though humorous and of advertising value, these signs often carried a moral and safety message important to travelers.

Modern automobile travelers to the West take for granted the technological and engineering improvements in their cars. The automobiles of the 1920s were crude prototypes of today's vehicles with their power steering, power brakes, air conditioning, automatic transmissions, air bags, and even geographic positioning systems. New hard and smooth surfacing of roads together with better and longer-lasting tires and more sensitive suspension systems enhance greatly travel comfort, safety, and security. These improvements, coupled with sexy styling, have made the automobile an extremely high-priority possession of all Americans, even cherished more than homes and wives. Manufacturers, workers, and economists now know that the automobile industry is the largest engine of the American economy.

The Concept of Scenic Roads

For many decades, aesthetes, landscape architects, and tourism promoters have touted the value of scenic roads. Important as is this groundswell of interest, implementation of sustainability has been and continues to be difficult. For tourism in the West scenic roads are of great tourism importance.

Local, state, and federal interest in scenic roads has an early history. As far back as 1886, the concept of a memorial scenic parkway was initiated by residents of Alexandria, Virginia.[42] By the 1920s most western states showed interest in scenic roads. The real push came in 1934 with federal legislation that mandated states to spend not less than 1% of their apportionment of federal highway moneys on roadside landscape beauty. Another significant movement for highway enhancement occurred during the administration of President Lyndon B. Johnson when his wife, Lady Bird, lobbied for the Highway Beautification Act of 1965. This act provided new funding for roadside beautification. Some states were reluctant and complied only when threats of withdrawal of funding were made. The feasibility of a national scenic highway system was undertaken by the Federal Highway Administration in 1973–1974.

Roadside billboards have been a continuing contentious issue, defended by advertisers and despised by aesthetes including landscape architects. The issue of sign comprehension by drivers was researched and published in 1971 as *Street Graphics* by the American Society of Landscape Architects Foundation.[43] It proved that the amount of information a driver could absorb and comprehend at normal speeds was extremely limited, rendering extensive wordiness and masses of signs virtually unintelligible. Not only are signs often bad business because they do not carry intended messages, they also frequently hide beautiful roadside vistas. In spite of many attempts toward eradication in the West, many roadsides have become cluttered with ugly billboards and signs.

A major problem of all scenic road sustainability has been the maintenance of landscape place values throughout the road corridor. The corridor includes many private lands whose owners believe that they have the right to use their properties as they wish. Even though this is a guaranteed American right, so has been the general public good. Among the techniques employed to mitigate this conflict are the following: wider than normal rights-of-way; outright acquisition of corridor areas; fee acquisition and leaseback with controls to adjacent owners; acquisition of scenic or conservation easement; local zoning control; scenic highway corridor reservations; designation of special conservation or corridor districts; comprehensive planning; and restrictive covenants in deeds. Desirable as these techniques may be, they are very difficult to implement because of the problem of extending the public weal over private property rights.

Land use impacts of all highways continue to challenge designers concerned with the entire corridor, not just the roadway. Researchers in Wisconsin made an evaluation of three techniques that had been used to evaluate impacts.[44] Although they concluded that there was merit in each approach, application would be difficult because lay citizens would not be able to understand the technical process. Esoteric techniques have their place but they are sterile if they ignore input from those impacted by highways, such as local property owners.

In 1991 the Intermodal Surface Transportation Efficiency Act (ISTEA) gave strong federal support and promise of $155 billion for a variety of roadside enhancements. Included were: facilities for bicycles and pedestrians, acquisition of scenic easements and scenic or historic sites, scenic or historic highway programs, landscaping and other scenic beautification, rehabilitation of historic transportation buildings, preservation of abandoned railway corridors, control and removal of outdoor advertising, archaeological planning and research, and mitigation of water pollution due to highway runoff.[45] Major responsibility for carrying out the recommendations fell within the jurisdiction of metropolitan planning organizations (MPOs).

Meanwhile, a coalition of 150 groups, the Surface Transportation Policy Project (STPP),[46] was created to lobby for implementation of ISTEA. In the first 3 years after authorization very little had been accomplished except for creating plans. The main reason cited was the high expectation compared to the ability of states and local communities to follow through. With political changes in the makeup of Congress, there was much doubt regarding implementation even though a few projects had been started. Criticism was leveled also at a shift in goals from ease of travel access to volume capacity ratios of vehicle use, but there was evidence for the first time that states were engaged in a broader concept and better long-range planning.[47]

Although ISTEA had promised many amenities important to tourism, little overt emphasis was actually placed on tourism. An editorial by the director of STPP finally made this linkage, emphasizing the need for highway policy concerning historic sites and structures, place quality protection, and scenic values often blocked by billboard pollution.[48] Others in this same issue cited the negative influence on tourists of the "crudscape," sameness of franchise strips, and lack of scenic roads.[49] But, in spite of lobbying and rhetoric toward extension of ISTEA, it was blocked in 1997. It had become bogged down in federal versus local politics. Even so, states had become more aware of issues beyond mere traffic counts when decisions on highways were to be made. They were finally realizing that the amenities along the entire corridor were as important to travelers as only access.

After much acrimony on both sides of the issue, the Transportation Equity Act for the 21st Century (TEA-21) was passed by Congress and signed by President Clinton on June 9, 1998.[50] This act authorized federal spending of $217 billion on highways. Of this, Arizona was to receive $408 million; California, $2.4 billion; and Oregon, $324 million. Of course, there were many strings attached to these for every state, such as allocation between highway construction and the Congestion Mitigation and Air Quality Improvement (CMAQ) program and the new Transit Enhancement program. Under this enhancement program, the following were the main eligible activities: historic preservation, rehabilitation and operation of historic mass transportation buildings and facilities, bus shelters, landscaping and scenic beautification, public art, pedestrian access and walkways, bicycle access including bike storage facilities and bike-on-bus racks, transit connection to parks within the transit service area, signage, and enhanced transit access for persons with disabilities.[51] If implemented by states and communities these projects could be a positive force for tourism. Only the future will show the extent of application of this new legislation.

Airlines and Controls

In this democratic market-economy nation, there has been much vacillation regarding public-private relations on airlines. Contrary to many other countries, airlines began as private enterprise, although many were subsidized heavily as mail carriers. But since 1938 the federal Civil Aeronautics Board (CAB) exercised control over air fares, routes, and many details of service until its demise in 1978 with the airline deregulation act. Arguments against the CAB included excessive delays for bureaucratic approvals of any sort, denial of competition, and a stranglehold over fares.

Immediately after deregulation, a spurt of new smaller air carriers emerged, providing needed low-cost service to areas not reached before. For several years all airlines experienced great growth. In recent years, however, many of the smaller carriers died out, leaving Southwest Airlines as the only major survivor. It became the opinion of many in the 1990s that deregulation was not accomplishing its hoped-for objectives. The large carriers continued to monopolize, fares went up, and many communities were no longer served. The Department of Transportation (DOT) began receiving many demands for reinstating regulation. The future of air access tourism in the West depends greatly on balancing public-private relations, resulting in some control, but perhaps not as stringent as the older federal regulations. Since September 11, 2001, the air transport issue has shifted dramatically from overcapacity to increased security and business recovery. The fear of air travel is gradually being overcome, but huge financial deficits will take longer to overcome. It is in the selfish interest of the tourism sector to resolve this issue, requiring new commitment and understanding of how all components of the tourism system are interrelated and planned in concert.

Tents to Homogenized Franchises

In response to the surge of camping travelers in the 1920s many local townspeople and rural ranchers became tourist business entrepreneurs. The side lots of filling stations, the land at road intersections, the front lots of residences, and land near grocery stores became sites for catering to these new customers. With no standard plans or specifications these places varied greatly in site design, some offering neatly laid out sites and central kitchen and toilet facilities and others merely a free-for-all in muddy open space. Some communities on travel routes had begun to offer their city parks to travelers. The slow speed of autos and poor road conditions forced travelers to seek services rather frequently en route. As a result, roadsides soon became proliferated with service stations, hog dog stands, and campgrounds. The going rate in 1929 was $0.25 for camping and $1 to $1.50 for a cabin.

This period of the late 1920s in the West gave birth to a new form of traveler accommodation—the tourist cabin, followed by the tourist court and motel. Cabins were tiny and offered little more than bed space; water supply and toilet facilities were elsewhere on the lot. These first structures were built of whatever material was handy—adobe, block, log, stone, frame and clapboard. These were clearly a new form of architecture, the very antithesis of hotels. Throughout the rapid expansion of motel development, personal service by the owner-manager to the automobile traveler prevailed but without the hotel frills of attendants demanding tips and more formal dress in the lounges and dining rooms.

In this prefranchise era, each place was so individualized that travelers often inspected several before making a choice, often poking the mattress to test its resiliency. Travel historian Warren Belasco observed, "tourists were indefatigable comparative-shoppers for whom the roadside was one elongated cut-rate bazaar."[52] The burst of automobile travel in the 1920s was the beginning of an entirely unprecedented landscape/business principle. No other business had been so firmly founded in geography and the power of the tourist-oriented landscape.

By the 1920s, most hotels had been located near railway stations whereas these new tourist court services were located along highways. For years hotel owners fought this new upstart of highway accommodation rather than remodel or relocate to meet this new travel market segment. Today, the franchise motel that offers some of the traditional hotel services but caters to automobile travelers has replaced most of the camping and tourist cabin services along highways. It can be said that the West was both father and mother of the motel as we now know it. But some travelers begrudged the demise of older hotels in the heart of small towns where locals and travelers could meet. The observation from the solo sojourn of one traveler, "No matter how you built it, the motel remains a haunt of the quick and dirty, where the only locals are Chamber of Commerce boys every Thursday. Who ever heard the returning traveler exclaim over one of the great motels of the world he stayed in? Motels can be big but never grand."[53]

The motel, like all creative inventions, passed through several mutations before reaching today's popular accommodations, not necessarily grand but serving the traveling public well. The clustering of cabins in the 1940s and 1950s came to be known as a motor court, often arranged in a horseshoe layout to make the greatest visual display from the highway. *The Tourist Court Journal*, founded by Hill C. Gresham and Bob Gresham in 1937 at Temple, Texas, monthly published a variety of tips for owner-managers—front desk and business techniques, signs, beds and bedding, lighting, floor surfaces, and maintenance. Because owners were also operators, a reader's column, "Courteously Yours," contained comments on "how-to" issues. Because motel growth was most rapid in the Southwest and West, they became prototypes for motels across the country to the East.

In the 1940s, as the architecture of travel lodging changed from the cluster of separate units to compact buildings, the term motel became the dominant descriptor. Favored first were highway locations near cities; downtown came later. Probably the characteristics that catapulted motels into preference over older hotels by the mass automobile traveler were easy access from main highways, no tipping, and the owner-manager's caring hospitality. Architecturally, designs of roadside facilities for food and lodging reflected the wildest of whims of the developers. There were places simulating wigwams, an elephant, miner's hat, bottle, fish, covered wagon, and even the famous Brown Derby, established in Los Angeles in 1926.[54]

One of the major hurdles that motels had to overcome was an early reputation of clandestine love affairs and gangsterism. Although most of these new overnight facilities were legitimate, the press played up the occasions of sensational murder and sex. A few entrepreneurs paid off the mortgage quickly by operating a "hot-pillow joint" (hourly rentals) and then switching to family travel trade. Some prudish developers insisted that the layout provided for observation from the front desk of all comings and goings of guests. Others in those days insisted on guests showing their marriage licenses before allowing them to register. In Michigan, where automobile license plates were coded by counties, some motel operators refused any guest with a local plate. An example along Route 66 was dubbed "St. Louis's little sin," the Coral Court Motel, a suburban landmark built in 1941 that soon developed a reputation of

In the 1920s, automobile service stations provided engine and tire repair, oil, battery and radiator water as well as gasoline. The customer saw clearly in the calibrated glass tank on top the amount of gasoline being delivered. Conversation with the attendant often included a variety of travel information. (Source: David LeBleu, Chevron)

a roadside brothel.[55] It took many years of diligent and well-managed effort by motel business developers throughout the nation to remove this impediment.The fascinating history of the motel has been well documented by historians Jakle and Sculle.[56]

The major lesson of motel development, in the West as elsewhere, was its innovative feature of personal service.The original Mom-and-Pop establishments provided close and friendly hospitality for tourists. In recent years, with greater franchise and megacorporation ownership and control, quite some distance from individual business management, the quality of service has deteriorated.As motels grew generally they became more impersonal,with desk clerks and other employees more concerned about wages than service.That unprecedented era of true hospitality was an outstanding period in western lodging and food.

In the 1920s autocampers generally prepared their own meals using white gas camp stoves or open campfires.This was done not only for economy but for convenience.Travelers were then at the mercy of "greasy spoon" restaurants, catering to a rough class of itinerants and a few locals. In small towns throughout the West, the best meals for residents were prepared at home, and dining out was reserved for church suppers and club meetings. In recent decades this has been reversed with the dominance of better quality dining out for both markets. But it was the autobound individuals who stimulated the concept in the 1950s of "drive-ins," with service directly to the car window. Even before, diners, often art deco train-car-shaped buildings with Formica counter tops and Naugahyde seats, had become popular with tourists as well as residents. A major innovator was Roy Kroc, whose first McDonald franchise was begun in 1955. The McDonaldization of fast food service is now well known throughout the world as well as in the US. Keys to success appeared to be a new efficiency, calculated and standardized production, predictability, and quality control. It has been called an adaptation of Fordism (assembly line mass production using standardized parts) to the food business.

One of the first responses to the great surge of automobile travel in the 1920s was the gas station. Most often in these earlier days it was truly an automobile service station, offering parts and repairs as well as gasoline, oil, and water, especially fixing flat tires that were so plentiful. By 1920 there were about 15,000 gas stations in America and historians have called the gas station a "cultural icon central to the American people."[57] Today most of the auto services have been dropped and "full service" pumping of gas and checking other fluids has been replaced by primarily "self-service," often with convenience stores attached.

The story of business response to tourism has been one of free enterprise, the true hallmark of American philosophy. The first response to autocampers was to use the highway corridor as the prime location tendon. The roadsides became proliferated with small businesses of lodging, food, and especially souvenirs. Even the first cabins and tourist courts responded to volumes of traffic, no matter where, as the prime location criterion.

It wasn't until the 1950s that motel investors began to recognize that rural areas, in spite of high pass-through traffic volumes and cheap land, were poor locations compared with places closer to travelers' destinations, primarily cities. Highways and automobiles had improved sufficiently to allow higher speeds, increasing the reluctance of travelers to make many stops as in the past. Then, with the coming of the Interstate System, standards prevented roadside businesses, forcing exit use to nearby communities, the best locations for travel businesses. When the functions of tourist businesses are examined more closely, it is discovered that all actually serve two markets: resident and traveler. Even hotels frequently provide banquet, restaurant, bar, and retail sales to local residents as well as travelers. However, this lesson of planning and location has not been fully grasped by urban planners and tourism developers.

Unfortunately, the powerful reality of tourism over the last several decades has not yet entered the agenda of city planners, whose preoccupation is exclusively with residents. Certainly, there is strong reason for favoring the locals because it is their taxes that support the infrastructure and many amenities. But as long as travelers are promoted, do come in great numbers, and make substantial expenditures, especially taxes, it would seem prudent to include their interests and needs in city planning. This is yet to happen. As a consequence, tourist services are located willy-nilly, with no guidance and reference to their relationship to resident needs. Too often, new tourist businesses select sites that gain a NIMBY (not-in-my-backyard) reaction from residents. Community–tourism development relationships are a relatively new arena of research. It is not a question of limiting the opportunities for the establishment of private tourism businesses, but rather a matter of integrating tourism with the community so that both objectives, resident and tourist, are reached.

The chaining of America grew rapidly after World War II, especially in the 1960s. The newest dimension of tourist services in the West was the uniformity and tedium of the business landscape. At the same time that better travel service businesses proliferated, they homogenized the design of all places. Travelers now see the very same place features they left back home: shopping malls, housing tracts, and franchise travel services. Modern idea transfer, communication, distribution systems, and franchising have proliferated sameness from coast to coast. Lodging and food services, especially, have succumbed to the marketing axiom of brand identification—a McDonald's appears the same in the West as the East. Modern processes of growth have provided an abundant cornucopia of standardized travel services that satisfy a huge travel market but tend to dilute the uniqueness of place. Such standardization has encountered some regional backlash, such as the difference of food preference near the Mexican border compared with ethnic desires in Washington State. Here and there brave entrepreneurs have created individualized and localized tourist service businesses, against the grain of general trends. This landscape and building design issue is a challenge to all designers, planners, and developers of future tourist services in the West.

From Cow Towns to Tourist Towns

The many waves of economic and population changes over history have left their mark on western communities. Geographical differences within the West contributed greatly to community diversity in response to farming, ranching, mining, commercial fishing, and timber harvest. Added to this was ethnic diversity in support of these differences in economic focus. And, through it all, there has been the western cowboy theme, a true western icon that grew from legend and myth as well as historic fact.

The rugged shoot-out mentality for conflict resolution that dominated western communities for generations has been difficult to change. Even today, Texas has a town called Cut-and-Shoot. Because of the boom in western tourism all communities have had to adjust, and not always gracefully. Great shifts have taken place in lifestyles, attitudes, cultural tenacity, governance, and principles of land use.[58] A very successful and currently active case of balancing resource protection with development is the Jefferson County Open Space Program along the Front Range of the Rocky Mountains, west of Denver. Since its initiation in 1971 it has fostered preservation of 50,000 acres of open space land and historic sites, protected vegetation and wildlife habitat, and established many parks. This case is testimony to effective adjustment to development and environmental change through local action.

An aid in understanding this local area backwash from development, including tourism, is to group emerging and often conflicting constituencies into several categories. Tourism promoters tout the economic benefits regardless of the negative impacts. More and more development becomes a public good. Environmentalists are often polarized against all development, such as for timber harvest, extractive industries, destruction of wildlife habitat, and urban sprawl. Governmental resource management agencies vary in their policies on tourism land use. Some encourage outdoor recreation development while others foster wilderness protection. Not to be overlooked are the western Native American populations. They view land and its use generally not as an economic commodity but within their own cultural beliefs and traditions. The many issues of assimilation into dominant societal patterns have become even more complex over the years. Added to all these categories are the diehard traditionalists who adhere to past rugged individualism and resent all newcomers, especially tourists.

A critical common denominator for all these constituencies is the land. Western geography had everything to do with the past and continues to dominate the future. Preoccupied with exploitation over many decades, these lands have been worshipped, admired, abused, and defaced. At the same time that new tourist business has been an economic boon to many western communities, they now face new and difficult challenges. Little consideration was given to the finite quality of land.

The Interstate Highway system and expanded air travel not only created a new market demand for tourist services but also changed tourist geography. Interstate roads often killed established tourist businesses when communities were bypassed. Masses of automobiles, RVs, and tour busses have glutted community streets, pushing pedestrians away, converting downtown into touristy shops, and often eroding the social context of the community. Slow to react to these many impacts by tourism are the elected officials who represent local taxpayers and often have a limited understanding of the many physical and political results from tourism growth.

Sustainability of Place

For both resident and visitor populations of the West, the sustainability of place is essential. For today's functioning system of tourism, communities fulfill a critical place role, more than they ever did before. All travel modes have termini at cities. Cities contain a great number of travel attractions, such as convention centers, trade centers, sports and entertainment arenas, cultural and historic attractions, festivals and events, homes of friends and relatives, and basic travel services and infrastructure. Virtually all of these are amenities important to residents as well.

The concept of sustainable community is not a mere philosophical overlay; it is a political, social, economic, and physical necessity for tourism as well as local quality of life. If this fact is accepted and action implemented, several new programs may be required. How communities handle and recycle waste may require improvement, not just for aesthetics but for economy. How communities guide land use for visitor and resident activity may need revision and even implementation of new policies and programs. The several aspects of the community's infrastructure, such as water quantity and quality, police, fire protection, traffic control, and lighting, are as important to visitors as to residents. Urban sprawl and the flight of business from downtown are of concern to both tourists and local citizens. Beatley and Manning have studied sustainable community development in depth and refer to it as *The Ecology of Place*.[59] They cite especially significant new examples in the West as containing features of sustainability: Laguna West housing in Sacramento; Suisun City, Silicon Valley, San Jose, Richmond City, and Mountain View in California; Boulder, Colorado; and Portland, Oregon. Communities that implement policies of sustainable development have fewer negative impacts and instead provide positive results for residents and visitors alike.

From a tourism perspective, rivalries among neighboring communities are often a major deterrent for sustainability. Often they share area amenities, resources, and access. Unless these communities cooperate there can be land use degradation, water pollution, traffic congestion, and other impacts that bridge jurisdictional boundaries. Unfortunately, once the scenic beauty of an area is gone, this asset can be restored only with new investment in design and landscape change.

For much of tourism, restoration is a better option than allowing older development to deteriorate. The place quality of location is often so strong that recycling, especially for historic sites, is a desirable option. Sustainability of communities is influenced greatly by several external factors: policies of distant tour operators, changes in air access, and, for international travelers, changes in monetary exchange rates, as well as internal factors such as land use controls, development ethics, and tradition of environmental viability.

Some observers have put forth the concept of "limits of acceptable change," an idea well suited to growth adaptation of tourism to communities.[60] This concept is an admission of potential negative consequences of tourism growth, both physical and social. Such concern over the negative side often creates polarization between developers and residents. This situation begs the introduction of conflict resolution, moving on toward planning and management that can resolve issues. Acting as a catalyst for this function is an appropriate role for landscape architects and has been utilized in many instances as cited throughout this book. This process brings opposing forces together to take positive steps toward resolution: clarify issues, research information, create alternative solutions, and finally agree upon an acceptable solution.

Another approach to tourism's expansion in communities, according to tourism researchers, has been the application of exchange theory. For example, there may be a threshold beyond which the local quality of life is perceived as eroding, suggesting the halt to any more tourism expansion. This process can help resolve sociopsychological issues as well as concerns over the environment. Resident response to tourism development may follow a sequence of embracement, tolerance, adjustment, and withdrawal.[61]

This author has contended that communities generally have three options as they look toward tourism growth opportunities.[62] One option is *prohibition*, complete refusal to any more tourism growth. Because of the popular conception of tourism as positive economic impact with no pitfalls, this option is seldom implemented. To do so would require rigorous land use control, seemingly contrary to the religion of free enterprise. But today there are hints of curtailing sprawl and even demarketing of tourism where capacities are being exceeded.

A second option, most frequently used, is *capitulation*, accepting any new development anywhere, and with no constraints. Any proposal for a new hotel, restaurant, or attraction is accepted with no consideration of how well it is adapted to existing location or capacities of transportation, water supply, waste disposal, policing, and fire protection. The result is usually a chaotic pattern of development that is less than satisfactory for either tourists or residents. Unfortunately, this has dominated western tourism development.

A third option, just beginning to be implemented, is *planned adaptation*. This option does not refuse the potential for tourism development but rather gives it some studied guidance. Here the community studies land resources, existing infrastructure, market trends, and adaptation to the local area. This option requires leadership, input from tourism planners and designers, and involvement of publics to be impacted and those developers best able to implement plans.

One researcher has proposed the use of a Downtown Tourism Impact Scale (DTIS) for guidance on decision making.[63] This scale measures behavioral and attitudinal perceptions of residents regarding adaptation of downtown to tourism. A refinement of this approach would encompass not just downtown but all components of the supply side of tourism: attractions, transportation, services, information, and promotion. The purpose would be to obtain the public reaction and guidance for how each component can best be developed locally. Increasingly, over several decades, techniques and practices have been available in the West to reduce negative impacts of tourism.

This review of community change in the West offers mixed conclusions. In the beginning decades of tourism the commercial drive toward satisfying a new travel demand brought new life to many communities. But when a massive tourism growth wave is combined with new population by the millions, the undertow places great stress on the environment and upon the community's ability to cope. These changes have now produced a complicated array of issues, an extraordinary challenge of connectivity, and search for common ground for western tourism.

The Governed West

Because the West in the frontier period was dominantly public domain, it fell to a variety of public agencies, federal and state, to manage this vast region. Throughout this period of 70 years, agencies such as the Bureau of Reclamation, Bureau of Land Management (BLM), US Corps of Army Engineers, FS, and NPS have inherited custody of millions of square miles of territory. Although recreation and tourism were not specifically identified as responsibility at the turn of the century, new regulations of the General Land Office in 1902 did provide for permitting uses such as for sanitariums and hotels, especially at locations of mineral springs.[64] But, according to Chief Gifford Pinchot of the newly formed FS in 1905, these land uses were incidental to the main purpose of economic utilization of forests. Sustainable development of activities, projects, and tourist facilities was not then a part of government policy.

National Park Service

The NPS grew out of many years of political debate, starting with the establishment of Yellowstone National Park in 1872 and ending with its own autonomy as a federal agency in 1916. Because it is a governmental agency it is subject to the annual whims of Congress and many constituencies throughout the country. In spite of the many outside pressures from year to year, the NPS has performed an amazing role of keeping the park areas in reasonably good shape for these many decades. Although erosive forces have taken their toll, the basic resource assets of the parks remain intact. This is testimony to the dedication and professionalism of park staff who have held fast to basic resource management principles in face of changing politics and spectacular increases of visitors.

From the very beginning of the national park movement, landscape architects have been major players in policy as well as design. Founder of the profession of landscape architecture, Frederick Law Olmsted, is credited with language of the National Park Act of 1916 that encompassed resource protection as well as public use.[65] In his mind these two functions, often cited as conflicting, were actually compatible. In spite of anticipated impacts on resources by visitors, he believed a visiting public would support parks because of their visits.

Because the scenic values of the first national parks were so important, the first director of NPS, Stephen T. Mather, consulted landscape architects such as Frederick Law Olmsted, Jr. and others for advice on planning in order to perpetuate natural aesthetics. By the 1920s landscape architects such as Daniel R. Hull and Thomas C. Vint and others were major forces in the planning of national parks.

The American philosophy and practice of landscape architecture was influenced greatly by the vast and undeveloped open space of the West and the opportunities for major parks. Designers of this period were influenced also by predecessors such as Andrew Jackson Downing. His landscape gardening designs that emphasized land forms and plant materials were prototypes for extensive park design of forest areas and natural resources of the US. Today these principles would be labeled sustainable because resource protection was essential and yet compatible with human use. Landscape architects of this period were developing a philosophy directed heavily to design with the objective of scenic enhancement and appreciation.

However, large masses of public use and their land planning were not translated into NPS planning. Large outdoor gatherings for fun and entertainment and the need for crowd control were not new even in 1872 when Yellowstone National Park was established. Even before the turn of the century, Coney Island was extremely popular. The St. Louis World's Fair of 1904 demonstrated many lessons of planning and design for masses of visitors. It seems strange and short sighted that it has taken over eight decades for many resource managers to recognize that handling masses of visitors is part of their responsibility. The public use dimension, a major policy statement in the enabling act of national parks in 1916, has paled in significance compared to the biological protection dimension.

Because the first travelers were wealthy, there was response by park leaders in the form of high-scale lodges located directly within the parks. This beginning of visitor services of food and lodging should have been a clue to the need for establishing full-service communities adjacent to parks rather than within them. The environmental mess that tourists were creating was beginning to be recognized as early as 1916 in Grand Canyon National Park when the ugly sounds, sights, and odors of trash, steam engines, mules, and offal had become offensive. The issue of planning for visitor service continues to be a challenge for park planners and managers.

Because the management of the parks has been dominated by foresters and biologists, their training and interests became primarily resource protection, one major mandate of the NPS. However, an equally important mandate was and continues to be public use. Because management of masses of visitors was outside the training and interest of park managers, it has been difficult for them to accept this role. They had wished it would go away. At a tourism–park conference in the 1980s, a national park superintendent was heard to quip, "You guys want to bring more people into the parks. My job is to keep them out!" Fortunately such an exclusive policy was not mandated and has not been followed by all managers, but it suggests a major resistance on the part of some for the handling of visitors.

Related is the issue of services desired and needed by visitors. It seems appropriate to this author to ask the question: Why wasn't it clear from the very start of the NPS in 1916 that visitors would desire and need services such as interpretation, transportation, lodging, food, and even souvenirs and entertainment? Even though the agency saw its role primarily as resource protection, it held a responsibility for planning for visitor services even if not on their land. For a nation founded in a market economy and free enterprise it should have been obvious that at entrances to parks there must be service communities. Such communities would have their own autonomy, providing governance for needed infrastructure of power, water, waste disposal, police, and fire protection. Private enterprise would be free to establish a diversity of businesses to meet a variety of market needs, from luxury to economy.

But it didn't happen. Instead, NPS in 1916 made a decision of monopoly for services within the park, a decision that would not provide a diversity of market need nor allow free enterprise to be free because of many architectural and policy decisions on products and services. These businesses, called concessions, have experienced a rocky history throughout these many decades. Politically it seemed difficult for NPS staff to reach out to nearby communities to provide needed planning guidance for a visitor need equal to resource protection.

There seems to have been three main reasons why the concept of service community nearby was not promoted from the beginning. First, and perhaps the greatest, was a *philosophical* barrier. National parks were created by government on the belief that this decision was in the interest of the public weal. This policy was then taken literally to mean that private enterprise was incompatible with park purposes. Throughout the history of the park and recreation movement in this country, their professionals have held a dim view of the private sector: that profit making taints public welfare and is evil. This attitude seemed a paradox because only through a thriving economy from business and industry did government agencies receive their financial support. Profit making can be called a social good because it provides products and services for the public, creates jobs and income, builds wealth for future investments, and covers the expenses of doing business, such as insurance, maintenance, and costs of retooling or relocating to meet market changes and employee fringe benefits. In early parks, however, policy did yield to the wealthy tourists of the time by providing monumental hotels and high-class service within the parks. Even though a system of concessions has continued for many years, the philosophical dichotomy remains between many public resource agencies as well as the NPS.

A classic example was the bitter controversy over Walt Disney Enterprises' proposal to build a major ski resort in the Mineral King Valley on national forest land northeast of Bakersfield. It was a beautiful area surrounded by mountains with snowfall adequate for winter sports. The issue started when ski enthusiasts from Los Angeles sought development in the San Gorgonio area. The Sierra Club, a strong environmental advocacy group, opposed this location as being too near and recommended the Mineral King Valley.[66] Later, Disney gained governmental support to build an access road to the proposed site, removing the first obstacle for development. Immediately, the Sierra Club reversed its position and began a vigorous fight to stop the project. Their lawsuit was carried all the way to the Supreme Court. It became clear that the issue was not even environmental because Disney's plans contained many safeguards. It was simply a hate for private enterprise, resorts in particular. This is an example among many over these years where philosophical differences kept governmental park policy in conflict with commercial development.

A second difference has been *aesthetics*. It must be admitted that the design of service business in the 1920s was less than aesthetically pleasing. Each individual owner could and did build his own structure as he pleased, often creating a garish hodgepodge of land development. For national park administrators, they preferred a uniform rustic or naturalistic design theme for all structures within and near the park. Log and stone became the standard building materials, even for signs, shelters, steps, toilet facilities, and overlooks as well as lodges. Such a policy of appropriateness was another wedge between private enterprise and public park management. From the NPS perspective, this aesthetic difference translated into belief that all commercial development was bad even though well-designed services to visitors were needed and could be supplied by private enterprise.

Much of the objection to commercialism stems from the often ugly and cluttered gateway communities to national parks and forests. These communities are responding to the demands of travelers with tourist development. But too often there is little building or land design guidance. The businesses serve a needed function but there is no excuse for shoddy and poorly planned tourist business zones. Professional designers and planners have been available to produce functional and yet beautiful development but have not been asked often enough to prevent eyesores. Apathy on the part of community leaders and officials, not the need for commercial facilities, is the cause of the problem.

A third impediment for working together with private enterprise was a park policy of *geographic homogeneity*. This policy was derived from governmental ownership and that all land within the boundaries of parks should be given uniform treatment. The error of this policy stemmed from the geographic fact that all land within the park is *not* the same—there may be mountains, valleys, forests, deserts, and a great variety of ecosystems. The boundaries were set by Congress and seldom reflected boundaries of ecosystems. Some areas were devoid of rare or fragile environmental assets and could be given the landscape label of "hardened sites." Such sites might support buildings without any threat to natural forces. Some sites are closer to highway access and therefore require priority consideration for visitor services. Not all land characteristics are homogeneous throughout the park, demanding different land use and management policies for different areas, but this has been difficult to accomplish in the West.

To a degree, these differences in land characteristics within park boundaries were recognized in the early 1920s when park designer Thomas Vint advocated two major zones: a nonvisitor wilderness zone and a development zone. Although not clearly stated, this policy was followed in the preparation of the master plan for Mt. Rainier National Park in the 1920s.[67] Sustainability was a major concern by designers Frank Kittredge, Ernest Davidson, and Thomas Vint. A later plan (1940) delineated three zones for this park: wilderness, research, and developed. Developed areas were located primarily along access roads and at gateways.

Several planners have advocated park plans that place a full-service community at the edge of the park, shuttling visitors into and out of the resource area on terms agreeable to NPS. Landscape architect Richard Forster, in a publication of the International Union for Conservation of Nature and Natural Resources in 1973, described the merits of a two-zone concept whereby the resource core remains inviolate while services are provided in a peripheral zone.[68] He expanded this into a three-zone pattern with an outdoor recreation zone in between the resource and service zones. In all his recommendations, he emphasized the need for management to monitor use to determine limits of carrying capacity. In *Vacationscape* five concentric zones are advocated: protection zone, wildland low-use zone, extensive outdoor recreation zone, tourist use and interpretive zone, and a service community zone.[69] Because aesthetics of commercial tourism establishments seemed to be of greatest concern to environmentalists, this problem should be solved if communities engage in better planning and design. These concepts have been slow to be adopted in practice in the West as elsewhere.

At the same time that the West benefited from federal and state governmental land use protection measures, local residents have increasingly felt disenfranchised.They have been concerned about policies and management practices that impact them for which they have very little influence.This concern is well founded not only on governmentally managed lands but also on private property. For example, the 1960s saw a flurry of federal acts that were environmentally well meaning but again moved decision making to Washington, DC. Here are some of these acts that impinged on local land use for tourism: Wilderness Act, 1964; Land and Water Conservation Fund Act, 1965; Concession Policies Act, 1965; National Historic Preservation Act, 1966; Clean Air Act, 1967; Wild and Scenic Rivers Act, 1968; National Trail System Act, 1968; National Environmental Policy Act, 1969.[70] It is no wonder that conflict between local residents of the West and governmental agencies has increased dramatically over the last seven decades.

It has taken a long time for each side to recognize the value of coordinating development. It wasn't until the Reagan administration and the appointment of Priscilla Baker as director of tourism within the NPS that some communication began. The first among her several conferences of tourism and national parks was held in 1988 in Biloxi, Mississippi. At this conference, the author shared a panel with the superintendent of Dinosaur National Monument, who was to relate his great success of working with tourism interests in nearby communities. He had received more funding, volunteer assistance, and greater support for resource protection. However, when queried about his anxiety before making his presentation, he answered that his regional director was in the audience who demanded that he stay in his park! Because of the leadership by Baker in this period several conferences brought tourism and park interests into new beginnings of understanding.

Early on, the NPS recognized that the automobile would have to be dealt with. In 1919 a new function was added, the establishment of a Landscape Architecture Division with Charles Punchard as its head.[71] The purpose was to accept the new trend of automobile penetration of park lands but to design roads to capture outstanding vistas and scar the landscape as little as possible. He provided scenic turnouts for visitors to stop, view, and photograph scenes. Images from these points became the fodder for a flood of postcards, travel brochures, and tourist snapshots.

But because of unprecedented growth in popularity, park areas began to show wear and tear in the 1980s. It was clear that millions of automobiles and people were overwhelming NPS management. This situation stimulated many outcries by citizens and organizations. Among these was a list of threats identified by writer Robert Cahn in 1982.[72] His list included inappropriate development on adjacent lands, pollution of waters, mineral exploration and extraction, logging nearby, and air pollution. The 1980s were filled with pronouncements severely critical of park management. In his "Un-Greening of Our National Parks," traveler and author Michael Frome accused Secretary of Interior Watt's policies as encouraging nonprofessional management, poor preservation of resources, and lack of private sector initiatives to save public funds.[73] Frome went further by advocating a 10-point plan for rescuing the dilapidated park system: 1) limit visitor use, especially for outdoor recreation; 2) close Yellowstone for a 5-year rejuvenation; 3) protect solitude areas; 4) reduce automobile access; 5) reevaluate all concession businesses; 6) deemphasize lodging within parks; 7) buy up in-holdings; 8) provide full funding for parks near urban areas; 9) list and restore pertinent historic sites; 10) adopt a strong clean air policy.

Further to the park dilemma and needed changes was the NPS's own "State of the Parks Report—1980" prepared by Gary Gregory, natural resources manager.[74] In his report were included the following major threats to the integrity of the park system: 1) aesthetic degradation; 2) air pollution; 3) physical removal of resources; 4) encroachment by exotic animals; 5) physical impacts from visitors; 6) water pollution; and 7) impacts from park operations. These are just a few of the overt expressions of concern over the growing pressures on the nation's parks, a critically important spin-off from gargantuan growth in tourism.

By the 1990s it was clear that threats to the western parks were not being dealt with, internal organization was not functioning well, and personnel morale was at an all-time low. Partial remedy took place with three major changes in national park policy. The first was the Native American Graves Protection and Repatriation Act of 1990 that required Indian remains found in archaeological digs to be returned to cultural descendants. The second, "Science and the National Parks," asked NPS to base policy more firmly upon scientific study. The third was the result of a conference focused on a 75-year review identifying needs for change in NPS policy, "The National Parks for the 21st Century—The Vail Agenda." Six major strategy recommendations evolved from this conference: 1) stronger resource protection; 2) access and enjoyment without impairment of resources; 3) education and interpretation on park values; 4) proactive rather than reactive leadership; 5) engagement in scientific research; and 6) increased professionalism within the organization. Ideal as these may be, only time will demonstrate how effectively they will be implemented in the face of so many political, traditional, and constituency constraints.

As the volume of visitors has increased over these several decades, the issue of people movement, especially private automobiles and tour buses, has become increasingly critical. But the people dimension has not been given as high a priority as resource protection by NPS, even though both purposes were clearly stated in the original mandate of 1916. Increasingly, groups outside the bureaucracies have pushed for better solutions. As a consequence, in November 1997, the issue of automobile congestion within western national parks was addressed jointly by Secretary of the

Interior Bruce Babbitt and Secretary of Transportation Rodney Slater.[75] Three parks were singled out for "demonstration" improvements: Zion, Yosemite, and Grand Canyon.

For Yosemite, major improvements in handling masses of tourists were influenced greatly by recommendations of the Wilderness Society in 1992. The General Management Plan of the NPS in 1980 called for many changes but by 1990 none had been implemented. The Wilderness Society then picked up on this issue and launched a major project to stimulate action. Funding was obtained from True North Foundation and assistance was obtained from national park staff, state and local governments, and professional designers and planners. Together they made a detailed study of the problem and developed a recommended solution. Among the landscape architects were Ervin H. Zube, Peter Dangermond, Jr., Bobi Lyon, John Reynolds, Donald M. Fox, and Louis G. Alley.

This Yosemite plan made several specific recommendations for improved transportation: 1) establish periphery parking; 2) provide intermodal transfer to the Valley Shuttle System; 3) expand bus linkage with anchor cities; and 4) establish visitor services at the periphery of the park.

The US Forest Service

Of equal significance throughout this history of the West is the role of the federal FS. Considering that the major policy focus of this agency has been on timber production and watershed management, it should not be surprising that it took many years to accept landscape architects as staff members for site design of facilities and services. Even so, a thorough history of the early years of the FS proves the influence of site designers as early as 1919 when landscape architect Arthur H. Carhart was hired by the Rocky Mountain District.[76] Already, recreational uses of FS lands had shown the need for good site planning of trails, picnic areas, and campgrounds. Carhart's first major outdoor recreation plan was for sites in the San Isabel National Forest in southern Colorado. A local nonprofit organization, San Isabel Public Recreation Association, an outgrowth of the Pueblo Commerce Club, helped him on this project by raising funds. This concept of collaboration between a private organization and the FS for recreation planning became a model for other communities.

In spite of this successful precedent, further expansion of landscape architects in FS was not accepted by the administrators. Carhart remained the pioneer and fostered the enlargement of the standing committee on parks of the American Society of Landscape Architects (ASLA). But the animosity between NPS and FS made it difficult to convince Congress of the need for landscape architects in both services. Miffed by the lack of support, Carhart resigned the FS in 1922 and joined the private practice firm of McCrary, Culley, and Carhart. For several years, recreation planning responsibility fell back on foresters who frequently obtained advice from leading landscape architects, such as Frank Waugh and H. R. Francis. Throughout the history of park and tourism development in the West, landscape architects have played a major role. Landscape architectural educator David C. Streatfield describes their function as, "Their work is rooted in a profound respect for and celebration of place. Their designs interpret place as bio-physical processes, and as intertwined acts of cultural will and transformation."[77]

In President Roosevelt's New Deal era, in collaboration with the Civilian Conservation Corps (CCC), the FS greatly expanded its role in recreation and engagement of landscape architects. An example was the hiring in 1935 of landscape architect Ernest E. Walker to head the Washington recreation staff and the commissioning of Albert D. Taylor, then president of ASLA, to make a study of recreational problems and needs in national forests. Soon the more primitive development of sites was modified to include more modern facilities such as showers and flush toilets. Some even surpassed the NPS in design quality for winter sports areas, resorts, organization camps, and other tourist facilities, so that by the end of World War II the FS was a leader of recreation facility design and development. By 1939, the FS had developed 23,000 camping units and 30,000 family picnic units.[78] Thus, recreation development policy became of equal significance in the FS to past forest development.

Today the FS has difficulty in coping with its many issues other than maintaining forest crops. Intensive visitor use, especially within a day's drive of metropolitan centers such as Los Angeles, San Francisco, and Sacramento, presents many traffic, parking, trampling, and litter problems, similar to those experienced by the NPS. A second challenge is law enforcement such as reported in 1996 by Mitchell: over 7000 felony-level violations, including growing marijuana, timber theft, and even murder.[79] Some growers of cannabis patrol their lands with machine-gun-equipped guards. Rescue from remote areas, cliffs, and snowbound mountains also adds to the management issues of forest managers. Arguments over balancing timber production with resource protection continue.

The West now contains an abundance of lands now declared as part of the National Wilderness Preservation System that resulted from a Congressional Act of 1964. Among other stipulations, that act defined such places as "where the earth and its community of life are untrammeled by man, where man himself is a visitor who does not remain." These lands include portions of areas managed by the FS, NPS, National Wildlife Refuge System, and the BLM. Because these wilderness areas are open to limited tourist use, such as for hiking, backpacking, camping, and canoeing, some areas of more intense use show signs of litter and environmental erosion. To reduce such negative impact, some managers require quotas and advance reservations by lottery, an attempt toward sustainability. Many advocates today cite the need for even increased public use to foster greater awareness and support for resource protection. However, tour guide companies object to present controls as being too restrictive. Arguments continue over this issue.

A study of campers in a western wilderness area revealed major difference of opinion of impact between users and managers—the latter much more critical of environmental damage.[80] The camper groups included hunters, horse riders, Scouts, hikers, and Sierra Club members. All were much more tolerant of areas with bare ground, perhaps because they needed space for tents and separation from others. Research of four national forests in California revealed that managers still adhered to past values of resource protection rather than visitor use.[81] Their actions toward outdoor recreation could be characterized as reactive rather than proactive. Even though this was not necessarily federal policy, it was the way it was carried out on the land.

The governmentally owned and managed West is a powerful and complex force of greater significance to tourism today than ever in the past. And it is on these lands that environmental degradation continues to challenge managers.Among the issues today are soil compaction and erosion of vegetation from trampling, motorboat discharge pollution, desecration of cave sites, excessive deterioration of resources from off-road vehicles, and threats to wildlife habitats.[82] Resource managers are increasingly aware of these impacts and are implementing new control measures.

Environmentalism

Dams: Blessings or Blunders?

Today, millions of visitors to the West enjoy the abundance of thousands of acres of water for boating, water skiing, fishing, swimming, and aesthetic appreciation from shoreline development of resorts, condominiums, and campgrounds. Significant is their water for drinking, cooking, bathing, washing, and toileting. Millions of others who live there are grateful for ample water supply, not only for their living but also for industry, agriculture, and other economic development. It is because of the absolute essentiality of water to tourism in the West, today and in the future, that the following discussion of river impoundments and dams is presented.

Although environmentalists have questioned the wisdom of dams in the West for generations, only now is there a serious groundswell of antireservoir sentiment. Perhaps the earliest controversy surrounded San Francisco's proposal in 1905 to dam the Tuolumne River in Yosemite, creating a huge reservoir in the Hetch-Hetchy Valley. Ever since, dam proposals have been met with cries of opposition, citing major upsets of natural and cultural resources. These reservoirs have often inundated villages and valuable prehistoric artifacts, introduced water seepage into adjacent land, and destroyed needed niches for wildlife and plants. All these resources are valuable for many tourism developments that cannot be substituted by water recreation.

Probably the most comprehensive documentation of this bittersweet history is *Cadillac Desert*, researched and written by Marc Reisner.[83] He clearly describes how the blessing of water in the West has come at a very high price, not merely in economic terms but in cultural and natural resource losses as well. He traces early beginnings of trouble because the Homestead Acts stimulated settlement of the West with no regard to the blatant fact that the land had limited water sources. Then, after the fact of settlement of millions of people, they immediately expected others to provide them with needed water. This great demand then stimulated engineers, public agencies, and politicians to employ "chicanery, subterfuge, spies, bribery," and strategies filled with deceit. No matter the methods, tourism as well as settlement today is at the mercy of water resource managers who are just beginning to recognize the difficulty of reaching water sustainability. One of the many difficulties is the huge mass of mud silt that has accumulated behind dams that now puzzles everyone regarding its removal.

Indication of today's concern is revealed in the headline, "Deconstructing the Age of Dams," that appeared in the October 27, 1997 issue of *High Country News*.[84] The many ill effects of dams and reservoirs are now being identified, not only by nature lovers but also by agricultural producers and biologists. Slated for deconstruction are dams such as in Butte Creek, Elwha River, White Salmon River (Condit Dam), Similkameen River (Enlo Dam), Lower Snake River, and Colorado River (Glen Canyon Dam).

Of course, this issue is highly controversial. Very vocal are proponents and opponents for the concept of removing the Glen Canyon Dam on the Colorado.[85] Proponents argue that even more water would be available if the 30 points of dams and diversions on the Colorado were removed. The Lake Powell reservoir has a shoreline greater than the West Coast and loses about a million acre-feet of water due to evaporation and seepage into surrounding sandstone. And some claim that some day this will be an academic issue when the reservoir silts up and the river flows over the dam. As of 2003, a 4-year devastating drought has lowered the level of Lake Powell to almost one half, which is a major threat to water supply for Las Vegas and Los Angeles. Political and legal conflicts are increasing, often called "water wars." Environmentalists, however, are delighted to see renewed exposure of Indian rock art and ruins, caves, natural arches, and beaches.

Tourism's future lies in the hands of those who seek compromise and resolution to this critical issue. The huge economic value of tourism's dependence upon western water resources may disappear if a solution is not found.

Disneyfying America

Because the focus of this book is on environmental issues, it should not be construed that tourism encompasses only those activities based on cultural and natural resources of areas and regions. The last seven decades have demonstrated phenomenal growth of created attractions, especially in the West. It is no exaggeration to credit Disneyland, built in 1952, as the incubator of major theme parks in America. So-called amusement parks with roller coasters and midway scams were well entrenched in the East many years before. Electric parks, accessible by trolley car at the edges of major cities, were popular at the turn of the century. Then, as automobile and air access grew, these parks waned in popularity. The concept of a full-blown entertainment complex did not appear until the Disney innovation.

The major breakthrough of Disneyland was a new standard of business. Up to this point, commercial recreation had a shady reputation—socially degrading activities, poor maintenance, and not suited to families. The leisure pundits adhered to the belief that only government-sponsored recreation could be wholesome, of high quality, and suited to young people and families.[86] The creative mind of Walt Disney and his planners, designers, and managers changed all this. Disneyland demonstrated for the first time that entertaining and worthwhile activities, high standards of safety and maintenance, and socially valuable objectives could be accomplished in a commercial operation. Design elements included mass people movement, spatial walkways and plazas, attractive structures, colorful landscape use of plant materials, integrated signage and guides, and fanciful activities. The hallmark of management was not only courtesy but also impeccable maintenance. Lore states that no cigarette butt remained on walks longer than 20 seconds.

Throughout the West, over these seven decades, an outstanding array of man-made attractions has multiplied tremendously. Even so, attractions founded in natural and cultural assets continue to provide major travel appeals of the West.

Toward Sustainability

As tourism grew to be a major economic and social power in the West, so did friction mount between the public sector, a huge land owner in the West, and the private tourism sector, a producer of $120 million and employer of some 2 million people a year. The concerns between public and private sectors involved are more critical in the West than elsewhere. Ninety-three percent of all federal lands in the US are found in the 13 western states where travel and tourism constitute a major economic force. Nearly one third of all people employed in the US tourism economy work in the 13 western states.

In the 1990s, a major effort of conflict resolution was launched with the establishment of the Western States Tourism Planning Council (WSTPC).[87] This represented the first multistate consortium on cooperation between the public and private sector of tourism. The agreement of purpose among many representatives and several innovative summit meetings demonstrated a new understanding of tourism issues in the West and challenges for improvement. This huge and productive effort was facilitated by the tourism consulting firm of Hunt and Hunt (Kristin DeNure Hunt and John Hunt).

The Memorandum of Understanding (MOU) of WSTPC included 13 federal agencies and 7 western state government tourism offices (Alaska, California, Nevada, New Mexico, Oregon, Utah, and Washington). The purpose was to coordinate tourism goals among the many federal and state tourism agencies and to foster travel and tourism in America's West with the following goals:

- Enhance the experience of visitors.
- Support the long-term economic viability of the travel and tourism industry and communities that serve these visitors.
- Protect and, where appropriate, restore the natural, environmental, cultural, and historical resources that are the foundation for tourism.
- Respect the needs and values of those people who live in the West.

More specifically, the WSTPC believes that the following purposes represent the best interests of people in the West at the same time tourism is fostered:

- Optimize the contributions of tourism to economic prosperity and full employment.
- Make tourism universally accessible and ensure that present and future generations are afforded adequate tourism and recreation resources.
- Contribute to personal growth, health, education, and intercultural appreciation of the western states' geography, natural and human resources, history, and ethnicity.
- Encourage the entry of international visitors by positioning the western states as a major international destination, to enhance understanding and goodwill.
- Promote quality, integrity, authenticity, and reliability in all tourism and tourism-related visitor services.
- Preserve the historical, natural, and cultural foundations as part of the west-

ern states' development, and ensure future generations an opportunity to appreciate and enjoy the West's rich heritage.

- Ensure the compatibility of tourism with other western states' interests and values.
- Encourage the development, collection, analysis, and dissemination of data to measure accurately the economic and social impact of tourism to and within the western states to facilitate planning, marketing, and management in the public and private sectors.
- Harmonize, to the maximum extent possible, all government activities in support of tourism with the needs of the general public and the tourism industry.

It should be noted that a plank in this platform relates to sustainable tourism development by recognizing the need for perpetuation and interpretation of the natural and cultural resource foundation of tourism in the West. Further to this cause are the following statements of the WSTPC:

- Federal resource and land management agencies are dedicated to the wise use of the nation's natural and cultural heritage. Encouraging responsible travel and tourism on public lands is an appropriate way of furthering the public's knowledge, awareness, and appreciation.
- Travel and tourism to federal lands provide significant, economic, educational, and recreational benefits for the United States in general and the rural communities in particular. Federal lands provide an important component of the travel and tourism opportunities which appeal to traveling United States citizens and international visitors.
- The visitors and the rural areas of the United States can be better served by the cooperating organizations working together toward mutually developed objectives. These objectives contribute to the sustainability of local communities through the protection and management of America's public land heritage now and in the future.
- The federal government and the states will work in a coordinated manner to develop and distribute information, and participate in community activities that enhance understanding about the use of travel and tourism to diversify the economic base of the community.
- The western states and the federal government will provide educational programs that enhance their ability to manage travel and tourism activities in balance with sustainable management practices in order to protect natural, environmental, historical, and cultural resources.

An example of the work of the WSTPC is the Western Summit on Tourism and Public Lands: Seeking Common Ground. The Summit was a gathering of tourism industry leaders and the key stewards of the West's public lands. The goal of the Summit dialogue was to identify and prioritize issues, generate strategies, and create coalitions to enhance the delegates' ability to meet the needs of users of public lands and contribute to the sustainability of communities through the protection and management of the West's public lands.

Delegates to the Summit included federal and other high-level public land managers and policymakers and key leaders from both the public and private sectors of the tourism industry from the 13 western states. This included the states of Alaska, Arizona, California, Colorado, Idaho, Hawaii, Montana, Nevada, New Mexico, Oregon, Utah, Washington, and Wyoming. In attendance were national leaders from the US Departments of Agriculture, Interior, and Transportation, and the Environmental Protection Agency, the National Governors Association, the Western Governors Association, Native American organizations, and national tourism organizations.

The objectives of the Summit were: create a lasting environment that promotes cooperation and mutual understanding about the opportunities and roles of public lands and tourism in fulfilling human needs, and develop strategies and actions that will help to meet the needs of people and contribute to the sustainability of local communities through the protection and management of America's public land heritage now and in the future.

The Summit was convened because:

1. The interests of the tourism industry and public land management are becoming increasingly intertwined.
2. America's public lands hold a unique position in the heritage of the West.
3. Many of the places held in public trust are among the prime destinations for travel and recreation.
4. These western lands and the values they hold define the spirit of America.
5. The mission of public lands stewards is to provide human use and preserve resources.

Delegates presented information and led discussions on many topics pertinent to tourism in the West, such as policies of federal agencies and the opportunities for better cooperation between the public and private sectors. Identified were five major tracks: *improved public access, infrastructure, fees and management, the environment*, and *information and marketing*.

An insightful summary of the interlacings between public and private entities and the need for sustainable tourism development was the 14-page White Paper on Environment (1996). Among the issues cited as grounds for closer public-private resolution are: air pollution; water shortage; threats to resources from mining, timber harvest, oil production; erosive grazing and agricultural practices; population dispersion and urban sprawl; and destruction of viewsheds. These combine to create concern over capacity issues and tourism glut. Recommended are creative partnerships between tourism and resource management to resolve these issues and work together toward sustainable development. Much of the burden for this action falls on tourist business enterprise that generally is not vocal regarding the necessity for sustainable development.

Emphasized in this paper is the need for stronger cooperation between public and private interests to reduce air pollution from all sources and especially from industry that impacts public agency land used by tourists. Tourism must take the lead in water conservation. And, very important, is better study and implementation of capacity control. The private sector has an obligation to assist public agencies in applying visitor capacity limits before erosion of resources takes place. Special effort must be applied to visitor activities of high impact levels, such as snowmobile and cross-country skiing, hiking, power water craft, and backcountry activities. Businesses have the opportunity to provide interpretation that will orient visitors on best behavior and acceptance of rules. Sustainability must be measured environmentally, economically, and socially.

Other papers issued by WSTPC include: Infrastructure on Public Lands, Access to Public Lands, Financing & Fees on Public Lands, and Marketing Information on Public Lands. The creation of this important council with its representation from both public and private sectors of tourism in the West is the most innovative and important event ever in the history of tourism in this region. The mechanism for future sustainability is there. Only future action will demonstrate sincerity of purpose in the West.

Future Challenges

If tourism in the West is to survive as it should and perhaps even grow, this review of the past suggests several challenges facing designers, planners, and developers. Over these seven decades great strides have been made in the development of tourism. Transportation, tourist facilities, and the level of sophistication have increased dramatically. The travel impediments encountered by the early autocampers have now been removed. The diversity of tourist experiences has proliferated way beyond those of the 1920s. Communities and residents of the West have come to enjoy the gigantic increase in employment and local economies. For all these benefits from growth of tourism, credit must be given to leaders and practitioners from all three development sectors: governments, nonprofit organizations, and commercial enterprise.

As one looks to the future of tourism in the West, however, there are several very important challenges facing the *enablers*—planners, designers, and developers—in their attempts to restore paradise. Unless these are dealt with, the future does not look bright. From this examination of tourism in the West, major conclusions are offered in Chapter 11, "Meanings for the Future," including: *assets, constraints*, and *opportunities for better future development.*

The next several chapters focus on four major western destinations, their past and present as well as difficulties and opportunities for new sustainable development. Because of mass production of the automobile, a massive boom in western travel occurred in the 1920s. As a case example of this period, a narrative of the author's autocamping trip throughout the West in the summer of 1929 is woven into the remainder of the book. Many lessons can be observed from this examination of the evolution of tourism in this bountiful region.

Endnotes

[1]Many books and journals are now available: Ritchie and Goeldner, *Travel, Tourism, and Hospitality Research*; Kahn et al., *VNR's Encyclopedia of Hospitality and Tourism*; Gee et al., *The Travel Industry*; Keiser, *Principles and Practices of Management in the Hospitality Industry*; Spears, *Food Service Organizations: A Manage-*

rial and Systems Approach; Lockwood, *The Management of Hotel Operations*; *The Cornell Hotel and Restaurant Administration Quarterly*; *International Journal of Hospitality Management*, and many others.

[2]See Lindberg and Hawkins, *Ecotourism: A Guide for Planners & Managers*; Boo, *Ecotourism: The Potentials and Pitfalls*; Wight, "The Greening of the Hospitality Industry: Economic and Environmental Good Sense," in *Tourism: State of the Art*; Smith, "The 4-H's of Tribal Tourism"; and other sources on topics of adventure, nature, and cultural tourism.

[3]Dann, G. M. S. (1996). *The Language of Tourism—A Sociolinguistic Perspective.* Oxon, UK: CAB International.

[4]Gunn, C. A. (1972). *Vacationscape: Designing Tourist Regions* (1st ed.). Austin: Bureau of Business Research, University of Texas (and 3rd ed., 1997). See also Burkhart and Medlick, *Tourism: Past, Present and Future*; Young, *Tourism: Blessing or Blight?*; Matheison and Wall, *Tourism—Economic, Physical, and Social Impacts*; and Mill and Morrison, *The Tourism System*.

[5]Dulles, F. R. (1964). *A History of Recreation: America Learns to Play.* New York: Appleton-Century-Crofts.

[6]Bryant, V. M., Jr. (1992). In Search of the First Americans. In *1993 Yearbook of Science and the Future* (pp. 8–27). Chicago: Encyclopedia Britannica.

[7]Kittredge, W. (1996). *Who Owns the West?* San Francisco: Mercury House.

[8]Stewart, E. C., & Bennett, M. J. (1991). *American Culture Patterns* (p. 114). Yarmouth, ME: Intercultural Press.

[9]Schmitt, P. J. (1969). *Back to Nature* (p. 4). New York: Oxford University Press.

[10]Jackson, J. B. (1994). *A Sense of Place, A Sense of Time* (p. 155). New Haven: Yale University Press.

[11]Schmitt, ibid.

[12]Schmitt, ibid.

[13]Donovan, F. (1968). *Wheels for a Nation* (p. 159). New York: Thomas Y. Crowell.

[14]Mann, W. A. (1998). Journals of Early Explorers in the Pacific Northwest. In *1998 Annual Meeting Proceedings* (pp. 168–171). Washington, DC: American Society of Landscape Architects. Also: unpublished paper by Mann, "Capability Brown in the Wilderness: Late Eighteenth Century and Early Nineteenth Century Travelers and Their Writings About the Trans-Mississippi Landscape" (1998). Athens, GA: University of Georgia.

[15]Etulian, R. W. (1974). The Historical Development of the Western. *Journal of Popular Culture, 7*(3), 719.

[16]Steinbeck, J. (1945). *The Red Pony* (p. 129). New York: Viking Press.

[17]Belasco, W. J. (1979). *Americans on the Road: From Autocamp to Motel 1910–1945* (p. 27). Cambridge: MIT Press.

[18]Grosvenor, M. B. (1979). A Long History of New Beginnings. *National Geographic Magazine,* 156(1), 18–29.

[19]Pomeroy, E. (1957). *In Search of the Golden West—The Tourist in Western America* (p. 203). New York: Alfred A. Knopf.

[20]Wood, D. B. (1987). Fold Up the Zagelmeyer, rev the Model A. *Christian Science Monitor*, September, 25.

[21]Lee, R. F. (1974). *Family Tree of the National Park System* (pp. 10, 18–19). Phila-

delphia: Eastern National Park & Monument Association.

[22]Many sources cite the principle of encouraging visitors to national parks, including: Ise (1961), *Our National Park Policy—A Critical History*, Baltimore: Johns Hopkins Press; Runte (1979), *National Parks and the American Experience*, Lincoln: University of Nebraska Press; and Sax (1980), *Mountains Without Handrails*, Ann Arbor: University of Michigan Press.

[23]Kaufman, H. (1967). *The Forest Ranger: A Study in Administrative Behavior.* Washington, DC: RFF Press.

[24]Holbrook, S. H. (1947). *The Story of American Railroads* (p. 11). New York: Bonanza.

[25]Bryant, K. L. (1974). *History of the Atcheson, Topeka, and Santa Fe Railway* (p. 329). New York: Macmillan.

[26]Garrison, L. A. (1983). *The Making of a Ranger* (p. 210). Salt Lake City: Howe Brothers.

[27]Jackson, J. (1979). *Man and the Automobile* (pp. 34, 80). New York: McGraw Hill.

[28]Dulles, F. R. (1959). *America Learns to Play* (p. 315). New York: D. Appleton-Century.

[29]Kihlsted, F. T. (1990). The Automobile: A Bridge Between Engineering and Architecture. In *Roadside America* (pp. 3–14). Ames, IA: Iowa State University.

[30]Coates, L. (1981). Ford's Plan Still Suits to a 'T.' *Enroute*, November, 26.

[31]Sedgwick, M. (1971). *Veteran and Vintage Cars in Color* (p. 124). New York: Viking Press.

[32]*Automobiles of America.* (1974). Motor Vehicle Manufacturers Association of the United States.

[33]Wagar, R. (1933). *Golden Wheels* (p. 140). Cleveland, OH: Western Reserve Historical Society and Cleveland Automobile Club.

[34]Owen, C. (1979). *The Grand Days of Travel* (p. 199). Exeter, England: Webb & Bower.

[35]Tobin, G. A. (1974). The Bicycle Boom of the 1890s: The Development of Private Transportation and the Birth of the Modern Tourist. *Journal of Popular Culture, 7*(4), 835.

[36]Quaife, M. M., & Glazer, S. (1948). *Michigan: From Primitive Wilderness to Industrial Commonwealth* (p. 288). New York: Prentice-Hall; and Chater, M. (1928). Michigan, Mistress of the Lakes. *National Geographic,* 53(3), 269–325.

[37]Concrete Highways and Public Improvement. *State Highway System, 13*(4), 84.

[38]Hugill, P. J. (1982). Good Roads and the Automobile in the United States 1880–1929. *Geographical Review, 72*(3), 327–349.

[39]Lamb, D. (1993). *A Sense of Place* (p. 83). New York: Times Books.

[40]Partridge, B. (1952). *Fill 'er Up!* (p. 81). New York: McGraw-Hill.

[41]Rowsome, F., Jr. (1965). *The Verse by the Side of the Road* (p. 89). Brattleboro, VT: Stephen Greene Press.

[42]*Scenic Byways.* (p. xiii). (1988). Washington, DC: US Department of Transportation.

[43]Ewald, W. R., Jr., & Mandelker, D. R. (1971). *Street Graphics: A Concept and System.* Washington, DC: American Society of Landscape Architects Foundation.

[44]Horowitz, A. J., & Hansen, E. R. (1985). *Assessment of Land Use Impacts on High-*

ways in Small Urban Areas. Milwaukee: Center for Urban Transportation Studies.

[45]General Guidelines. (1993). *Transportation for Livable Communities* (Notebook for regional conference). Washington DC: Federal Highway Administration.

[46]*Surface Transportation Policy Project ISTEA Year Four.* (1994). Washington DC: Surface Transportation Project.

[47]Handy, S. (1995). Highway Blues: Nothing a Little Accessibility Can't Cure. *STPP Progress,* 5(1), 3-5.

[48]Dittmar, H. (1996). Sustainable Travel and Tourism. *STPP Progress,* 6(6), 1.

[49]Keillor, G. (1996). In Search of the Real America. *STPP Progress,* 6(6), 3-4.

[50]Maguire, M., & Vespe, F. (1996). Handling the Double-Edged Sword of Tourism. *STPP Progress,* 6(6), 5.

[51]Thompson, E., & Kientz, R. (1998). *TEA-21 User's Guide.* Washington, DC: Surface Transportation Policy Project.

[52]Belasco, W. J. (1979). *Americans on the Road: From Autocamp to Motel, 1910-1945* (p. 138). Cambridge: MIT Press.

[53]Moon, W. L. H. (1982). *Blue Highways.* Boston: Little, Brown.

[54]Andrews, J. J. C. (1984). *The Well-Built Elephant and Other Roadside Attractions.* New York: Congdon & Weed.

[55]Hirsch, J. (1988). Old-Fashioned Sin in a New Light. *New York Times,* July 20.

[56]Jakle, J. A., & Sculle, K. A. (1996). *The Motel in America.* Baltimore: Johns Hopkins Press.

[57]Jakle & Sculle, ibid, p. 132.

[58]From *Community in the West,* S. Tchudi (Ed.). (1999), Nevada Humanities Committee, including "Mending Babel's Walls," by A. B. Inoue; "Building and Subverting Community in the New American West," by A. Chiaviello; and "Walt Disney vs. Wallace Stegner," by E. Bateman. Other sources include *Who Owns the West?* by Kittredge; *Wilderness Preservation and the Sagebrush Rebellion* by Graf; and *Where the Bluebird Sings to the Lemonade Springs: Living and Writing in the West* by Stegner. Also: Closed to Development, by Kathi Grider, *Landscape Architecture,* 93(5), 44.

[59]Beatley, T., & Manning, K. (1997). *The Ecology of Place.* Washington, DC: Island Press. Among the many references to the West as a special place: *A Sense of the American West* (1998), J. E. Sherow (Ed.), Albuquerque, NM: University of New Mexico Press, and *Magic Lands: Western Cityscapes and American Culture After 1940* (1992), J. M. Findlay, Berkeley, CA: University of California Press, Berkeley.

[60]Sidaway, R., & van der Voet, J. L. M. (1993). *Getting on Speaking Terms: Resolving Conflicts Between Recreation and Nature in Coastal Zone Areas in the Netherlands: A Literature Review and Case Study* (p. 309). Wageningen, Netherlands: Agricultural University.

[61]See also: Getz, D. (1986). Models in Tourism Planning: Towards Integration of Theory and Practice. *Tourism Management,* 7, 21-32. Milman, A., & Abraham Pizam (1988). Social Impacts of Tourism on Central Florida. *Annals of Tourism Research,* 15, 191-204. Ap, J., & Crompton, J. L. (1993). Residents' Strategies for Responding to Tourism Impacts. *Journal of Tourism Research,* 32(1), 47-50.

[62]Gunn, C. A. (1997). *Vacationscape: Developing Tourist Areas* (3rd ed., p. 7). Washington, DC: Taylor & Francis.

[63]Snepenger, D. J., et al. (1998). Is Downtown Mainly for Tourists? *Journal of Travel*

Research, 36(3), 5–12.

[64]Tweed, W. C. (1980). *Recreation Site Planning and Improvements in National Forests 1891-1942.* Washington, DC: Forest Service.

[65]A very comprehensive history of involvement of landscape architects in the National Park Service is *Wilderness by Design* (1998), by E. Carr. Lincoln: University of Nebraska Press.

[66]Sax, J. (1982). *The Compromise Called For* (p. 63). In E. Connaly (Ed.), National Parks in Crisis. Washington, DC: National Parks & Conservation Association.

[67]Carr, ibid.

[68]Forster, R.A. (1973). *Planning for Man and Nature in National Parks.* Morges, Switzerland: International Union for Conservation of Nature and Natural Resources.

[69]Gunn, C. A. (1988). *Vacationscape: Designing Tourist Regions* (2nd ed.). New York: Van Nostrand Reinhold.

[70]Dilsaver, L. M. (Ed.). (1994). *America's National Park System—The Critical Documents* (p. 269). New York: Rowman & Littlefield.

[71]Cahn, R. (1982). The Conservation Challenge in the '80s. In E. Connaly (Ed.), *National Parks in Crisis* (p. 11). Washington, DC: National Parks & Conservation Association.

[72]Cahn, ibid.

[73]Frome, M. (1982). The Un-Greening of Our National Parks. In E. Connaly (Ed.), *National Parks in Crisis* (pp. 25–54). Washington, DC: National Parks & Conservation Association.

[74]Gregory, G. (1982). State of the Parks 1980: Problems and Plans. In E. Connaly (Ed.), *National Parks in Crisis* (pp. 75-90). Washington, DC: National Parks & Conservation Association.

[75]News release from the US Department of Interior, "Transportation, Interior Announce New Partnership to Handle Transportation Needs in Parks for 21st Century." November 25, 1997.

[76]Tweed, W. C. (1980). *Recreation and Site Planning and Improvements in National Forests 1891-1942.* Washington, DC: Forest Service.

[77]Streatfield, D. C. (1995). Regionalism in Landscape Design. *Process Architecture,* 125, 20-21.

[78]Tweed, op. cit., 26.

[79]Mitchell, J. G. (1997). On the Line of Fire: Our National Forests. *National Geographic,* 191(3), 58–87.

[80]Shelby, B., & Shindler, B. (1990). Evaluating Group Norms for Ecological Impacts at Wilderness Campsites. In J. Gramann (Ed.), *Proceedings—Third Symposium on Social Science in Resource Management* (pp. 65-67). College Station: Texas A&M University.

[81]Dennis, S. (1990). Outdoor Recreation Policy on Four Southern California National Forests. *Proceedings*, ibid., 165–166.

[82]Goudie, A. (2000). *The Human Impact on the Natural Environment* (5th ed.). Cambridge, MA: MIT Press.

[83]Reisner, M. (1986). *Cadillac Desert: The American West and Its Disappearing Water.* New York: Viking.

[84]Reisner, M. (1997). Deconstructing the Age of Dams. *High Country News*, Octo-

ber 27, p. 1.

[85]Joseph, P. (1998). The Battle of the Dams. *Smithsonian*, November; States Compromise Over Water Use (2000), *Bryan-College Station Eagle,* 126(209), 1. Booth, W. (2003). Environmentalists Seek to Drain Glen Canyon Dam. *Bryan-College Station Eagle,* 129(117), B4. Hettena, S. (2003). Water Wars Could be in West's Future. *Bryan-College Station Eagle,* 129(124), B3.

[86]Dole, C. E., & Twardzik, L. F. (1973). *Elements of Park and Recreation Administration* (3rd ed.). Minneapolis: Burgess.

[87]Excerpts drawn from many WSTPC documents available from www.wstpc.org as of August, 20, 2000.

Chapter 2

1929 Western Tour: Part I

The following eight chapters alternate between the 1929 western autocamping journal and historical assessment of tourism planning and development over seven decades in the following destinations: northern Arizona, northern California, Oregon and Columbia River, and Yellowstone. The purpose is to assist the reader of today (likely two generations removed from the travel of the 1920s) to gain insight into similarities and differences and especially the challenges for future planning and development of tourism in the West.

This chapter encompasses the motivations and preparations for the Gunn family's western autocamping trip as well as a log of each day's travel from Michigan through northern Arizona. Of interest to the reader is comparing this narrative with the description of tourism change and challenges for this destination as described in Chapter 3.

The Gunn Family Setting

This personal anecdote by the author is presented to provide a case study of an autocamping tour of a typical family in the 1920s. This narrative is the author's elaboration of the terse log notes made on the trip. Review of this narrative illustrates the significance then of what we now call the overall tourism system, the role of the environment, the beginnings of development, and the precursor to the concept of sustainability. To set the stage, a brief description of family status and preparations for the trip are offered here (and in first person).

The Gunn family in 1929 could be placed in the modest lower middle class and consisted of my mother, Lila (48), a housewife and a one-time teacher; father, Fred (50), formerly a carpenter and teacher, then postal dispatcher; my brother, Lauren (17), and myself (12). The simple two-story box-like home had been built by dad in about 1910 and was located outside Grand Rapids, Michigan, just a mile from the small town of Grandville.

My father, like thousands of others in suburban and rural America, was caught up in an insatiable desire to travel. In spite of limited family funds from a job of about $1,000 a year, he bought his first car, a Model T Ford, in 1921 and took the family on a camping trip to Michigan's Upper Peninsula. Later, in a new 1925 Model T Ford, a

The Gunn autocamping experiences began as soon as we had our first automobile in 1921. Our next trip was in a 1925 Model T Ford to Michigan's Upper Peninsula. Here we are camping in a farmer's field near Stevens Point, Wisconsin, where we learned to cope with mosquitoes. At left, holding the tent rope, is the author.

similar but expanded trip was taken. I remember that the lean-to tent attached to the side of the car was insufficient to keep mosquitoes out. It was on this trip that only a crude map offered minimal guidance, causing dad to comment, "I think we've gone north far enough and we had better turn east." Rural roads then were merely two gravel or sand tracks with grass between, and when my brother and I needed to relieve ourselves we merely lifted up the floor boards.

By 1929 dad had dreamed of a more major trip, one throughout the West. For this adventure he had saved up a total of 6 weeks of vacation and sick leave. As plans were being laid, there must have been considerable stress between my mother and dad. It had been only a year or two since the house was wired for electricity so we could have a bathroom inside with running water. A new hand-fired coal furnace had been installed to combat Michigan's winters. To forego these marvelous conveniences for 6 weeks of primitive camping, sleeping on the ground, cooking on a camp stove, and enduring extremes of heat and cold, must have been a severe test of the marriage. But stoicism never allowed this to show.

Now that I am an octogenarian, images of waterfalls, prairie dogs, bear, deer, wildflowers, mountains, and lakes obtained on our trip of 1929 are still clear to me. My many travels throughout the US and over a dozen foreign nations have never quite reached the memorable imprint of this camping trip to the West. Before this adventure, my world understanding didn't go much beyond my home territory near the little town of Grandville, Michigan. So, for the first time, and as a 12 year old, I learned about the differences and similarities of people and their settings—accents, ethnic groups, occupations, traditions, and local response to these new tourists invading their territories. Perhaps even more important was what this trip did to and for us as a family. This camping togetherness had its ups and downs. Our thrill of adventure, our arguments over travel plans, our mutual support of each other, the conflict and differences among us, but most of all our feelings of wellness and accomplishment after it was over are still stuck in my memory. Certainly, the speed, comfort, and convenience of travel today that offer so many more destination opportunities with ease are a tribute to our technical and scientific progress. But one wonders if the extra effort, difficulties, and stress of automobile travel in these early years may have added a dimension of richness that never can be duplicated in the future.

Retrofitting

Because autocamping became popular before auto designers knew about it, owners made many modifications to their autos. Dad was no exception. On several previous jaunts he had observed that most of these new travelers and their autos were ill-prepared for road travel. Gear was stored outside carelessly and often soaked in the rain or fell off the car due to poor tying. He vowed he would retrofit the new 1928 Model A Ford to avoid all these pitfalls. One must remember that this was long before vans and recreation vehicles such as motor homes were available.

Being a carpenter, he used the space between the bottom of the car doors and running boards to create storage boxes with hinged lids. These small cabinets stored

Typical autocampers of the 1920s, the Gunn family strikes a pose before our 1928 retrofitted Model A Ford. From left: mother (Lila), brother (Lauren), dad (Fred), and the author (Clare). In the summer of 1929 this was our home on wheels for a 6-week tour of 8575 miles from Michigan throughout the West.

canned goods, utensils, and many small necessities for camping. In this model of car there was a space of about 16 inches between the radiator and front bumper. A blacksmith was hired to shape iron bars to support a storage box in this space for pots, pans, and water pail. Cars then had no trunks so dad purchased a "Kari-Keen"[1] trunk that could be bolted to the rear. By lowering the metal lid, the storage space was tripled but then mother had to make an oil-cloth cover to keep out the rain.

This space contained our heavy canvas 9 by 12-foot umbrella tent and many of the larger items. Dad had purchased the tent at Coye Tent & Awning Company, Grand Rapids, for $35. The back seat was removed and layers of bedding served as a cushion. Even though this car had glass windows, as protection against rain, on hot days, and there were many, the open windows drenched us in dust, resulting in frequent wash-ups and fuzzy snapshots.

Even though these many features provided for weather-proof storage, one more concession to mother was required. She refused to sleep on the ground so dad bought a steel fold-up bed frame that made into a skimpy two-person bed about a foot off the floor of the tent. But this presented a storage problem, being 6 feet long and about 4 by 6 inches when collapsed. Again engaging the blacksmith, C-clamps were attached to the front bumper. The folded bed frame and the tent centerpole, weather-proofed when wrapped in a canvas bag, were then secured in this space. The proof of all this preparedness was that it worked for the entire trip. The only damage occurred when a bear in Yellowstone National Park pawed off the locks and hasps of one storage box and smashed open cans of fruit, but we always wondered how he could read the labels and not get vegetables.

Motivations

Our travel motivations were likely similar to those of most autocampers of the day. For some time, magazines had featured ads of train travel to the West. Tales from returning relatives and friends certainly provided plausible testimony. Without doubt the retelling of their experiences embellished greatly the photo album evidence. Sprinkled throughout these albums were snapshots of western wonders but usually dominated by smiling and happy travelers in the foreground, subtle proof of the ease and great joys to be derived from a western trip.

Another motivation may have been the anecdotes set down in 1910 in a 104-page booklet by my Uncle Joe (Dr. Joseph Heasley). The story of his trip, from Grand Rapids, Michigan, to Yellowstone and the West by train and carriage included enticing statements such as, "On all sides of us we have beautiful lakes and rivers filled with mountain and rainbow trout. . . . The rivers with their falls, cascades and rapids whose clear sparkling waters are filled with fish, add enchantment to the surrounding. . . . The forests are enlivened by the stately elk, the nimble deer and the sluggish and awkward bear."[2] For me, there may have been more prophesy than he realized when he dedicated this book to his nephews and nieces. His statement in the Preface read: "Should the opportunity so avail itself that you may have the pleasure to visit some of Nature's wonders, I trust that you may find them as I have tried to picture them to you." My first exposure to these wonders was on the 1929 automobile trip.

Reflection suggests another motivation by my parents—a broadening experience for "the boys," as Lauren and I were always referred to. This was an era when it was typical for parents to wish for their offspring a better life than theirs of the past. And so, even though we were of modest means, considerable denial and frugality gave us many of the "better things of life," such as taking us to concerts, lectures, and putting us through college, a first for our relatives.

We represented a mix of two other travel motivations. The new ability to travel long distances in your own personal vehicle created the "getting-there" type of tourist. The objective was to make the most miles per day and reduce stops to the minimum. Some days we actually made over 300 miles, a major accomplishment for the cars and roads then. A second type was the "see-and-do-the-most" tourist. Dad's itinerary had scheduled both types for our trip. At times we wanted to get to our next destination as quickly as possible, but based on his preinformation dad had scheduled in many destination objectives. After all, we were not in a race but rather on an adventure.

Our Autocamping Days

I think I know why nearly all of the 8575 miles were driven by my brother. Dad had learned to drive on a Model T Ford. It had three foot pedals: clutch, reverse, and brake. The transmission was ahead of its time using planetary gears. The clutch pedal went from high to neutral and to low gear as it was depressed. Spark (timing) and accelerator levers were conveniently mounted on the steering column. The right pedal, as now, was the brake. But the new Model A Ford had a clutch pedal and gear shift stick, never fully mastered by dad through the rest of his life.

By this time in dad's camping career he had developed a circus roustabout's routine. Each evening we would seek out a town near a selected campsite to purchase groceries for the evening meal and next day's breakfast because we had no refrigeration. He usually selected paid rather than the free public campsites because they were less congested and, as he put it, "kept out the riff-raff." Sometimes he used grassy sites beside filling stations or country school houses because they provided water and privies. Of course, we used the public sites in the national and state parks we visited.

Pitching and breaking camp were carried out with military precision. Each one of us had his own assignments. As soon as we found our site, my brother and I set up the camp stove for mother and pitched the tent. Dad was sent after water so the meal could be started. But due to dad's neighborly gregariousness, much time was absorbed comparing travel tales with other campers at the common well. There were exchanges of comments, such as: Where are you from? Which route did you take? Did you run into that horrible detour? How many flats have you had so far? Where are you headed? After Lauren was unsuccessful in his attempt to get dad and water, I was sent, and usually accomplished as little. But finally we would enjoy a fine meal, review our day's experiences, and make plans for the next day as the sun went down. Early bedtime meant early rising the next morning. After a quick breakfast, we took down the tent and stored all gear and were on our way within 1 hour of waking. Except for mother's internal thoughts, this routine did not seem a hardship and became an accepted tradeoff for the fun and enrichment of travel. Actually, we felt superior to our fellow campers who were less experienced and poorly prepared. Still, it must be remembered that this was long before aluminum tent poles, Velcro, light-weight camp chairs and tables, propane, polyethylene foam pads, poly/cotton sleeping bags, light-weight poly/canvas tents, nylon bags, pop-up tent frames, and foam-insulated coolers. About the only camping items that have carried over these seven decades are Thermos bottles and Coleman stoves and flashlights.

Travel Observations

My brother's engineering mind conceived of the need for keeping a log of this trip. Perhaps he was also influenced by reading the adventures set down in ship logs of early pirates. Because he was busy with all the driving, the task fell to mother, not too thrilled about the idea. However, in spite of rough riding she was able to jot down a cryptic list of roadside features of interest, miles traveled, clock times, car maintenance, and some of the humorous aspects of the trip. Along boring roadside scenery, often the Burma Shave sequence of signs would enliven our spirits: "Every shaver now can snore six more minutes than before, by using Burma Shave."[3] In light of today's travel, her notes offer a quaint and naive account of our impressions.

A dominant note in the log is an assessment of farming quality of the land, which of course came from their background but would not be typical of today's travelers unless they were farmers, ranchers, or agricultural scientists. Comments such as the following occur frequently: fruit country, vineyards, poor farming region, mushroom farm, fox ranches, combine drawn by 16 horses, much corn and wheat, potato fields, poor land with nothing on it, herd of black cows, cherry orchards, dry land farming, sheep, good crops, horses running loose, fields of head lettuce, irrigated land, orange groves, fig trees, and corn higher here than at home.

A regular entry into the log describes the ever-present plague of car trouble. The 29 flat tires are cited along with comment on the delays and distractions they caused. Typical of travelers of the day, we had our own tire repair kit containing inner tube patches, rubber cement, and "boots," large patches placed inside the casing for most stone bruises. Major blowouts required replacement of the tire and sometimes repair of the wheel rim. The many stops for adding radiator and battery water, oil, and gas, and lubrication jobs took time away from our sightseeing but were accepted as necessities of travel by car. In those days gas pumps were tall with a glass tank on top scribed with lines indicating gallons and fractions thereof. A hand lever was used by the attendant to pump gasoline from an underground tank up into the glass jar; then it slid by gravity through a hose and into the car. The fuel capacity was small and service stations were so infrequent in some stretches of the highway that extra planning was required to avert further time delays for rescue. It was clearly evident that the production of automobiles and their ownership had far exceeded the development of highways and car services. Testimony to the rugged construction of these cars, however, was that the only major breakdown on our trip was when brakes failed.

Because this trip was only 2 years after Lindbergh's spectacular flight across the Atlantic, airplanes and airports were novelties and were cited whenever we saw them.

Such a roadside scene hardly warrants any traveler interest today unless on a fly/drive trip and looking for the car rental return lot. In these 1920s, the principal airplane activity was using World War I surplus biplanes for showing off—barnstorming. Dare-devils would stand on the wings as the planes did barrel-rolls and loop-the-loops and fatal accidents were not infrequent. Passenger air travel was in its infancy. Intercity air travel had to wait for engineering and technical improvements that later led to the indestructible Douglas twin-engine DC-3 in 1936, followed by jet engines and much more rapid, safer, and the extremely popular air travel of today.

Very frequent entries are comments about road conditions, mostly bad. Mother jotted down many notes such as: detour 9 mi., poor roads, miserable road, very hilly, slow and long grade, boards laid on clay road to prevent sinking in when wet, lots of rocks, ford a dry river bed, held up for road work, and drove through fresh tar that took many hours of scrubbing with gasoline to remove. Oiled road surfaces represented the first major improvement over primitive dusty and muddy roads. Detours in those days were really rerouting along another route that often doubled the mileage. The many times that road conditions were mentioned bear testimony to how conscious we were of them and how states had not yet caught up with road travel demand.

Contrary to today's Interstate travel, in our log of 1929 there are many citations of cities and towns we passed through that became important for their attractions as well as for services. In Illinois, for example, the coal mines near Braidwood, Alton Limited train near Chenoa, a race car going 35 mph around a race track near Lexington, and a tree planted in honor of Theodore Roosevelt by Troop 28 of Bloomington became points of interest. A very recent innovation that caught our attention from the roadside was radio transmitters, such as for WIBW and WREN (Lawrence, Kansas), KDYL (Salt Lake City), and WSBT (South Bend). Of course, this was long before cars had radios.

But probably the most frequently cited roadside impressions were images of landscape beauty. Because our experience was very limited, we were already conditioned toward great expectations and were primed toward these observations. Some key log entries illustrate this dominance of our travel experience: many meadowlarks; sagebrush; yucca; Colorado blue spruce; beautiful blue, red, and yellow flowers in field; dramatic snow-capped mountains; pinion trees and nuts; extensive forest; Douglas fir; wild roses and red lobelia; beautiful white poppies; blackberries in bloom; the most wonderful canyon yet; yellow lupine; 11 kinds of flowers; oyster beds; heron; daises; redwoods; cascades; waterfalls; and deer and bear. These brief comments may seem trite today as the population is saturated with even more grandiose and scintillating adjectives in travel advertising—magazines, newspapers, direct mail promotion, radio, TV, Internet, and guide books. But, in the context of the times, these were very important to us, as they were for most of these new touring tourists.

As a personal note, there is no doubt in my mind that this trip, even at the impressionable age of 12, had a subliminal influence on my 50-year career of study, teaching, consulting, and writing about tourism. Our family's grounding in nature and our appreciation and enjoyment of it certainly has had a lasting impact on my concern over environmental issues, especially as applied to tourism.

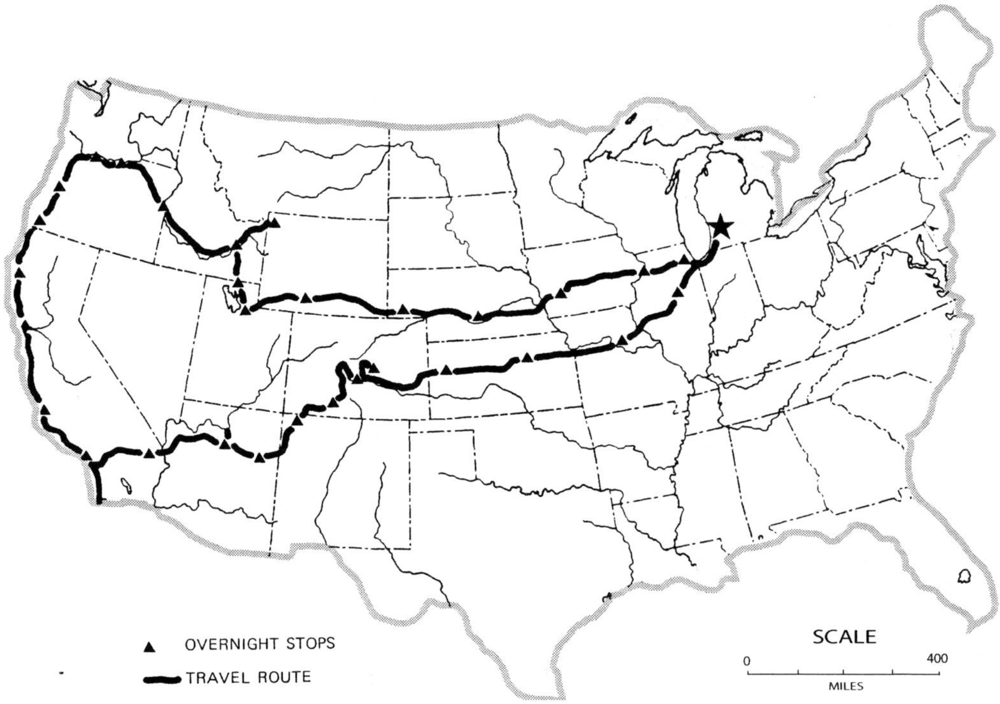

Illustrated is the route and overnight stops on the 6-week Gunn autocamping tour of 8575 miles from Michigan throughout the West in 1929. Campsites included service stations, fields, schoolyards, parks, and commercial campgrounds.

Our spirits were a mixture of hope and fear as we readied ourselves for this 6-week travel adventure to the West. Never before had we seen mountains, vast forests, bears, the Pacific Ocean, or deserts, nor had we ever ventured away from home that long. This was to be the most extended trip ever for our family of four. The trip traversed 16 states from Michigan to the Pacific coast and return, a total of 8575 miles, and was accomplished in 45 days. We camped every night with exceptions in Canon City, Colorado, and Pasadena, California, when we stayed with friends and a few nights when the weather drove us into a tourist cabin. Perhaps more meaningful statistics include having 29 flat tires and wearing out a set of brakes and three sets of tires, normal tradeoffs for camping trips then.

Because travel was slowed by low car speed and bad roads, a 300-mile day was a major accomplishment. Based on what we called our shorter shakedown camping trip to Washington, DC, in our brand new Model A Ford during the summer of 1928, dad had gained experience on preparing the itinerary for the western trip. His predictions were correct because we met all our travel objectives. It took us 5 days to get to our first destination, Colorado. After 3 days sightseeing around Colorado Springs we spent days 9 to 13 traveling out of Colorado, through a corner of New Mexico and to the major attractions of northern Arizona. Days 14 to 18 brought us through the heat of southern California and to Pasadena. A quick trip to Tijuana (to say we had been in Mexico) and back along the California coast northward to Portland, Oregon, took days 19 to 23. We traveled along the Columbia River and on to Pocatello, Idaho, on days 24 to 29. Yellowstone National Park and Salt Lake City were our objectives from days 30 through 35. It then took us days 36 to 41 to cross Wyoming, Nebraska, and Iowa and on to La Grange, Illinois, where we rested with relatives for days 42 through 44 before returning home on the 45th day.

The Journey Begins

Following is the author's reconstructed daily log of the Gunn family's autocamping journey in the summer of 1929 in a Model A Ford, from Michigan through northern Arizona. Other legs of the autocamping trip are presented in Chapters 4, 6, and 8.

On **June 29** we leave the house at 6:30 am and reach La Porte, Indiana, by noon, a distance of 151 miles. Points of interest we observe along the way include: Kalamazoo River, grape vineyards, fruit orchards, a mushroom farm, cross first state line, stop to fix our trouble light, and make our own picnic lunch. A detour of 3 miles then takes us to Valparaiso, passing fox ranches, and then at the state line of Indiana-Illinois had a flat tire. We travel poor roads through Chicago Heights and stop for gas in New Lennox, 17.9 cents a gallon. A stop in Joliet is needed for directions to Bloomington. For the rest of the day our observations included: good farming areas, high overpass over railroad, coal mines, a racing car, and arrived in Bloomington at 6:15 pm. Here we get groceries, buy postcards, and pitch camp.

At 6:45 am, **June 30**, we turn our watches back 1 hour, break camp, and travel further into Illinois, passing extensive plains and a site of brick kilns and corn higher that at home. We join Route 66 and after Atlanta observe pretty countryside, short telephone poles, and cross Kickapoo Creek, a name that gives us a hint of Native American occupation of this place in history. Then, after Lincoln we see a 70-foot coal mine operation of the Brewerton Coal Company, the court house where Lincoln first practiced law, some pottery kilns, and again are impressed with the prevailing landscape of plains. We stop to check battery and get gas, see a huge grain elevator, cross Wolf Creek and Sangamon River, and become increasingly uncomfortable with the rising temperature. As we pass through Springfield we see the Illinois Watch Company, the capital building, and then move out into more plains. By now we have left Route 66 and traveled on US 36, Ill 10, and back to US 36.

A flat bottom river steamer, *The Bold Eagle*, a back wheeler, takes us across the Illinois River in 25 minutes. We encounter several detours and the land becomes very hilly, making the car work very hard. At 35 mph we pass many other cars. At Louisiana we stop to buy postcards and eat a picnic lunch on this very hot day. Soon we pass the colorful Stark Nurseries and continue through very hilly land. At Bowling Green the land begins to flatten out again and we are surprised to find a short and narrow strip of concrete road. Then, over a hard clay road, boards had been laid to keep cars from sinking in the mud when it rains. On these rough roads our speed slows to 15 mph. We camp near Midway, Missouri, after a day of 278.4 miles.

On **July 1**, with rain threatening, we break camp at 5:30 am and between intermittent rains we are glad to travel on pavement for awhile and soon stop for gas. After crossing the Missouri River we stop for restrooms at Boonville and soon stop for breakfast indoors. Soon after traveling over hilly roads the rain begins to pour very hard as we pass through Sweet Springs—rain drops so large we think the pounding will break the windshield. As we approach Kansas City we see a Chevrolet factory, the Hotel La Salle, immense railroad yards, Loose Wiles Biscuit Company, and soon our noses tell us we are passing Armour's Meatpacking Company.

After crossing the state line into Kansas, we observe many beautiful churches in Kansas City. Soon, out of the city, we stop for gas and are impressed by the rolling hills of good farming country. Highlights of our roadside sightseeing are potato fields, the campus of the University of Kansas at Lawrence, WREN radio station, and after crossing the Arkansas River we have lunch. We are lucky again to have some good paved road and pass a sign admonishing travelers "Don't Park on the Slab." At Topeka we see the capital building and soon are happy to see sunshine again and stop for some ice cream. After passing great stretches of wheat fields we come to Manhattan where we are told this is the geographical center of the United States and the first capital of Kansas. After nearly 2 hours of nothing but wheat fields as far as we can see, we find a camp site at Abilene. The camp is on low land abundant with fire flies. Lauren captures a jar full that sparkles with light.

After fixing a flat tire we break camp on **July 2** and move on through Lindsborg, LaCross, and Dighton. We can't seem to find a campground anywhere and finally camp free in a rancher's field at Leoti, after a day of 269 miles. This is the first we had heard the slow western rancher drawl and found it quite funny and interesting. Along the way we had observed not only much wheat but also 45 dead rabbits, many mead-

Blasting road tunnels through rock, such as this 1929 example near Royal Gorge, Colorado, was a major engineering accomplishment in the 1920s. Of course, rocks sliding from the mountainsides contributed to many flat tires from stone bruises.

owlarks, salt wells, and many mirages, all new experiences for us. As we stop to fix a tire we see a humorous sign, "Dr. Blades, Physician, Surgeon."

On **July 3** we break camp at 6:50 am after a good rest. The remainder of the travel across Kansas is dominated by sparsely settled plains that change into desert with sagebrush and yucca. We reach the state line by 8:05 am. Then the landscape becomes even more deserted as we travel on through Towner and Eads. No houses are visible for at least 2 miles and we are taken back in history when we actually see a covered wagon. At Sugar City we wonder where the name came from, get gas, and stop for lunch. Here we see some irrigated land and the first trees we've seen for over 200 miles. By the time we reach Ordway we are at an elevation of 4700 feet and begin to see mountains in the distance. At Pueblo we have another flat tire but are excited about our first glimpse of Pikes Peak to the north. After fixing the tire and filling the radiator that seems to want to boil out the water we cross the Arkansas River, observe an oil tank farm and several cherry orchards. We are weary after our travel of 247 miles and at Canon City are delighted to see friends from Grandville, the Secords, who are kind enough to house us as we camp beside their house.

July 4 and 5 are spent sightseeing, led by our friends, the Kings and Secords. We thrill at the sight of the Royal Gorge, eat along the Arkansas River, climb a mountain, drive along the Skyline Drive, drive through a long tunnel, and hear many tales about mining in the region. Mr. King worked with mining around Leadville. Brother Lauren was sick for a while but recovered. Here mother takes advantage of the hospitable facilities and washes and irons clothes.

[*Throughout the trip, we were dressed well, an extraordinary accomplishment considering dusty roads and roughing it in the many settings. Dad was always in a white shirt and often wore a tie. And this was long before deodorant antiperspirants. There was no such thing as casual camping attire. Perhaps the significance of this is the need to carry your home customs with you wherever you go. The pleasure of meeting friends at destinations is as significant today. This enables the traveler to gain better insight into the attractions of the area. The feeling of security to be in the hands of someone you trust cannot be ignored.*]

Before we head west dad wants to make a loop drive north and return to see the area around Colorado Springs. So, on **July 6**, we leave our friends, stop for battery water, and head into the mountains, giving our Ford a good workout. We are thrilled and awed by the mountains, rocky gorges, open space, Colorado blue spruce trees, and old gold mine operations. As we stop for gas in Victor at an elevation of 9717 feet we see the Victor mines and the log notes that we are in "sombrero country." By the time we reach Cripple Creek it is lunch time and we shiver with cold. On our way again, now in Pike National Forest, we pass through a long tunnel, and the Clyde settlement. The beautiful blue, red, and yellow roadside flowers help ease our tension over the spiraling mountain road where we peek over the edge and see the curvy road we just went over. At Rosement we top a 10,000-foot crest. Then, after Duffields, the narrow road takes us through tunnel after tunnel as we work our way down slowly past Fairview where we soon encounter toll gates. After paying a fee of $1.00, "well worth the price," we are taken through another tunnel that frames the most spectacular hotel we have ever seen, the Broadmoor. After passing North Cheyenne Mountain, Garden of the Gods, Balanced Rock, and Steamboat Rock, we travel over some very rugged terrain hoping to see Green Mountain Falls, but were disappointed. Finally, weary after a sight-filled day, we find a pleasant camp site at a filling station in Colorado Springs and enjoy a good night's rest.

[*In our appreciation of the many aesthetic spectacles we probably had only cursory understanding of who owned and managed them. At that time we knew that the conservation ethic had been responsible for establishing national parks and monuments.*]

Sunday, **July 7**, we are able to get a key made to replace one we lost and also get one of the storage clamps mended. At Florence we have a flat tire—punctured by a big nail. We find a garage that is open and get it fixed. Also discovered that because of the elevation, we had boiled out much of the water and needed to refill the radiator. It begins to rain very hard as we travel in the Sangre de Cristo Range. We drive over Poncha Pass at 8945 feet elevation. We pass snow-capped mountains on our left all along the way to Saguache at 7748 feet elevation. We make sure we record these elevations because we will need to tell our friends back home about these mountainous adventures. Then we pass irrigated croplands and arrive at a pleasant campground at Del Norte on the bank of the Rio Grande.

A beautiful morning on Monday **July 8** greets us as we break camp and stop to buy a water bag for future use across the desert. This seemed silly at the time because we had no idea regarding its function for cooling in the heat. Here we realize that we

Pausing after a rigorous climb to 10,000 feet over Wolf Creek Pass in our Model A Ford, dad stops to let the car cool down and to snap this view of grazing sheep in the nearby meadow.

have traveled 1854 miles from home, an unbelievable accomplishment for us. We know we are really in the West when we see a cowboy. Along the way we are pleased to see pinion pine, white poppies, wild roses, lobelia, blue columbine, and yellow lupine. Now in the Rio Grande National Forest we soon cross the Rio Grande at South Fork and pass by fields of head lettuce, the S. Fork Ranger Station, Trout Creek, and begin again a mountain climb on a twisty one-lane road with the mountain on the right and deep valley on the left. The sign "The Gift of God is Eternal Life" is not very reassuring at this point. Then the many sights and scents tell us we are immersed in Nature's finest—Douglas fir, yellow pine, wild roses, red lobelia, blue and lavender flowers—and we pick some beautiful white poppies. Now in the San Juan Mountains, we go by Park Creek Camp Ground Cabins in the Woods, blackberries in bloom, Box Canyon with deep gorge and rushing water, and at Lake Fork we believe this is the most wonderful canyon yet.

Not far from the snow line (and this is July!) we see wild iris, blue columbine, yellow lupine, and after eating some wild strawberries found enough snow to make a few snowballs. Dad then takes a picture of valley, sheep, and stream way below. Our trusty Ford then struggles up to about 11,000 feet at Wolf Creek Pass. Here mother counts 11 kinds of wildflowers as we stop to catch our breath and see a beautiful waterfall along gulches 3000 feet below. On the mountainside there was evidence of an avalanche that had ripped out a ribbon of trees. There seemed to be waterfalls everywhere as we drove on past Wolf Creek Campground, West Fork Ranch, to Pagosa Springs where we stopped for a welcome trout dinner at 75 cents each. After the Great San Juan River we buy gas at the exorbitant price of 30 cents a gallon.

After crossing the Denver–Rio Grande Narrow Gage Railroad we take a picture of Chimney Rock and move on through many ranches, often seeing prairie dogs alongside. Soon we encounter a series of road detours, the first since Missouri, and as we cross the Animas River we reach out and slap a cow on the behind. After crossing the state line into New Mexico we seek out a campsite at Aztec but even though we are travel weary we visit the Aztec Ruins, after dad cashes a check. These ancient ruins plunge us back in history, many rooms, burial chambers, main kiva, and several others where a central fire is surrounded with worship space. A museum helps us understand this ancient civilization as we view pottery, woven apparel, and war implements. As a naive 12 year old, I imagine I am surrounded by the ghosts of these ancient people.

July 9 then finds us on our way across the northwest corner of New Mexico. Here we see Shiprock and know we are in the Navajo Indian Reservation as we move on to Gallup. After a rain shower we cross the state line into Arizona. Moving along Route 66 we observe that the desert geography of this corner of eastern Arizona is in great contrast to the mountains around Colorado Springs. Rather than a "welcome" sign, we are greeted by an arch over the highway inscribed "You are now leaving New Mexico, come again." Pink rock cliffs flank us on the right and on the left we see Indians tending sheep. We pass the little village of Lupton, named after railroad man, G. W. Lupton. After a fruit quarantine inspection, we are initiated into desert storm country, first sunshine, then sand storm at Houck, followed by pouring rain. We aren't aware of potential quicksand hazards and ford several creeks where the water is over a foot deep, threatening our well-enclosed storage compartments. A note in mother's log, "Who said the desert was hot and dusty?" We are glad that our Ford pulls us through several treacherous mud holes. At Navajo we get gas and finally the sun comes out. Because a flooded river denies us access to the Petrified Forest, we have to be satisfied with display of specimens at a tourist information lodge. Meanwhile, the weather has enhanced our impressions of that strange and colorful landscape of the Painted Desert.

That night, July 9, 1929, we camp at what is said to be the first tourist camp in the nation, the White Grocery Auto Camp in Holbrook, the town named after the railroad developer. In its Wild West heyday, it was known for a famous gunfight.

The next day, **July 10**, learning that roads were again passable, we visit the spectacular display of crystalline trees, the Petrified Forest. Playing the typical tourist we pick up and also purchase specimens such as a polished paper weight to incite envy amongst our friends on return to Michigan. Of course this wasn't without objection from mother, who kept reminding us of how these specimens were robbing valuable storage space throughout the rest of the trip.

Back in Holbrook we purchase two pies at 25 cents each and push on to Winslow and beyond. We are both fascinated and worried over this part of our journey. Along the way, the scenic variety from red rocks to scrub cedar, the visual splendor of a spectacular plant with huge white blossoms, and the contrasting black soil peak our interest. But appreciation is interrupted frequently by thunder, rain, flooded road, and many flat tires from stone bruises. As Michiganians, Winslow fits our image of what a Western town should be: on the railroad, frontier architecture, and cowboy atmosphere. Here we indulge in pineapple buns and coffee. Not far away we view Meteor Crater through the clouds. This is said to be one of the largest and best protected craters in the world. It is hard to imagine the impact of this extraterrestrial mass that scattered fragments over a 100-mile radius and dug a hole 600 feet deep and almost a mile across. Many times we had to ford the inundated roadway and headed into a rainstorm. After stopping for lunch at the roadside to beat the rain we pass through Padre Canyon in Coconino National Forest and mother sees a large morning glory-like bloom on a ground-hugging plant.

Our thirsty Ford needs gasoline frequently and so we stop at the little settlement of Winona. At the time all we can see is a store and campground. The topography begins to change and soon we pass through Flagstaff, actually along a paved road! After changing a tire we pass by Agassiz Peak and San Francisco Peak on our way to Williams. We learn that the town was named after an original fur-trapping settler, Bill Williams. In the 1880s he was an adventuresome eccentric, more at home with friendly Indians than those of his own kind. Although by now the town has begun to refine itself, we can sense its reputation as a stereotypical Wild West town.

On the north edge of Williams and after fixing two flat tires from stone bruises dad finds a spot for us to camp for the night. Simple cabins furnished with a bed or two, a water pitcher and bowl, and maybe the luxury of a mirror were for rent at $1.00. However, because we had all our camping gear we camp for 25 cents here in Tom Cureton's Auto Camp. He boasted good mountain water, hot showers, electric lights, and clean wood.

The next day, **July 11**, we drive over a very rough road in the rain as we pass by hundreds of prairie dogs and rabbits. The road does turn into pavement as we ap-

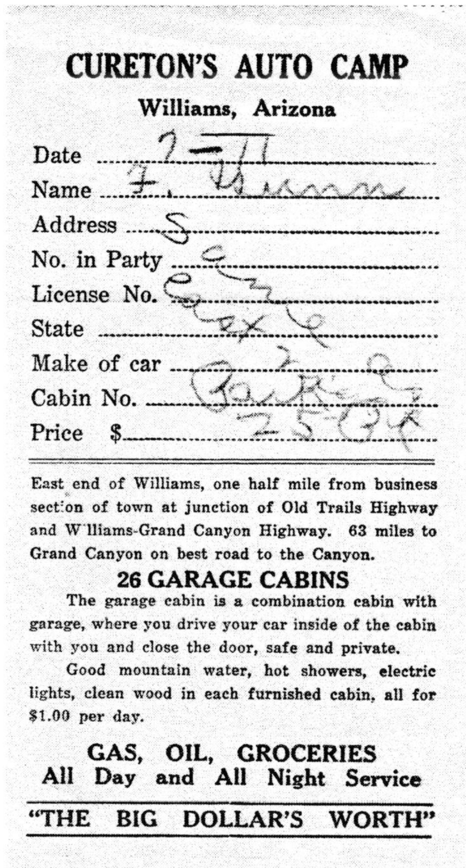

CURETON'S AUTO CAMP
Williams, Arizona

Date ....
Name ....
Address ....
No. in Party ....
License No. ....
State ....
Make of car ....
Cabin No. ....
Price $..........

East end of Williams, one half mile from business section of town at junction of Old Trails Highway and Williams-Grand Canyon Highway. 63 miles to Grand Canyon on best road to the Canyon.

26 GARAGE CABINS

The garage cabin is a combination cabin with garage, where you drive your car inside of the cabin with you and close the door, safe and private.

Good mountain water, hot showers, electric lights, clean wood in each furnished cabin, all for $1.00 per day.

GAS, OIL, GROCERIES
All Day and All Night Service

"THE BIG DOLLAR'S WORTH"

Typical in the 1920s were campsite charges of 25 cents for tent space and $1 for a cabin. Cabins usually contained only beds with a hand water pump and privy facilities elsewhere on the property. A few furnished cabins were beginning to appear. Illustrated is the receipt for our camping at Cureton's Auto Camp, Williams, Arizona.

proach the Grand Canyon, a major objective of our trip. Mother capsules our feelings as we stand at the brink, "beyond our imagination; no words can express."

Our visit includes the Powell Memorial, Pima Point, Hermit Trail, Yavapai overlook, a museum, Yaki Point, and Grandview Point. We are fascinated by the yucca, lizards, horned toads, and wind-bent trees along the trail but mostly by the awesome vistas of the canyon walls and the Colorado River with Phantom Ranch far below. We regret that our time is so limited here but the impressions are indelible. We are proud of the political decision that set the area aside for resource protection and public use. We feel that the El Tovar Hotel, originally built in 1905 with Fred Harvey as its first concessionaire, catering to the wealthy tourists of that day is out of our class so we pass it by. The museum helps us understand the history of this place and even displayed tracks of extinct animal and plant life of millions of years ago.

[*I can agree with those who believe the Grand Canyon is best appreciated in retrospect.As an impressionable 12 year old in 1929 nothing in my childhood, not even* National Geographic Magazine *pictures, had prepared me for it. As I looked from side to side and up and down I was completely baffled by the immensity of the scale. The 100-foot hill in back of our home in Michigan, our favorite winter sledding slope, was no match for this huge, colorful, and rugged gash in the earth.*]

We stand at the rim in silence, struck dumb by the length, breadth, and depth of this mountain in reverse. Pinnacles, peaks, and stepped slopes of variegated coloring could not be translated into words.And the only way to register our impressions was to try to grasp them in our minds. Dad's box camera with black-and-white film was incapable of any reasonable imagery.

We return to Williams to get back on Route 66 for the next western leg of our trip. Here Lauren posts on July 11, 1929, a 1-cent postcard to his friend back home, Joseph Javinsky, who is in charge of the transmitter for radio station WOOD, Grand Rapids, Michigan. The call letters were originated by the owner of Stiles Lumber Company, then producers of prefabricated structures and owner of the station. The transmitter "shack" and antennas were located just outside Jenison, only a few miles from our home. Many times, as I accompanied Lauren's visits to the shack, my duties were sweeping out the wet-cell battery room filled with shelves of large glass jars of sulfuric acid solution and electrodes. These powered the station with direct current. Lauren's interest in this new phenomenon of radio was a major reason for our observation of radio stations on the entire trip.

As we break camp at 7:07 am, Friday, **July 12**, our minds, even though filled with the remarkable images of the Grand Canyon, are now turned toward our next major objective, California. But there are many miles yet to go. Our first town west of Williams, Ashfork, occurs after traveling through rolling cedar-studded topography. As we drive along in open desert country we can see Mt. Floyd (elevation 7449 feet) in the distance to the north. We are reminded of the historic past when we observe a pack train on a desert trail nearby. At Seligman, another railroad town, we change time.

Our road takes us through Audley and cactus-strewn desert, and we soon enter the Hualapai Indian Reservation and wonder how they could possibly survive on this parched land. We stop at Peach Springs and buy some groceries. The town name seems to be derived from peach trees that resulted from pits planted by Mormons on their early travels. Although our business is welcome we are very self-conscious of our foreign status here. We see a baby strapped to the back of a woman and receive blank stares from Indians sitting about. This Indian dominance continues as we drive on, noting the Truxton Canyon Indian school at Valentine. For years this was headquarters of the Indian agent and the town was known as Truxton Canyon. Here we know we are in the midst of vast desert lands, mesas, and buttes tempered by sagebrush and yucca plants. Early settlers named the next town Hackberry, believing their mining efforts would be as prolific as a nearby tree and spring. Apparently mother didn't find the groceries she needed at Peach Springs and we stock up again at Kingman, another railroad town where we stop for groceries and have lunch, probably peanut butter and pickle sandwiches. Our log states that we saw "a yucca tree with a dingus on top," whatever that might mean.

As we push on the heat gets more intense and we realize we are entering a different geography as we climb for 4 miles up and over Sitgreaves Pass. Now we are in old mining territory—Tom Reed Mine, Vivian Mine, and Gold Road Mine. Our tourist sightseeing abilities are increasingly dulled by the weariness of the afternoon heat as we finally cross the Colorado River to California at Needles, named after peaked mountains in view. Here we take on ice and ice water and for the first time notice palm trees in residential areas.

Comment

Comparison between this journey in the 1920s and modern tourism in this same region as described in Chapter 3 reveals great similarities and also differences. The power of attractions such as Grand Canyon, Petrified Forest, Painted Desert, and Indians remains. Of course, in these seven decades better tourist services and visitor interpretation are great improvements. Today's visitors, however, are much more diverse than the narrow niche represented by our family. And mass tourism is showing great wear and tear on the resource. Planners of future tourism here face many challenges to overcome these issues. The Gunn autocamping travel log continues in Chapter 4.

Endnotes

[1]Kari-Keen advertisements appeared in early issues of *Detroit Motor News*, such as (1925) Vol. 11, p. 30.

[2]Heasley, J. (1910). *A Summer Vacation in Yellowstone National Park* (p. 8). Grand Rapids, MI: Author.

[3]Rowsome, F., Jr. (1965). *The Verse by the Side of the Road* (p. 16). Brattleboro, VT: Stephen Green Press.

Chapter 3

The Northern Arizona Destination

For more than a century, the spectacular Grand Canyon of the Colorado River has been a major wonder of the world. When ancillary attractions such as the Painted Desert, Petrified Forest, Meteor Crater, and San Francisco Mountains are added, it is easy to understand why the northern corridor of Arizona has grown in its appeal and is now inundated by millions of visitors.

Even before white settlement of northern Arizona, its strange geological and landscape place characteristics had appeal to the natives. Hopis made regular pilgrimages to these special places where salt oozed from the rock. They mined clay and were awed by that huge gash in the rock caused by eons of erosion by the Colorado River.

Later, white prospectors sought the minerals that seemed to be abundant: silver, gold, lead, copper, and asbestos. Uranium became an important export in the 1960s. The wild, raging river that challenged Maj. John Wesley Powell in the late 1800s has since been tamed by dams upstream. Many other changes in the environment have taken place over the last 70 years, not only by tourism but by many other kinds of development. Much of the "old west" lure remains but the landscape character has changed dramatically.

The story of changes in tourism since the boom of autocamping in the 1920s demonstrates the complexity of taming the many-tentacled beast called tourism. Its many rewards are accompanied by erosion of both natural and cultural resources of the region, paradoxically the very foundations for its appeal. The following review of accessibility, Indians and settlement, touring appeals, erratic planning and design, and roles of public and private developers shows why there is modern concern over environmental impacts and the need for a new policy of sustainable planning and design throughout this world-class destination.

The Desert Barrier

The insatiable appeal of the West and particularly northern Arizona preceded the ability to get there. This fact was contrary to the later axiom of promoters that new rail and highway access was the sole stimulant of the economy. As with most automobile travel of the 1920s in the West, it took place on crude roads built primarily along early pioneer trails. Route 66 across northern Arizona roughly paralleled the several wagon trails and the Atchison, Topeka and Santa Fe Railroad laid down before. This road had grown out of the historic Beale's Road of 1857, the first major improvement to link the East and West.

Beal's Road was dubbed the "Lightning Dromedary Express" because it was built with camels imported from Cairo and Smyrna.[1] Lieutenant Edward Fitzgerald Beale had become interested in the possibility of using camels for this task after reading Abbe Hue's *Travels in China and Tartary*. Beale brought this idea to the attention of Senator Jefferson Davis. In the last days of the 1851 session of Congress Davis fostered an amendment to an army appropriation bill to develop a wagon trail approximately along the 35th parallel across Arizona. After bringing in 75 camels through Indianola, Texas, he reported, "I have tested the value of the camels . . . and have marked a new road to the Pacific."

Even though an historic event, this innovative trail blazing across the desert was met with many adversities, such as attack by Indians, scarce water supply, rocky arroyos and canyons, and the demand for building catch basins to water stock. Beale's enthusiasm for the use of camels was dampened greatly when he discovered that the mule skinners of the day hated the camels. Even though the road was completed, the use of camels was abandoned because the handlers couldn't speak to the camels in Arabic and the camels couldn't understand English.[2] For many years afterward locals blamed the wandering camels for spooking their horses as they crossed the desert.

In spite of the great difficulties encountered by Beale, he could not help but admire the beauty and natural assets of the places he passed through. He extolled the virtues of the spectacular scenery of mountains, forests, and desert and how his road would provide new access to that wonder of nature, the Grand Canyon of the Colorado.

The next major improvement in travel West was the Atlantic and Pacific Railroad following its land grant of 14 million acres signed by President Andrew Johnson in 1886.[3] Lewis Kingman, J. E. Early, and H. R. Holbrook laid out the line roughly following Beale's Road. A major obstacle was a 250-foot-deep gash in the landscape, Canyon Diablo, west of Winslow. This barrier of nature forced a routing around the canyon. It wasn't until 1947, after a takeover by the Atchison, Topeka and Santa Fe (Santa Fe) that a major bridge was built over the canyon, cutting out many miles of the original detour. The Santa Fe ran its first train to Los Angeles on its own line, May 31, 1887. To the railroad across northern Arizona must be attributed the establishment of most pioneer towns that still remain.

But real train tourism fame for this part of Arizona came when the Santa Fe began an association with Fred Harvey, a spectacular developer and promoter of tourist services. After a series of kitchen and pantry jobs and several bouts with illness, this young immigrant made an unprecedented proposition to the Burlington Railroad. His concept was to build a series of eating houses along their route to replace the abominable local fare then available to the elite train travelers. They sarcastically not only turned him down but also suggested he take his daft idea to the Santa Fe. He did, and built a food-lodging empire with no peer that lasted for decades. His impeccable care of foods and superb managerial skills were especially significant in catapulting the Grand Canyon region into an outstanding tourist attraction. He had virtually a monopoly with his Harvey Houses in Winslow, Williams, Ash Fork, Seligman, and Kingman. The civilizing of the West is attributed to him.[4] The relationship between Harvey and Santa Fe was based on a gentlemen's agreement rather than a legal one.

Another innovation of this entrepreneur, Harveycar Motor Cruises, was undoubtedly the first major establishment of motor coach tourism in America. These tours used White Co. buses with Packard engines and provided tourist access to the Navajo and Hopi Indian territories as well as the Grand Canyon. Only women couriers were hired to provide guide service and were selected on very rigid criteria: women college graduates; 25 years of age; willing to learn the history, politics, sociology, anthropology, geology, and arts of the region; a speaking knowledge of Spanish; social grace; and ability to meet and guide all kinds of tourists.[5]

As the railroad had pushed through Williams, construction workers had been followed by gamblers, saloon keepers, and prostitutes.[6] The nearby forested mountains provided excellent cover for desperados who lived off stagecoach holdups. Lawlessness, shootings, and "hop joints" of opium were thriving in the 1890s. Even in its heyday of train tourism, Williams had a grimy side as revealed by a description of 1902: "There is a wine joint up at the western edge of town that should be suppressed. No liquor is stronger than wine, but that is the vilest 'Dago Red' and would make a man assassinate his mother. This joint has been the source of many brawls."[7]

Early Arizona clearly had been a land of restless transients rather than settlers. People from the East came in great numbers but most moved on. Anticipating a fertile paradise, they met instead a hostile desert landscape fraught with many hazards, even more serious than scorpions, snakes, and lizards. Unyielding Indians who had occupied the territory for several thousand years defended this land against the massive white land takeover. This, together with unproductive soil and climate, meant that only the toughest and most stubborn immigrants would remain. Thus, the Arizona territory had gained the reputation as "the southwest corner of hell."[8] Only the most hardy men and women stayed on and soon found that their livelihood depended on gambling, rustling, and stagecoach robbery rather than legitimate agriculture.

Although these historic facts continue to provide ample fodder for voracious novelists and Hollywood script writers, a transition to a tourist economy and a more sedate lifestyle had already begun by the 1920s. Occasional remnants of the rough and rugged past remained but new motor camper services were beginning.

The Mother Road

Today's travel over I-40 is a magnum leap from tourist movement by autocampers in the 1920s. There was no official State Highway Department in Arizona until 1927.[9] The poor existing roads had been built by the counties with differing standards and with only minor assistance from the state. Route 66 was only 16 feet wide and surfaced with a minimum of gravel, terribly dusty in dry weather and often impassably muddy in rain. A few concrete structures were built over major water courses but corrugated steel pipes were used elsewhere for minor drainage. Gravel and concrete fords were used for dry washes and intermittent stream beds.

In 1928 low-cost surfacing of bituminous mix was started but lack of funds slowed actual construction. In 1929, out of a total of 21,666 miles of designated roads in

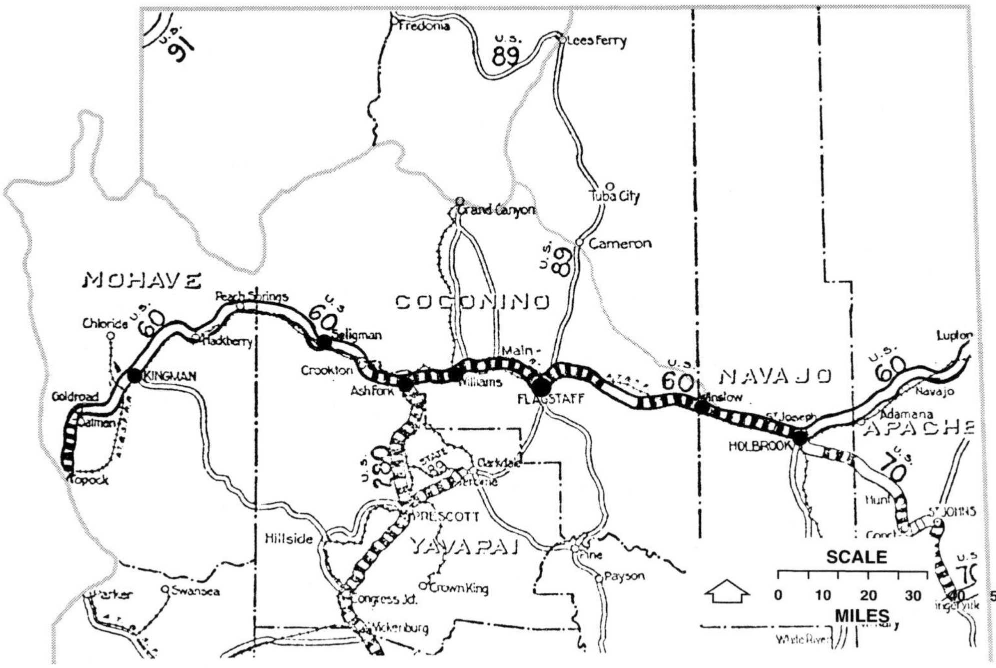

This 1926 road map of northern Arizona shows very few miles of "improved" (gravel surfaced) roads. US 60 later became the very important Route 66 from Chicago to the West. (Source: Arizona Highway Department)

Arizona, only 163 miles, mostly in the cities, were concrete; only 1784 miles were classified as "improved."[10] According to the official highway map of 1929, travelers were given many driving tips: 35 mph maximum speed on open country highways, don't forget to give proper arm signal, unlawful to coast with gears in neutral, vehicle coming from the right has the right of way so give it to him, don't carry luggage projecting more than 6 inches on the left side of the car, and don't throw glass, nails, tacks, wire, or cans on the highway.[11]

A tour guidebook of 1932 included special advice to tourists of this period in Arizona.[12] The tourist should have chains, a good jack, pump, shovel, small axe, stout tow line, can of gas, oil, and water. If stuck in the heavy deep sand of the dry washes, the driver is advised not to drive through in a jerky fashion or an axle might break. Using blocks of wood and a jack might be successful in getting you out. More difficult problems might require chains or a pull from a local team of horses. The assuring comment was made that the nearest Indian tribe can be relied upon to assist in such a dilemma. Special care should be taken when water covers the road—the authors had known cars to sink out of sight.

Route 66 has been dubbed "the mother road"[13] and is now cemented firmly into American lore. It was the prime collector of millions of midwesterners that then deposited them in that rich wonderland of the West. From Chicago to Los Angeles, this route also gathered up a string of pearls of attractions en route. Threading through the land of Lincoln, it then sliced through a diversity of small towns, rich agricultural lands, rivers and streams, the rugged Ozark Mountains, flatlands of the prairies, and the deserts and mountains of the West.

It came at just that opportune time in American history when adventure, life changes, inventiveness, and the search for new freedoms dominated society. In the 1920s, localities and regions still retained their cultural differences, now accessible for the very first time. It was in 1924 that the American Association of Highway Officials petitioned the US Secretary of Agriculture to designate a comprehensive nationwide highway system, eliminating the piecemeal labels by area trail associations.[14] After much political haggling, this road from Chicago to Los Angeles was identified as Route 66, although the origin of the number is not clear. Later, Phillips Petroleum adopted the number for its gasoline brand because of its popular recognition.

Over its history this road saw the complete strata of western-bound travelers: developers, settlers, drifters, writers, songsters, and tourists. Popularized by Jack Kerouac, John Steinbeck, Woody Guthrie, and Bobby Troup, this route took on a spiritual and romantic value like no other road in the country. "Get Your Kicks on Route 66" by Troup immortalized this famous passageway of 2400 miles from Chicago to Los Angeles. And not only were autocampers enticed to travel this route. In 1927, the Pioneer Yellow Bus Line began transcontinental passenger service along this road—5 days plus 14 hours.[15] It was along this road that the complete history of tourist business enterprise was written, from the first camp sites to the finest hotels and from local "greasy spoon" restaurants to the broad array of franchise and full dining establishments. In spite of being displaced by today's Interstate system, many organizations and public agencies are now actively engaged in the preservation of those segments of this "Main Street of America" that remain.

Among the many fascinating and informative writings about this famous road are *Route 66* by Susan Croce Kelly (1988) and *Route 66: The Mother Road* by Michael Wallis (1990). Kelly cites the Petrified Forest as one of the first major attractions along Route 66. Before restrictions on removing samples of the unique wood, entrepreneurs collected and sold tons of pieces at roadside stands near the park and in Holbrook.

Even in the Depression, travel on Route 66 increased, not only by typical autocampers but also by migrants who were driven out of farming because of severe drought in Kansas and Oklahoma. They hoped for a better life farther West. Cabins and motel businesses grew, often supplemented by food service, groceries, and souvenir sales with husband and wife doing all the work. In wartime, Route 66 travel dropped greatly but still saw many migrants traveling to California in search of war plant jobs. Truckers hauling war materiel did a great deal of damage to this poorly built road. The roadside businesses did not complain as much about the drop in numbers of travelers or shortages of supplies and goods as the increased paperwork caused by rationing. The only bright spot in the tourism economy was greater Indian production and sales of jewelry resulting from lifting the silver embargo by government.[16]

A second boom in travel on Route 66 came after World War II with a pent-up demand to exercise the new freedom to get in a car and go, anywhere as well as on this highway. Even though the roadway had deteriorated, entrepreneurs saw opportunities for building cabins and tourist courts as soon as materials became available. With ever-

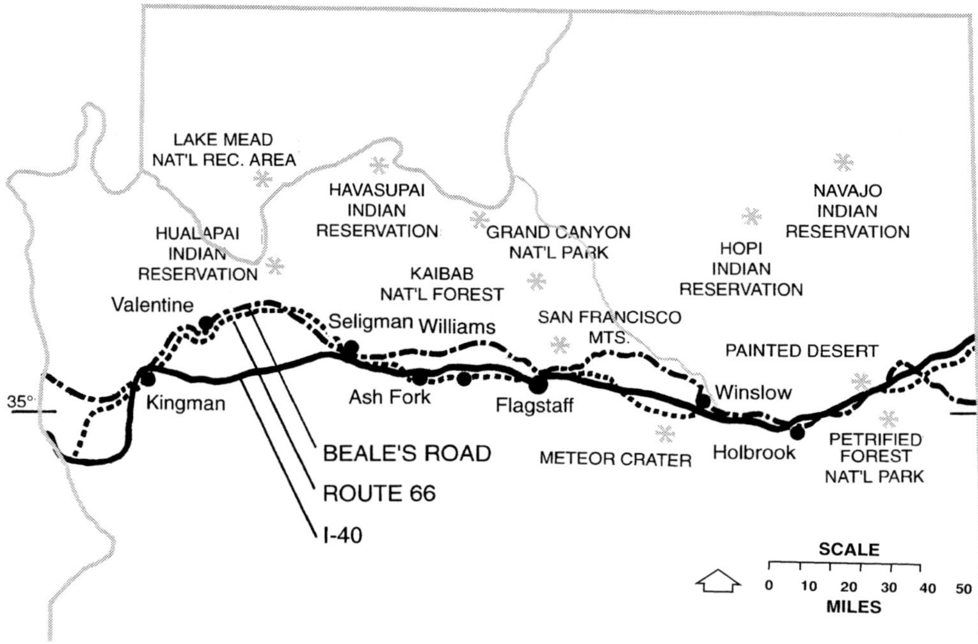

Even though Beale's Road of 1857 across northern Arizona lacked modern highway design sophistication, it established the basic alignment for all travel modes since. Shown is a comparison of Beale's Road, Route 66, and Interstate 40.

increasing amenities, these facilities soon became known as motels and boasted indoor plumbing, hot water, showers, better beds, air conditioning (from "swamp water coolers" to refrigerated air), and even television and swimming pools later on. Equally strong growth occurred with new restaurants and filling stations. The older "railroad hotels" had not been kept up and were not closely oriented to the highway traveler. The motels offered a new image of more personalized and less formal service.

Then, with the Interstate Highway System, authorized by the federal government in 1956, dramatic change was forced on all tourist enterprises. Even though greater volumes of automobiles could be moved more rapidly, implying greater demand for services, the location of these new highways often bypassed towns and destroyed roadside travel businesses oriented to the old Route 66. A new location near the Interstate highway demanded new investment, often beyond the reach of existing service business people. Although many communities almost became ghost towns, pride and persistence has prevailed, now capitalizing on nostalgia to bring tourists onto some old Route 66 sections.

Whose Land, Whose Culture?

This region of the US represents dramatic examples of human occupation for over 10,000 years.[17] Archeological study reveals that the earliest people lived off bison and mammoth and were followed by those who gathered plants as well as hunted. Gradually, over many centuries, nomadic life was modified by sedentary settlements depending on basic agriculture. Anthropologists cite this as the first great revolution in the history of mankind. Village life, organized ritualism, and creation of pottery, baskets, bags, and containers and the development of trade between groups are typical evidence of the high degree of civilization that took place here centuries before European occupation.

Over the many decades since white settlement of the West, it has been difficult for European descendents to understand the contrasting cultural background of ancient and modern Indians. And within their culture today, assimilation and especially adaptation to tourism has caused great stress. To the Indian, there was to be no accumulation of wealth and any gains by an individual had to be shared. Tourism, however, demanded private enterprise and those Indians who first began to sell objects and services became outcasts. Distrust and even animosity toward tourists stemmed from several sources. Early Spanish missionaries whose religious zeal and bigotry blinded their understanding of Indian culture tried in vain to stop the "snake dance" of the Hopi. Both the Hopi and Navajo resented and often prohibited visitors from photographing their private rituals and settings. So-called Indian trading posts along the highways were usually run by whites who often exploited the Indians and their artifacts. Major changes then took place in the 1970s that improved Indian tourism: civil rights movement, an Americana trend, greater demand for fine art, and improved self-determination of Indians.[18] In the 1990s there was a flood of articles and books exposing early racism in many forms and admission of pangs of guilt by white descendants. At long last the wrongs against Indians in early history were brought out in the open.

Revealing is the documentation of the history of Indian–NPS relations by Robert H. Keller and Michael F. Turek.[19] Over many decades along the Arizona strip, conflicting cultural conventions between white bureaucrats who dominate land ownership and management and Native Americans have made it difficult to develop and manage places for tourists in northern Arizona. Further complication has been fostered by another factor—decades of Mormon settlement. This trio of land use managers in this region has endured many years of racial bigotry, deceit, broken promises, and continuing animosity in the search for social and environmental sustainability, essential to tourism.

This continuing struggle is exemplified in the interpretive programs at Pipe Spring National Monument administered by the NPS. The NPS message on history emphasizes cattle and cowboys and attacks by Indians. The hundreds of years of Indian occupation and cultural development and especially later encroachment by and conflict with Mormons are not clearly told. One interpreter's experience revealed that he typically asked tourists to decide which of three versions they preferred to hear—that of the NPS, of the Mormons, or Indians. He had discovered that any version, when honestly told, would offend someone.

Adjacent to Grand Canyon National Park was another area of controversial management, greatly resolved by President Gerald Ford's Grand Canyon Enlargement Act of 1975. This transferred 185,000 acres of land from NPS to the Havasupai Indian Reservation, marking the end of a long conflict over jurisdiction. A peace-loving people, this plateau tribe had held a long-time and intimate place relationship with their land that had been encroached upon by NPS for park use and by American settlers for mining, ranching, and railroad development. Barry Goldwater is credited for this important land exchange, but it came against opposition from the Sierra Club and other environmental groups.

This act spelled the end of NPS mismanagement of these lands where campgrounds were overrun, massive amounts of trees were cut, campfires eroded the land, litter was accumulated, and sacred places were burned and burial grounds were raided.[20] Important as this land transfer was, the many strings attached to the act continued to be a source of Indian irritation. Even though today's tourists may not be able to enjoy the slick modern conveniences seen in other NPS sites and have to ride horseback 8 miles to Supai Village, the area remains Indian. Although NPS might have made Havasupai Canyon into a cleaner and safer place (a white perspective), the area is homeland for a people who now maintain their own standards and values.

After several decades of adaptation, many Indians today are heavily involved in profit-making tourism services. Native crafts have been so stimulated and increased in quality that they are collector's items rather than merely tourist souvenirs. Much of the upgrading was influenced by Inger Garrison (wife of national park veteran, Lemuel A. Garrison) through her many seminars and personal counseling. These improvements have given rise to such organizations as the Navajo Arts and Crafts Guild, Hopi Arts and Crafts-Silvercrafts Cooperative, Hopi Enterprises, and Havasupai Tourist Enterprises.

Well known today are the many instances of new Indian income from casinos. But these ventures have resulted in mixed outcomes. Some people object to them on a moral basis, citing gambling as addictive. Indians within Arizona's Tohono O'odham Reservation object to their own Indian neighbors' proposal for a casino on the Punta de Agua site.[21] The conflict centers on the issue of preservation of important ancient artifacts buried at the site, perhaps over 700 years old. After archeologists removed the remains of 22 people, protests resulted in the Native American Graves Repatriation Act of 1990, requiring the return of such remains to tribes. The issue is not so much the ethics of extracting moneys from tourists as it is one of cultural resource sustainability. This is just one of many illustrations of the complexity of reaching toward tourism environmental sustainability.

The Navajo Indian Reservation includes 25,000 square miles in northern Arizona, the largest in the nation. The rich cultural heritage is protected by over 15 national monuments, tribal sites, and historic sites.[22] But this protection has come at great cost to the Navajos. The establishment of the Navajo National Monument by the federal government in 1909 was made with good intentions—protection of ancient artifacts that otherwise might be destroyed. However, this was the beginning of major threat to the Navajo culture and what Rothman calls the expanding power of governmental imposition of authority upon the Navajos.[23]

Poverty continued and was exacerbated severely by the governmental stock reduction program of the 1930s, making life even more difficult for the natives. Even though the National Monument employed a few locals, most remained as paupers of the government. Then the greatest invasion of their culture came with the building of new paved roads, giving access for masses of tourists of an outside culture. Even

Navajo tour guides did not perform according to the expectations of white visitors because of entirely different values.

As the Navajo were pushed into a money economy, everything changed for them, now expressed in a clash of values between older and younger generations. Tradition prevents individual accumulation of wealth, resulting in a horizontal distribution of income to extended families. Navajo cannot own property, a cherished right of other Americans, making it difficult to establish businesses in order to obtain income. Especially acute is the attitude of young people who are bored with the old ways. Researcher Michael J. Francisconi has found that neither the Bureau of Indian Affairs, boarding schools, nor missionaries have done as much to destroy Navajo culture as has television. Over many decades, the issue of cultural clash has diminished slightly but, as in all aboriginal populations around the world as they are thrust into an industrial age, there continues a high degree of stress as adaptation to tourism takes place.

Monument Valley, an area of natural rock sculptures in a desert setting, has been the locale for many Hollywood western films featuring stars such as John Ford and John Wayne. Such movies helped to foster western lore, much to the enjoyment of viewers. The Monument Valley Tribal Park, located just south of the Utah border, has been popular for both domestic and international tourists and is available only by horseback or four-wheel drive vehicles, led by Navajo guides. Adaptation to tourism is made also with the sale of turquoise jewelry, kachina dolls, woven rugs, and other crafts. The natural land sculptures and landmarks such as the Mittens and Three Sisters are favorite targets for visitor photography. Nearby is Navajo National Monument, established by Presidential Proclamation in 1909. This site includes several of the best-preserved and most elaborate cliff dwellings known. For sustainability reasons, tours to Betatakin Ruin in the canyon are limited to tours of no more than 24 people and only when led by a ranger. Also available only on foot or horseback and led by a Ranger is Keet Seel, the largest cliff dwelling in Arizona. Inscription House, once available to tourists, is now closed for preservation reasons, a true act of environmental sustainability. However, tension continues between tourists, NPS staff, and Navajos.

The Hopi Reservation, surrounded by Navajo land, includes the town of Old Oraibi, said to be the oldest continuously inhabited community in the US. Hopi adaptation to tourism is exemplified by their engaging a planner, Michael E. Kelly, to facilitate a plan.[24] Their concern was primarily to improve their economy but only when it does not interfere with religious privacy and local initiatives. Based on local interviews and workshop meetings, an inventory of attractions was prepared, a market survey was developed, and major issues of tourism were identified. A major recommendation was that each community had a right to set its own goals and objectives regarding adaptation to tourism, from rigid control to open hospitality. Following are the main recommendations:

- Establish a centralized location for visitor information.
- Develop informative brochures.
- Establish a Web presence.
- Develop signage policies.
- Increase and improve overnight accommodations.

- Build on cooperative relationships with other tribes.
- Agree on a broadly based vision.
- Agree on the role of Tribal Government.
- Initiate designation of Highway 264 as historic and scenic.
- Designate scenic and recreation areas.
- Invest in off-Reservation facilities.

In addition, a Visitor Code of Ethics was prepared. Centered on behavior that respects Hopi traditions, this code asks visitors to refrain from picture taking and note taking except where allowed, walk on designated trails, do not interrupt ceremonies, and do not remove any artifacts. The Hopi are demonstrating their sophisticated planning for maintaining their cultural foundations and yet adapting to tourism—true sustainability.

The case of the Acoma Pueblo Indian site just west of Albuquerque, New Mexico, illustrates typical tribal concerns over tourism development.[25] This anthropological research again endorsed the ambivalence among tribes themselves—some seeking tourism and others resisting tourist use of their sites. The Pueblo Indians at Taos, New Mexico, with its five-storied pueblo, is on the National Heritage List and attracts millions of tourists. However, the Hopi and Zuni have been very wary of tourism and have refused to invest in gambling casinos. At Acoma the Zunis use the major pueblo as their tribal ceremonial center with Mission San Esteban del Ray of 1640, named as a National Historic Landmark. A visitor center, built in 1970, and its museum give visitors a general view of their culture over many centuries. Because of natural clay soils, excellent pottery is a popular handicraft. Although tourism is difficult for them to manage, they are finding that it can support many important local social programs that help sustain their heritage. One writer, however, believes the casino emphasis where wholesomeness is a mask for stultifying tourists is doomed to failure in the future.

Native American populations find themselves hampered in their efforts to become assimilated into society through development of tourism. One survey of Indian Tribal Governments in the Southwest revealed several major concerns.[26] Because Indian tribes cannot tax property as do communities in general, they have no source of revenue to support important basic infrastructure, such as water supply, waste disposal, fire protection, police, and roads. Another continuing concern reported is tourist threat to Indian privacy and cultural protection. They resent commercialization of their rituals and artifacts and invasion of their sacred sites by archaeologists. Finally, they reported the need for better signage and the development of visitor interpretative centers that present truthful information about Indian culture.

A very special but perplexing attraction of 130 square miles in northeastern Arizona is Canyon de Chelly. It became a national monument of NPS in 1931 because of its unusual geological, ecological, and cultural features.[27] A narrow stream bed threads through spectacular rock walls that depict over 200 million years of geological change. The reddish sandstone is often streaked by seepage of colorful minerals, as if hand painted by a fanciful artist. The rare beauty of the canyon is heightened by variations in weather that create scenery of dramatic proportions, popular by both amateur and professional photographers.

The Navajo have tried for 60 years to get the NPS to return Canyon de Chelly to them, with no avail. They claim this area is the real soul place for the Navajo.[28] Throughout the history of park-Indian relations, differing agenda, priorities, and customs have maintained a stand-off situation. In spite of this, many NPS staff members have gone out of their way to assist Indians whenever they needed help. And, as Indians have increasingly become NPS staff members, they are gaining some understanding of the NPS position and practices.

Archeologists are still puzzled by clues of pictographs, petroglyphs, dwellings, and rock monuments left by the Anasazi from the first century to about 1300 A.D. Artifacts of ancient weapons, jewelry, and works of art reveal a high level of civilization by the early occupants. They were then followed by basket makers and pueblo builders who were eventually replaced by Navajo who now gain their livelihood from subsistence farming and hunting.

But, because the location is within native Navajo territory, there is frequent conflict with NPS management. A study in 1990 reported that there was great difficulty in resolving differences in values held by NPS, the Navajo Tribe, and visitors.[29] When bear roam into the area and threaten Navajo livestock and visitors, NPS has to trap them and remove them to remote locations. The Navajo's need for water conflicts with preservation of nearby flora and fauna. Often the privacy of Navajo people is invaded by curious tourists as they seek intimate contact with the native culture. It seems that it is impossible to establish and manage such treasures without conflict. The resurgence of Native American status and prestige is an important factor of tourism place development in Arizona and throughout the nation.

If this region is to reach even the minimum of sustainable tourism, greater progress toward accommodation between federal agencies and the Hopi and Navajo must take place. The policies and traditions of the NPS toward protection and visitor use of archeological and historic sites are well founded in their legal mandate. Managers and staff of these sites are well founded in their professional roles. At the same time, Native Americans are proving their right to the protection of their cultural heritage on these sites. New cooperation and accommodating measures must be applied to replace bickering with resolution of critical land use issues.

A Tour Critique

An analysis of this significant corridor across northern Arizona reveals its many changes and characteristics of the past that are important today. As tourists now enter Arizona from the east on I-40, they see the same pink rocks as autocampers did in the 1920s, then are greeted by the sign arched over the road, "You are now leaving New Mexico, come again." The little village of Lupton, named after railroad man G.W. Lupton, is now a ghost town. It is likely that modern travelers will see Indians nearby tending sheep and goats, the same as in the 1920s.

As the desert begins to take on strange hues, one approaches the Painted Desert, part of today's Petrified Forest National Park. A feature of the Painted Desert, then and today, is the Painted Desert Inn, built by Herbert D. Lore in 1924.[30] Then it contained a lunch counter, Indian trading post, six rentable rooms, and owner's quarters. In 1936, as the NPS took over a large portion of the Painted Desert and incorporated it into the Petrified Forest National Park, the Inn was included. After many reconstruction efforts and a short period of management by the Fred Harvey Company, the Inn is now primarily an interpretive center with a museum of rotating exhibits, demonstrations of rug and jewelry crafts, and a shop of crafts and books. At one time considered an architectural intrusion, the Inn has become an integral part of this very special landscape.

Today's visitors along this exceptional corridor of northern Arizona have much greater opportunities than before for learning about its special natural and cultural character at the many interpretive centers of the NPS. Exhibits, talks, tours, campfire programs, audio visual presentations, and demonstrations are professionally designed and managed techniques that help visitors understand and enjoy the area. Eleven national park areas in this region offer some kind of interpretation.[31] At many of these locations, the prehistoric cultural features as well as natural characteristics are interpreted.

Of course, the Petrified Forest holds the same fascination as it did in the 1920s. Although visitors and natives have decimated the site and shipped out tons of specimens over many decades, management has been able to retain enough evidence to convince tourists that they are in a very special place. Polished specimens in the visitor center show the beauty of radiant colors, resulting from being buried in volcanic ash millions of years ago. In this stretch of I-40, there are virtually no remnants of old Route 66. Petrified wood samples are on display and even for sale at the touristy town of Holbrook, just off the Interstate. The town still retains some of the early character, although the White Grocery Auto Camp, claimed in the 1920s to be the first tourist camp in the nation, is now gone. The concrete tepee motel, Wigwam Village, has been restored. The Navajo County Museum displays historic artifacts of the region.

Travel beyond Holbrook passes through a varied and scenic landscape, just as in the 1920s but now filtered through billboard hucksterism. An example is the huge sign of a jackrabbit at Joseph City.

The town of Winslow, the next point of interest, has intentionally retained much of its western frontier character of decades ago in spite of newer franchise tourist businesses at either entrance to the town. A sign lays claim to the corner that the Eagles sang about in 1994: "Standin' on the Corner in Winslow, Arizona." In 1990 the state of Arizona endorsed a $20 million allotment to the Arizona Heritage Fund. Locals tapped into this fund to establish an 11-acre area now named to the National Register of Historic Places, evidence of cultural sustainability. A significant piece of restoration has been La Posada Hotel, now an operating resort hotel, originally designed by the Fred Harvey Company's innovative and talented designer, Mary Cotter.[32] A classic of the Fred Harvey railroad hostelries, built in 1929 for $1 million, it contained 74 rooms, three restaurants, and eight acres of beautiful gardens. Later it housed the main Santa Fe office and was closed for 40 years. This newly restored hostelry now enjoys new travel market demand for cultural tourism.

As one travels on I-40 today on the way toward Flagstaff, there is no awareness of Diablo Canyon, once a major obstacle for both rail and road development. With effort, one can see the old Route 66 bridge and remnants of the old trading post of Two Guns. Once a campground and topic of the Route 66 song, "Flagstaff Arizona, Don't forget Winona," the settlement has virtually disappeared with only a small fragment of the old road remaining. Winona probably never would have appeared in song if it hadn't rhymed with Arizona.[33]

Legend has it that Flagstaff got its name from Boston colonists who stripped a pine tree and raised the American flag in 1876. The magnificent natural setting near springs at the foothills of San Francisco Mountains is as appealing today as it was over a century ago. Its real spurt of settlement began when the Atlantic & Pacific Railroad was established. By 1886, Flagstaff was the largest city on this line between Albuquerque and the Pacific coast. It became the center of trade and ranching for the entire region. Most prominent were the Babbitt brothers' trading posts and stores, many of which continue today.

But Flagstaff in the late 1800s became increasingly dissatisfied with the arduous journeys to Prescott, the Yavapai County Seat. Finally, after much political haggling, leaders of Flagstaff were able in 1891 to create a separate Coconino County with Flagstaff as its County Seat. As train tourists began to arrive in significant numbers, the locals made special effort to downplay the past image of harboring drunks and gangsters. Like many small towns of the West, the resident population began to fall into two groups: merchants and professionals, and ranchers and foresters.

In the 1920s Flagstaff exhibited an interesting population mix: cowboys with boots and spurs, lumberjacks, Indians, and whites. It was the building of Route 66 and the great influx of tourists ever since that have given Flagstaff its greatest economic boost. Today, some vintage motels still exist but franchise services dominate. The Hotel Monte Vista has been restored to the image of the "roaring twenties." One can now gain insight into the past of this region at the Museum of Northern Arizona. And the School of Hotel & Restaurant Management of Northern Arizona University has become a focal point for tourism study.

Even though the fanciful exaggerations of the original land speculators for this area were misleading, the basic resources of this place remain: mountains, forests, scenery, wildlife, Indians, and surrounding wonders of Grand Canyon, Oak Creek Canyon, and Walnut Canyon cliff dwellings. Throughout these many decades, the residents have evolved into a modern population that is carrying on traditions of fellowship, respect, courage, high standards, and ingenuity, as mass tourism grows.

In contrast to the desert land of eastern Arizona, the elevation and climate have produced magnificent forests north of Flagstaff, as beautiful today as 70 years ago. The Francisco Mountains were originally Hopi land called *Nuva-tukia-ovi*, the Place of Snow on the Very Top. This place was believed to house beneficent spirits, called Kachinas, often represented by doll-size figures. These dolls were used to indoctrinate children into the Hopi religion. Sometimes the Kachina spirit is played out by men in traditional colorful costumes as they perform special ceremonies in the plazas and kivas. Much of this land is now within the jurisdiction of the FS, but governing policies remain controversial. In recent decades, this delightful mountain region has attracted a great amount of tourist development, such as vacation homes, scenic drives, camping, mountain biking, game hunting, and winter sports.

Although a traveler can access the Grand Canyon from Flagstaff on a delightfully scenic tour, the more popular road remains from Williams. This town was named after the mountain-man, fur-trapping settler, Bill Williams. In the 1880s he was known as an adventuresome eccentric, more at home with Indians than other whites. For the early autocampers the town still had much of the rough frontier patina.

Typical of the early tourist courts throughout the West was the Bow B Ranch just outside Williams by local rancher Harold Greene in 1922.[34] As tourists began to squat overnight on his undeveloped land, they would often come to his house asking for water, milk, and eggs. Rather than chase them away as trespassers he saw them as potential customers. Soon Greene built a small store and added a gas pump. Then, with a spark of entrepreneurship, he built some open-sided cabins for shelter and called the place "Mountain Spring Ranch." Not to be outdone, another rancher, "Doc" Massey, living about 4 miles farther west, built a store and some log cabins and installed a gas pump. These two innovators of new travel lodging are credited with originating tourist cabins in Arizona, and perhaps the country.

Williams today has become a modern tourist town with motels, restaurants, and gift shops. The motels show evidence of lodging evolution over the years—remodeling, expanding, and developing new facilities. The city is recovering well from being bypassed in 1984 by the building of I-40 around the north side of town. As with many small towns dropped from travel flows with the new Interstate Highway System, Williams held a "funeral" celebration upon the demise of the last vestige of Route 66 between Chicago and San Francisco. But the highway would not die. Today, due greatly to the efforts of the Historic Route 66 Association of Arizona, this important scenic and historic corridor retains much of its original character, especially from Seligman to the Colorado River at Topock. At Williams, the old historic Harvey House Hotel was restored in 1990.

When I-40 planners were selecting alignment for the new highway, the decision was made to abandon the old Route 66 in western Arizona and strike out from Ashfork westward toward Kingman. This of course aroused much opposition by travel businesses in the communities bypassed. However, locals have now seen this as a blessing for their tourism, building on the nostalgic appeal of this longest remaining stretch of old Route 66. There is a renewal of community cooperation and spirit rather than doom. The behemoth 14-wheelers no longer roar through these towns with their exhaust fumes, shattering noise, and potential for disastrous collisions. Fortunately for modern travelers, restored and drivable portions of old Route 66 across northern Arizona now total about 300 miles but not in a continuous roadway. Much of the same appearance of the several communities along this route remain as seen by autocampers of the 1920s except as modified by contemporary franchise motels and food services.

For example, in Seligman, named after the pioneer Seligman brothers, bankers, and ranchers in the late 1800s, tourism has become their economic foundation. Old hitching posts and walks remind today's visitors of what autocampers saw in the 1920s. The old Harvey House railroad station has been converted to a restaurant and there is evidence of a strong desire for tourism sustainability.

A major force for preservation of remnants of old Route 66 has been the Historic Route 66 Association of Arizona, founded in 1987 by people from the area, led by Angel and Juan Delgadillo of Seligman.[35] Tourist teasing is as important to them as their food services and historic preservation.

As Route 66 passes through the tip of the Hualapai Indian Reservation the community of Peach Springs is seen. Continuing westward, the traveler comes to the remains of old Hackberry. Legend states that Mormon miners were inspired by finding a thriving spring and a Hackberry tree nearby. Surprisingly, it now houses the International Bioregional Old Route 66 Visitor Center and Preservation Foundation created by artist Bob Waldmire.[36] Nearby is Valentine, also known as Truxton, a one-time headquarters of the area's Indian agent.

About 30 miles farther west is the old railroad town of Kingman, now showing a monument to Beale. The old road through town is called Andy Devine Avenue, commemorating his origin here. Some of the older motels and cafes remain but now the town has an ample supply of franchise tourist services.

The World-Class Attraction

Even before 1900, it had been observed that mining, timber harvest, and wanton stealing of ancient artifacts were destroying major amenities of the Grand Canyon of the Colorado. The earliest efforts toward protection of this unusual area were directed toward making it a forest preserve (1893), game preserve (1906), and national monument (1908). Dr. Miller of Prescott is credited for the establishment of the Arizona Antiquities Association in 1895 with the main purpose of preserving Montezuma Castle.[37] This eventually led to the federal Antiquities Act of 1906. Between 1906 and 1970, 87 national monuments were created under this authority. But it was the rare combination of its many natural and cultural spectacles that finally established the Grand Canyon National Park in 1919. The first director of the NPS, Stephen T. Mather, in 1916 believed in encouraging public use. He produced several promotional publications in collaboration with senators, representatives, news writers, the General Federation of Women's Clubs, tourist organizations, and the National Parks Highway Association.[38]

Mather was a strong believer that public visits to national parks were of such social and personal value that they should be encouraged. By 1920, he had recognized that automobile travel would dominate the future and in that year dedicated his concept of tourist linkage of key parks of the West, the "National Park-to-Park Highway."[39] His plan was a 6000-mile-loop scenic drive emanating from Denver, passing over the Rocky Mountains to Grand Canyon, rolling on to California and up the Sierras to the Cascades, and then reaching on to Glacier National Park and back to Denver. Only 2000 miles of this route had been paved, leaving bad roads for the balance of the trip. Then the National Park-to-Park Highway Association, organized in 1916, became a strong vocal force for improved roads and signage. Other sources of promotion were the National Park Touring Association and several California auto clubs. Greater visitor use was a major NPS policy in these early years, not anticipating that eventually mass tourists would overwhelm the sites.

The fame of the region spread quickly with both train and automobile tourists—188,204 visitors during the 1929 season, an increase of 14% over the previous season.[40] NPS reported many improvements in services and facilities that had taken place in 1929, evidence of planning and design in response to more tourists.[41] Desert View Road had been surfaced with asphalt, a new Lee's Ferry Bridge was dedicated, and Bright Angel Trail was taken over from Coconino County. Other features included a "modern telephone system," many new campsites, and a ranger-natural-

In 1921 this long line of Harveycars serving El Tovar Hotel stands ready to take tourists along the South Rim of the Grand Canyon. Mass tourism had already begun, especially to western national parks. (Source: Cline Library, Northern Arizona University)

ist who provided interpretation talks and displayed exhibits in Yavapai Point Museum. Fred Harvey and the Santa Fe had made many improvements for visitors that year: cabins at Phantom Ranch, many new cottages and cabins, and new resident buildings. Two years before, Scenic Airways Company had begun sightseeing flights over the canyon.

For generations, writers, poets, artists, musicians, and photographers have tried to convey their reactions and meanings of experiencing the Grand Canyon of the Colorado, this bewildering and overpowering natural phenomenon. For most visitors the response is that verbalized by Irvin S. Cobb in 1913: "You stand there, stricken dumb, your whole being dwarfed yet transfigured."[42] The image is never fixed. It changes with vistas from different vantage points; with bright sun, cloudiness, or fog; and with periods of the day, especially the late sun that washes the rock faces in a rich palette of color. However, it must be recognized that human taste is not uniform and that a small number of tourists may be bored by the scene. One observer of tourists at the South Rim in the 1930s overheard a visitor exclaim, "Some hole!" followed by watching his tobacco spit vanish out of sight into the great canyon. And a sensitive visitor in 1927 observed, "My candidate for a reserved seat in a red-hot electric chair is the untutored biped, sans feathers, who insists on gabbing and pouring his wooden wit into your shell-like ear, wondering, mayhap, how many million tin cans it would take to fill up the Canyon, while you are struck dumb by the beauty before you."[43] One is reminded of Oscar Wilde's complaint in 1882 over the inordinate size of everything in America.[44]

Even in today's era of jaded tourists, the great majority are stunned by this huge geological and aesthetic gash in the landscape. However, based on interviews of hundreds of visitors to the South Rim, the tourists' perception of the Grand Canyon is influenced greatly by past experiences, movies, literature, advertising, and their own fantasies.[45] A small segment of visitors are not satisfied with this rich cultural and physical setting and would like to see more video arcades, beer, T-shirts, TV, and even the site where Thelma and Louise drove off the edge. NPS administrators have been plagued by many stunt requests such as a tightrope walk across the canyon, a vehicle jumping from the edge and carried by parachute to the bottom, and the zany "Bras Across the Canyon" (10,000 brassieres stretched across the canyon to protest the American obsession with appearances of women's breasts).

Of growing traveler interests are cultural attractions such as the many prehistoric sites within Grand Canyon National Park. Archeologists have identified over 2600 sites, representing a mere 5% of those believed to be within the park boundary.[46] This region was the meeting ground of several ancient cultures: Hakataya, Cohonina, Cerbat, and Anasazi. Although the Anasazi had occupied the area centuries before, their culture evolved rapidly after 1000 A.D. Along the South Rim, almost to the park's eastern boundary, are the ruins of the Tusayan Pueblo used by the Anasazi around 1200 A.D. Direct descendants of the Anasazi, the Pueblo Indians, occupied the area from 1600 A.D. to the present, exemplified by the Hopi villages. A tourism development challenge for the future is to identify, describe, and preserve the many fascinating aspects of these ancient Americans.

Even though the geology of the setting overshadowed natural science study at first, it was C. Hart Merriam, a scientist of the US Department of Agriculture, who observed the biological differences at the several layers of elevation of the canyon.[47] He put forward the concept of life zones, a major beginning in the field of ecology, areas in which certain species thrived best. Undoubtedly, this is one of the seeds that has germinated into stronger environmentalism in recent years and fostered the travel market segment now known as ecotourism.

Perhaps the first tourist operator here was John Hance, who really came to mine asbestos in about 1881.[48] His camp was about the only place to stay as tourists began to come by stagecoach. As he discovered that the high costs of mining would stop his venture, he began to accommodate visitors. The first hotel was built on Grandview Point by Pete Berry, called the Grandview Hotel. Even though Hance was then put out of business, his tall tales to tourists lingered on. A favorite was his story of strapping on snowshoes when the canyon was completely fogged in, telling the tourists it looked just right to cross to the north rim. He would leave them staring as he struck out for Yaki Point, where he said the crossing would be better.

As one visits the South Rim he is not aware of the social, political, and managerial issues involved here. What is now known as the Grand Canyon National Park was first established by President Teddy Roosevelt as a game reserve in 1906 but has been enlarged several times since. The FS controls large acreages in the Kaibab National Forest to the north and south of the national park. The Havasupai and Hualapai

Indians control vast acreages west of the park and along the south side of the Colorado River. Although dominated by a traditional livelihood of raising sheep and goats, their income is supplemented today by guiding hunters and rafters. Because the NPS has no control over these lands, some environmentalists fear degradation of resources, especially if mining and mass tourism are allowed to grow. The Hualapai already have an airstrip giving access to their costumed festivals for visitors, mostly from Las Vegas.[49] Much of the land across from these Indian reservations is within Lake Mead National Recreation Area. The huge Navajo Indian Reservation abuts the park land on the east. Nearby are a few private land holdings. Boundary and managerial disputes continue as these control groups try to work within their contrasting traditions and policies to iron out issues of conservation and public use.

Of course, the Grand Canyon has had many threats to its existence. Reisner reviews the period of Secretary of Interior James Watt, who gained the ire of environmentalists with his many proposals for dams across western rivers including the Colorado.[50] The Grand Canyon dam proposals excited the strongest opposition. David Brower, a self-educated nature lover who had become director of the Sierra Club in 1952, attacked many lobbyists. Based on his own adventure travel in the many reaches of the Colorado, he vowed that after he lost the battle against the Glen Canyon Dam he would dedicate his life to preventing any more dams. An argument by proponents for dams stated that tourists could gain greater appreciation of the Colorado River if seen from motorboats. This drew the ire of a Sierra Club member who asked whether we should flood the Sistine Chapel so tourists could get a better view of the ceiling. The tremendous growth of population, industry, and agriculture in the Southwest and the demand for more water has kept the damming of rivers a hot political issue for many years.

Although the major features of the Grand Canyon are the same today as in the 1920s, some changes are worth noting. Glen Canyon Dam, built in 1963, has dramatically changed the downstream flows that Powell knew in his historic trips. Flows are now intermittent depending on the demand for electrical power. There is less turbulence, less scouring of riversides, new permanent vegetation, and new bird populations. Native fish populations are gone but some endangered species of plants and animals are being sustained. But beaches are narrowing and some rapids are increasing because boulders are no longer removed by heavy flows. The introduction of burros for mining operations many years ago and their great growth in numbers since has resulted in crowding out other animals.

Coping With Escalating Visitors

Popularity has always been a concern of the park planners and managers. The NPS areas nationwide were visited by only four cars in 1895; by 8000 in 1900; 0.5 million in 1910; and 23 million by 1930.[51] Lon Garrison, assistant superintendent of Grand Canyon National Park in the 1940s, reported that there was never enough parking space, too many traffic jams, excessive demands on sanitation facilities, and inadequate space for camps and hotels.[52] The people problem has been exacerbated recently by concern over many more millions of visitors. In spite of the great growth in the popularity of theme parks in the West, travel demand for the natural and cultural features of the region continues to grow. Visitors to the Grand Canyon National Park have increased 24 times the volume of 1929, now reaching about 4.5 million.[53] Such a huge visitor demand on the features of the park has placed great stress on the management staff, whose growth has been very small by comparison.

Commendable in recent years has been greater emphasis by NPS on visitor management. For example, in 1992 a workshop of 35 professionals from the private sector and NPS determined five new policy directions for visitor use, especially at the South Rim of the Grand Canyon.[54] Agreed was the need for more and better *information* about the park, both preinformation and that inside the park. All *interpretive programs*—lectures, tours, maps, videos, games—should not only be expanded but designed to meet the diversity of ethnicity, origin, and national interests of visitors. Better planning and management must reflect the *visitor use patterns* to avoid excessive congestion, long waits, and poor access to services such as restrooms and provide for the best visitor experiences. To avoid environmental degradation and traffic congestion several *transportation modes* must be utilized. Finally, an *attractive and quality-built environment* will require new emphasis on location and design of structures and facilities that are compatible with resource settings. Application of these principles has been hampered by budget constraints.

NPS at Grand Canyon has expressed concern over recent deterioration of the visitor experience. For example, 1.5 million cars and 30,000 tour buses come to the park each year. Over 6000 vehicles daily compete for only 2500 parking spaces.[55] In addition, this area is new to most visitors, who often get lost or are unable to obtain adequate interpretive information. Overcrowded overlooks are eroding resources and also creating noisy and polluted settings in this dramatic landscape.

Innovative financial partnerships now promise new funding for NPS improvement, especially better access.[56] A Congressional approval in 1995 allows national parks to retain 80% of gate receipts. The TEA-21 Transportation bill offers funding for transportation and other site improvements. Nonprofit groups are raising funds for new projects. A joint venture with a private firm allowed a $150 million investment in a light rail system that keeps all visitor cars outside Grand Canyon National Park, an environmentally sustainable move.

Another proposal is a Grand Canyon View Information Plaza to be funded by several sources: Recreation Fee Demonstration Program, Federal Lands Highway Program, Grand Canyon National Park Foundation, and Grand Canyon Association.[57] This facility, designed to provide the visitor with complete orientation to the park, is to be located about 500 feet back from the rim. Included is a menu of the several ways to enjoy the park and particularly how to access interpretive transportation services. This user-friendly orientation facility will handle a peak flow of 4200 people per hour. Utility work was completed in 1999 and several phases are scheduled to follow: orientation building, visitor orientation display panels, bookstore, bike rental building (for wheelchairs, strollers, and bikes), educational exhibits, and road changes to accommodate light train transportation.

A greenway project with in-park transportation is planned to give visitors the experience similar to many decades ago but without the automobile.[58] The system includes access by nonmotorized routes and overlooks by means of foot, bicycle, wheelchair, and some horseback trails.

These new projects show good faith by NPS for resolving some of the visitor use pressure without resorting to rationing. However, extreme care must be exercised in the design and management of these systems if true environmental sustainability is to be accomplished.

Controversial has been the great growth of tourist flights over the Grand Canyon. In 1996 it was reported that over 600,000 visitors took such flights, 80% of which originated from Las Vegas, Nevada.[59] Because nature aesthetes had objected for years to noise created by these flights, the Federal Aviation Administration (FAA) approved a National Park Overflight Act in 1987. On October 10, 1996, a hearing was held on an FAA proposal to expand flight-free zones over the Grand Canyon, establish flight curfews (restricted times), and limit future growth of tour flights. The controversy centers on the overwhelming tourist satisfaction with the flight experience versus a small but vocal minority who believe their right to solitude is imperiled by these flights. Of course, the lobby of air tour operators and tourism economists is very strong. The issue is yet to be resolved to the satisfaction of all.

An overall assessment of Grand Canyon National Park is that management over these 70 years has been able to retain the basic values of the past and cope with monstrous increases in visitor numbers, and without a similar increase in staff. Some would argue that the area already has exceeded its capacity, especially during peak seasons, and that future planning may require implementation of controls if sustainability is to be a continuing goal. Assisting NPS in the resolution of people-problems and even financial support have been several nonprofit organizations.

Other Public Policy

Significant for tourism planning, design, and development of this region over many decades has been the role of the FS. Although its policies are quite different from the NPS, they are complementary today. Many decades ago it was the strenuous arguing within the Department of Interior and particularly NPS that caused a split between forest and scenic management, creating a separate FS in 1905. It was then placed under the US Department of Agriculture rather than Interior. Although tourists could care less about bureaucratic turf, FS lands have been of great importance to them throughout the West for many decades. Under the aegis of "multiple use" policies, FS functions have been identified as: to preserve and protect the forest within FS jurisdictions; to secure favorable conditions of water flow; and to furnish a continuous supply of timber.[60]

However, the application of planning strategies to reach these objectives has been difficult and controversial. Reactions from local residents and environmentalists regarding on-site development have often been in conflict with FS actions. As with all federal agencies, there is often a big gap between Washington policy and local application. Furthermore, all actions are susceptible to whims of local, state, and federal politicians.

Early on, the FS attempted to separate administrative guidelines for recreation areas, wilderness, and wildlands. Further refinement came with the Wild and Scenic Rivers Act, the National Trail System Act, and, in 1964, the Wilderness Act, establishing a National Wilderness Preservation System. The largest amount of land, some 1.3 million acres in 13 western states, was added to the wilderness system in 1978.

In the northern Arizona region, three national forests and their development are important to tourism there: Coconino, Kaibab, and Prescott. These contain many campgrounds, picnic areas, wildland trails, scenic vistas, dude ranches, pack trips, fishing areas, and hunting lands. These areas reflect the evolution of national forest policy over several decades, from forest management to multiple use, environmental awareness, and ecological responsibility.

Perhaps the greatest change in FS influence on tourism is recognition of geographical heterogeneity, that not all land is alike. The agency has found that public use of even wildland is not distributed evenly, that people tend to congregate at road heads and service centers.[61] In a way, this makes planning and management easier by concentrating people's services and controlling less intensive use in surrounding remote areas.

In the 1990s, tourists as well as environmentalists became increasingly critical of FS policies that seemed contrary to sustainability.[62] The FS response was to give greater consideration to wildlife (such as the spotted owl) and impacts on local community economic and social welfare. Both public and private forest land managers are now expressing greater concern over ecosystems, watersheds, and forest harvest and restoration techniques. This new forest management ethic is bound to strengthen the aesthetic and wildlife values of forests important to tourists and tourism.

The Bureau of Land Management (BLM), a major resource manager of 14.2 million acres in Arizona, is influenced by regional policy, outlined in *Recreation 2000: A Strategic Plan for California Recreation* in 1990. It has responded to recent tourism and recreation growth with a new policy agenda: maintain healthy ecosystems, serve current and future publics, promote collaborative leadership, improve business practices, and improve human resource management practices.[63] This agenda has grown out of BLM's Recreation 2000 Strategy Update (1995) that put forth emphasis on five recreation-tourism market niches: adventure, cultural/heritage, ecoeducation (nature), old West, and family fun. Nearly 9 million people visited BLM lands in Arizona in 1997. Only time will demonstrate how well BLM will be able to carry out its desired agenda toward tourism and environmental sustainability.

Toward Sustainability

Alongside the erosion of resources caused by tourism in northern Arizona are clues to positive efforts toward environmental sustainability, recently and in the past. Important has been the influence of conservationists, environmentalists, planners, landscape architects, and citizens dedicated toward extension of the cultural and natural resource foundations in this region.

Landscape architects and resource protectionists have provided substantial input to the success of Grand Canyon sustainability. In 1909, forest supervisor W. R. Matoon proposed minimum development along the South Rim, including a few rustic shelters at best vista points.[64] Matoon's successor, Don P. Johnston, teamed up with Aldo Leopold to develop a major plan for the area. They recognized and intended to eliminate major degrading impacts of the first tourists—offensive sights, sounds, unsanitary conditions, and inconvenient facilities. For Grand Canyon village, in 1917, they introduced a rudimentary zoning plan—a rim zone, accommodation zone, residential zone, commercial zone, seasonal camp zone, public campgrounds, and the stables zone. Soon the FS engaged landscape architect Frank Waugh to revise and expanded the earlier plan. When the park became a part of the NPS, administrative changes included hiring Charles Punchard as landscape architect who insisted that too great a variety of architecture would create a jumble of design.

In 1920, Daniel Hull took over the landscape architectural role and demonstrated great sensitivity to the existing natural features in his design work at Grand Canyon, true sustainability. His proposal for a village square located well back from the Rim included an administrative building and visitor center at the point where the rail and road access meet. His concepts set the pace for "naturalistic design," later called the Park Service Rustic Style, influenced greatly by Olmsted, and followed by NPS for many years.

After many delays, partly caused by the death of Fred Harvey Company's architect, Pierce Anderson, a new community plan was brought forward by Hull in 1924. This plan showed new orientation to automobile rather than rail access from Williams. His plazas, as open gathering spaces, have since been degraded into parking areas. Throughout this period, much landscape and building construction had been performed by the CCC that then came to a halt in 1942 when several of the New Deal programs were cut off. By then a great amount of sustainable design work had been implemented, including major structures, walkways, stone walls, fences, culverts, bridges, and a flagstone esplanade flanking the Bright Angel Lodge, much of which remains today. In all construction projects every possible effort was made to retain existing land forms and vegetation. Wherever replanting was necessary, indigenous plants were used. The influence of landscape architects such as Frank Waugh and others placed a permanent stamp on the landscape design of the Grand Canyon for visitor use.

By 1927, tourist traffic had already become a threat to the resource integrity of the park and of great concern to both designers and managers. Designer Vint tried to plan and keep road access to the minimum and only where visitor use could be controlled. He insisted on integrating the separate units into a design whole. The issue of high visitor volumes and how to maintain sustainability continues today.

Until the advent of the Interstate system that often plowed through geographical obstacles, such as arroyos and rocky mountains, the early roads were glued to the capricious landscape. First, they followed the railroads that had selected sites oriented to contours with the least topographical gradient, often along rivers. The right of way of early roads was comparatively narrow, only 60 feet for Arizona roads in 1927.[65] Because of relatively slow speeds and minimum budgets for construction, huge cuts through hills and massive fills were avoided. Although highway engineers are often criticized for such preoccupation with engineering details that aesthetics are ignored, some early road planners showed great sensitivity to landscape beauty, as an excerpt from a designer of 1928 demonstrates: "It should not, however, be permitted to bore ruthlessly through these areas so that the natural beauty of these spots will be seriously marred, and it is far better to have the location skirt such areas than to traverse them."[66]

Land design and structures of Grand Canyon National Park were influenced greatly by the classic set of design principles set down by Henry V. Hubbard and Theodora Kimball in their *An Introduction to the Study of Landscape Design*, published in 1917. These principles embodied sensitivity to the scenic values of the landscape and were influenced by earlier landscape architects such as Humphry Repton and Frederick Law Olmsted.

Beginning in 1919, the Grand Canyon Village had been laid out at the railhead and the Fred Harvey subsidiary of the Santa Fe Railway built the El Tovar Hotel here. The South Rim was considered the most dramatic scenic vantage point and a rim road was established. Innovative designer, Don P. Johnston, and Aldo Leopold recommended that the area be divided into seven land use zones, an unprecedented idea.

It must be noted that some sustainable design was being implemented in the Grand Canyon area as early as the 1920s, even though that label had not yet been invented. This design principle of preserving existing landscape features was derived from the earlier naturalistic design genre, which was in direct opposition to urban park principles that included geometric patterns, exotic plants, and obvious domination by mankind. To get the drives and buildings built, workers of the CCC were utilized. Other landscape architects who influenced early Grand Canyon design were Frank Waugh, Charles Punchard, Merel Sager, Daniel Hull, and Thomas C. Vint.[67] Even though some modification has occurred, much of Grand Canyon Village remains as it was in the 1930s. Of course, the mounting issue of traffic congestion continues.

For many years Arizona has been very active in one form of sustainability—its scenic road program. Spurred by the federal Highway Beautification Act and National Environmental Policy Act the state passed a law in 1982 authorizing the establishment of Parkways, Historic, and Scenic Roads.[68] An 11-step designation process was devised. The first step is initiation by any interested group, requesting designation by a special state advisory committee. A very important step is an inventory of natural, cultural, and visual resources. Descriptions of these factors provide the very foundation for justifying designation.

Because scenery implies vistas, an essential step is visual quality assessment that includes two elements. First is a landscape classification process that describes the landscape character—biotic communities, vegetative cover, landforms, and land use activities. Second is description of viewsheds from a series of vista points along the route. Several criteria are used by the committee to evaluate the proposals and make final decision on designation. As of 1993, 19 historic, scenic, or parkway roads had been designated in Arizona.

Similar to the establishment of scenic roads is involvement of nearby communities. Now considered an innovation by federal agencies, this policy actually had been stated by the director of NPS, George B. Hartzog, in the 1960s:

> In the early days of the park movement, the mission of the National Park Service was to manage the parks and its activities did not extend beyond park boundaries . . . today the Park Service can be considered a social institution, concerned with human as well as scenic and wildlife values. The national parks, like life, are meant to be lived, and in parks we can better understand, or perceive, our place in the universe. The ultimate test of the national park idea is its ability to respond to the urgent needs of society.[69]

Today, most professionals of federal agencies in Arizona strive toward this goal in their attempt to cope with mass tourism and pressure from so many constituencies, not typical of the 1920s.

In recent years, the consultant-only approach to planning and design of the past has been modified greatly. Experience has demonstrated that unless the people impacted by design are involved, it is unlikely that the plan will succeed. The newer approach recognizes the talent, interest, and capability of local people to provide valuable input to planning and design, even when led by specialists in design.

A case demonstrating how a local organization in Arizona acted as catalyst to bring environmental and developmental forces together to create a sustainable tourism development is the Rocking K Ranch of 6000 acres near Tucson. A plan involved a resort, hotel, and housing development. But environmentalists feared such development would threaten natural resources of adjacent Saguaro National Park. In order to agree on a mutually suitable plan, both the NPS and the ranch owners agreed to engage a conservation group, The Rincon Institute, to assist in planning a future that would be acceptable to both. By means of bringing community leaders, environmentalists, park officials, and the developers together, a solution was found that protects the soils and plant and animal life at the same time a high-quality development could move forward. Sensitive wildlife habitat on the ranch was acquired by NPS, riparian areas and steep slopes will not be developed, and overgrazed lands will be restored, still allowing well-planned sustainable development on the remainder of the Ranch.[70]

As another example, designer Steve Marino has created the beautiful Arid Zone Trees garden in Maricopa County.[71] Instead of adopting the popular array of exotic plant materials, requiring volumes of irrigation water, he chose native plants, such as mesquite, acacias, cacti varieties, and wildflowers indigenous to the Sonora Desert. This award-winning design sets a new pace for sustainability in a region of environmental stress for agriculture. The designer hopes that even in fallow farm lands, new plantings of palo verde trees, cacti, desert marigolds, and other native plants will demonstrate that beauty can be obtained if environmental factors are respected.

An excellent case of Indian tribal initiative, design, and catalytic action is Nature Park on the Lower Colorado River.[72] The 'Ahakhav area had been homeland for Mohave and Chemehuevi tribes for generations who based their livelihood on the riparian resources. In addition to the very important water resource, the area provided materials for shelter, food, baskets, medicines, clothing, dyes, and paints from native plants, such as willow, cottonwood, and mesquite. These early peoples had struck a reasonable balance between their lifestyle and the land. European settlement then changed all this with major environmental deterioration—introduction of exotic species, agricultural practices, and dams. This change was endured for some time until in 1994 a Mohave Indian, Dennis Patch, had a vision for major restoration. He was a prominent council member of Colorado River Indian Tribes (CRIT).

Patch learned that a landscape architectural student at Purdue University, Fred O. Phillips, had a strong interest and knowledge about the Lower Colorado Indians. He accepted their request for help and became project administrator of a plan for restoration and new development. He followed basic landscape architectural design principles in a process that began with detailed analysis of the area, its resources, and its people. He was assisted by Bertin Anderson of the Revegetation and Wildlife Management Center, and Dave Wegner and John Nagy of the US Bureau of Reclamation's Glen Canyon Environmental Studies Office. From conclusions reached from the land analysis, Phillips designed concept plans. The objectives of this project were very

An excellent example of sustainable land restoration is the 'Ahakhav Tribal Preserve along the Lower Colorado River, Arizona. Initiated by the Lower Colorado Indians and designed by landscape architect Fred O. Phillips, the project now includes a visitor center, picnic area, conoe rentals, interpretive trails, restored wetlands, and a replanted forest preserve. This creative plan has reclaimed cultural, historic, and environmental values to a badly eroded site. (Source: Randy Prentice Photography)

visionary. Nothing like this had ever been done—to tap state, federal, and tribal resources to create a nature park, restore a wetland, establish a native plant nursery, and improve Native American understanding of natural environments. All this appeared to be a dream, especially with no visible financial support. With considerable time and effort as well as many discouragements, the project finally gained acceptance. Phillips discovered he had talent also for preparing grant proposals. After a $2 million grant and in-kind service support were obtained, work began in 1997.

One part of the project was a seemingly impossible task of restoring a wetland that had silted up and was covered with cattails. With assistance from BLM, a 2.5-mile channel was dredged back to its original depth. This allowed the use of water control measures that replicated the original flooding. Marsh vegetation is now returning to the area.

The project also features a 4-acre day use area with a visitor center, picnic tables, barbeque pits, canoe rentals, and interpretive trails. Included in the project is a $10,000 'Ahakhav Native Plant Nursery.

Because the project designer was white, several cultural clashes occurred during the process of implementation. Although Indian leaders had initiated the project and were supportive, some contract workers resented taking orders from a white person and a skirmish ensued. These workers still carried anger, justifiably so, against the white dominance of Indians many years ago. Phillips believed so intensely in the project that he was able to carry on.

The result of this complicated but centrally focused project is not merely physical restoration of a deteriorated riparian site but also new innovation for tourism and recreation. It represents an entirely new attitude toward leadership and people power for environmental sustainability of both cultural and natural resources.

Although sporadic, today's development in northern Arizona shows new sustainable design effort. These and other cases are beginning to stimulate a new environmental and social awareness within the region.

The Challenges Ahead

The story of tourism development in northern Arizona over several decades reveals lessons of value to future developers. Even though the primary environmental settings of this region have endured much change, it demonstrates unfettered environmental exploitation and narrow bureaucratic control. Each segment of public and private development has gone its own way. The only common denominators have been visitors and the environment. Visitors and their activities cut across all development, and the natural and cultural resources form the foundation for all tourism. Lacking has been an understanding and implementation of tourism as an integrated and interdependent system.

The challenge then is to back away from the narrow perspectives of the tourism pieces and move toward a broader overview. From such a vantage point, many opportunities open up for better tourism in the future. Commercial enterprise can gain by stronger environmental protection because sustained natural and cultural resources are essential to business success. Communities can analyze their geographic resources and guide tourism growth with land use planning that integrates tourism with local resident needs and protects rather than erodes unique resources. There may be opportunities for restoration of many of the landscape values observed by the autocampers of 1920s.

A further challenge in this destination is to overcome the continuing racial tension between whites and Indians, especially within the NPS. Indian populations need to become more articulate regarding their personal and traditional values, especially toward land use. Their concepts of land resources are more closely intertwined with spiritual and personal beliefs and customs than are the concepts of whites. Whites are frequently considered intruders, not far from historic fact. Greater study of interrelationships important to tourism, greater education, and greater cooperation among the races are in critical need.

The past *is* past, and many of the travel conditions of the autocamping era of the 1920s are gone. But the tremendous numbers of visitors today are proof of the travel market's continuing interest in the region's natural and cultural resources. Critical today is the extreme tourism development impact on the environment, already showing great stress. If tourism is to progress in northern Arizona, it demands a new vision, a comprehensive view of where it wants to be in the future to avoid further erosion of its resource base. The responsibility for this future lies primarily in the hands of an agglomeration of public and private decision makers in all five components of the supply side: attractions, transportation, services, information, and promotion. Within all components in this region today are capable and experienced leaders and practitioners. But lacking is some mechanism for greater communication and cooperation among all the developers, designers, planners, and residents.

Now available in Arizona are two avenues for developing tourism in a more cooperative way. The many observations and recommendations prepared by The Western States Tourism Policy Council have merit for application in this region. For the first time, public and private tourism interests have agreed to work together toward a better tourism future.

Another source is The Arizona Council for Recreation and Tourism that also brings together the public and private sectors of tourism. Already, Holbrook, Peach Springs, and Page are involved. In Page, this program has produced several important recommendations: upgrade worker skills; improve customer service; obtain stronger community support and better access to financing; widen Route 89; acquire more robust air service, better telecommunication, and more visitor activities; extend business hours; establish better signs and information; obtain more cooperation with the business community; and create better access to Navajo and Hopi cultures.[73] At Peach Springs, an attractive 80-room lodge, new river runners, a wildlife conservation area, bus tours, and helicopter rides have been established. New signage, road improvements, and a Grand Canyon West airstrip have been added. In Holbrook, downtown has been refurbished with new sidewalks, curbs, street improvements, new streetlights, and extensive landscape enhancement. Included in this program is integration of tourism planning with the surrounding area.

If environmental sustainability is a serious and concerted goal, it would appear that two major issues must be addressed by the tourism establishment, including planners, designers, developers, and public and private sectors. First, the sheer volume of tourists may reach a level at which they, not the scenery or cultural features, become the dominant scene. Their mass presence and elements that come with it—trampling, noise, pollution, landscape erosion, and cultural clash—may outweigh the significance of the major attractions that began it all over a century ago. As remedy, it is doubtful if mathematical capacity formulas will be useful. Instead, a consortium of public and private interests, such as recommended by the WSTPC, will best be able to derive solutions adapted to each area of this important tourism corridor.

Second, environmental sustainability demands retention of resource integrity. Such an objective is not only protection of physical assets but also maintenance of the spiritual landscape expression of this phenomenal region. Such an objective can be reached only by annual accommodation toward consensus among the many entities that control and develop land. This necklace of pearls of attractions stretching from border to border is like none other in the world. Even the most jaded of travelers today feels the essence of this region as a special ethereal place. Throughout the history of this region, visitors have been awed by the intangibles of the many spectacles. In spite of many attempts to describe this place, from literature and art to today's advertising, it continues to defy such attempts. There is no substitute for experiencing it. Urbanized travelers of today cannot help but sense feelings of relief, tranquility, and spiritual refreshment.

It is for these very reasons that one must address the issue of how this special place fits into modern "malldom" and intensive special effects of sight and sound, now proliferated on film and in entertainment. Both public and private sector leaders of tourism face the monumental task of accommodating these millions of visitors without eroding the visitor's opportunity to be enriched by a visit to this very special piece of geography.

Alongside the great personal reward from a visit here, tourists are the same cultural beings they were back home in Chicago or Boston. At the same time they seek enjoyment and enrichment, they have the same habits and desires regarding creature services as they did back home. Commercial tourism developers, based on the traditional American foundation of free enterprise, have responded to these market needs with new lodging, food service, and entertainment. These are best located back at the gateway communities rather than intruding upon the major natural and cultural features of this region. At these communities, support is available from governance and management of infrastructure, perhaps the best location for intensive tourist services.

In spite of tremendous growth in numbers of visitors, the northern corridor of Arizona still retains its appeal. Credit for most of this continued destination lure must be given to the enduring management and staff dedication of several governmental agencies. Even though these entities have faced many budget and political challenges over the last seven decades, resource protection and sustainable development are continuing goals. In addition to the new light rail access, future visitor growth may require new policies of rationing, lottery, and other techniques of crowd control.

This region, particularly within government-owned attractions, has benefited from substantial design input by landscape architects. The early leaders of the profession were not only designers but also active advocates for national parks, such as Grand Canyon. From the very beginning, sustainability dominated design philosophy. The protection of rare and outstanding natural and cultural resources of sites was first in the design agendas of landscape architects. At times their vision and concepts were blocked by administrative, political, and popular decisions but eventually most have been implemented. Much slower over these decades has been the role of landscape architects in the private sector of tourism development. An emerging role of landscape architects is acting as catalyst for conflict resolution and producing land planning solutions to projects that were stalled. The opportunities are abundant for greater input for sustainable tourism in the future.

One opportunity for mass tourism development and resource protection is the establishment of visitor interpretive centers where tourists receive educational and stimulating information and yet make little impact on the environment. As acculturation takes place in this region, the old ways and rich heritage may be lost. Interpretive centers could be designed to offer pageantry and reenactments of early frontier life; museums containing artifacts, exhibits, videos; and lectures supporting the enlightening value of past history, such as the highly advanced cultural level of ancient dwellers.

In summary, local citizens of northern Arizona will gain when higher quality resource protection is balanced with better quality planning, design, and management of future tourism development.

Endnotes

[1]Among the sources describing Beale's Road are: Bowman, E. G., & Smith, J. (1979). *Beale's Road Through Arizona* (pp. 3, 9). Flagstaff: Flagstaff Corral of Werterner's International; and Rose, A. C. (1976). *Historic American Roads* (p. 57). New York: Crown.

[2]Trimble, M. (1977). *Arizona: A Panoramic History of a Frontier State* (p. 123). New York: Doubleday.

[3]Bryant, K. L., Jr. (1974). *History of the Atchison, Topeka and Santa Fe Railway* (p. 94). New York: Macmillan.

[4]Bryant, op. cit., p. 113.

[5]Thomas, D. H. (1978). *The Southwestern Indian Detours.* Phoenix: Hunter.

[6]Early Day Williams Rough Railroad and Cattle Town. *Williams News,* 90(32, Sec. 1), p. 5.

[7]Ibid.

[8]Sonnichsen, C. L. (1987). The Southwest Corner of Hell. *American West,* 24(5), 30–37.

[9]Arizona Highway Department. (1929). *History of the Arizona Highway Department.* Phoenix: Author.

[10]Concrete Highways and Public Improvement. *State Highway System,* 13(4), 84.

[11]Arizona Highway Department, ibid.

[12]Colton, H. S., & Baxter, F. C. (1932). *Days in the Painted Desert and the San Francisco Mountains, a Guide.* Flagstaff: Museum of Northern Arizona.

[13]Wallis, M. (1990). *Route 66: The Mother Road.* New York: St. Martin's Press.

[14]Scott, Q., & Kelly, S. C. (1988). *Route 66: The Highway and Its People.* Norman: University of Oklahoma Press.

[15]Lamb, D. (1993). *A Sense of Place* (p. 83). New York: Times Books.

[16]Scott and Kelly, op. cit., 79.

[17]Lister, R. H., & Lister, F. C. (1993). *Those Who Came Before* (2nd ed., p. 47). Tucson:

Southwest Park & Monument Association.

[18]Gilbert, B. (1973). *The Trail Blazers.* New York: Time-Life Books; and Deitch, L. J. (1977). The Impact of Tourism Upon the Arts and Crafts of the Indians of the Southwestern United States. In V. L. Smith (Ed.), *Hosts and Guests.* Philadelphia: University of Pennsylvania Press.

[19]Keller, R. H., & Turek, M. F. (1998). *American Indians and National Parks.* Tucson: University of Arizona Press.

[20]Keller and Turek, op. cit., 168.

[21]Miller, E. (1997). An Indian Casino Would Sit on Ancient Graves. *High Country News,* 29(16), p. 4.

[22]Tripp, S. (1995). *Arizona Journeys* (p. 39). Phoenix: Arizona Department of Transportation, Kingman, Arizona.

[23]Rothman, H. K. (1998). Pokey's Paradox. In H. Rothman (Ed.), *Reopening the American West* (pp. 90–121). Tucson: University of Arizona Press; and Francisoni, M. J. (1998). *Kinship, Capitalism, Change.* New York: Garland.

[24]Schroeder, P. (2001). *Hopi Tourism Marketing and Feasibility Study.* Phoenix, AZ: Practical Solutions.

[25]Smith, V. L. (1995). *The 4-H's of Tribal Tourism: Acoma, a Pueblo Case Study.* Presentation, Biennial Meeting of the International Academy for the Study of Tourism, Cairo, Egypt, July; and Kaplan, R. D. (1998). *An Empire Wilderness.* New York: Random House.

[26]New Mexico Indian Tourism Association. (1998). *Indian Interviews with Tribal Governments.* Santa Fe: New Mexico Department of Tourism.

[27]Supplee, C., D., & Anderson, B. (1985). *Canyon de Chelly.* Las Vegas, NV: KC Publications.

[28]Keller and Turek, op. cit., 205.

[29]Stoker, T. N. (1990). Parks and People: Biological Versus Cultural Diversity. In J. Gramann (Ed.), *Proceedings—Third Symposium on Social Science in Resource Management* (pp. 16–17). College Station: Texas A&M University.

[30]Hellikson, M. M. (1994). Correspondence of June 29 and paper "Painted Desert Inn, A Brief History," NPS, Pertified Forest National Park.

[31]*The Complete Guide to America's National Parks* (1988–1999). Washington, DC: National Park Foundation.

[32]*La Posada.* (n.d.). Descriptive brochure of Fred Harvey Hotel La Posada, Winslow, Arizona.

[33]Lamb, D. (1993). *A Sense of Place* (p. 213). New York: Times Books.

[34]Origin of Tourism in Williams. *Williams News,* 90(32, Sec. 1), p. 3.

[35]*Historic Route 66 Association of Arizona.* (n.d.). Descriptive brochure, issued by the Association.

[36]Jensen, J. (1996). *Road Trip USA.* Chico, CA: Moon Publications.

[37]James, G. W. (1917). *Arizona, the Wonderland* (p. 57). Boston: Page.

[38]Ise, J. (1961). *Our National Park Policy—A Critical History* (p. 196). Baltimore: Johns Hopkins Press.

[39]Carr, E. (1998). *Wilderness by Design* (p. 87). Lincoln: University of Nebraska Press.

[40]Annual visitation, 1915 to present, Grand Canyon National Park.

[41]Tillotson, M. R. (1929). Grand Canyon National Park. *Annual Report of the Direc-*

tor of the National Park Service (p. 77). Washington, DC: USGPO.

[42]Babbitt, B. (1978). *Grand Canyon—An Anthology* (p. 135). Flagstaff: Northland Press.

[43]Nelson, W. H. (1927). *Alluring Arizona* (p. 41). San Francisco: W. H. Nelson.

[44]Conrad, P. (1980). *Imaging America* (p. 62). New York: Oxford University Press.

[45]Neumann, M. (1999). *On The Rim: Looking for the Grand Canyon.* Minneapolis: University of Minnesota Press.

[46]Fishbein, S. (1991). *Grand Canyon Country* (p. 39). Washington, DC: National Geographic Society; and Lister, R. H., & Lister, F. C. (1993). *Those Who Came Before.* Tucson, AZ: Southwest Parks & Monuments Association.

[47]Babbitt, op. cit., 46.

[48]Babbitt, op. cit., 56.

[49]Fishbein, op. cit., 61.

[50]Reisner, M. (1986). *Cadillac Desert: The American West and Its Disappearing Water.* New York: Viking.

[51]Lee, R. F. (1974). *Family Tree of the National Park System* (p. 16). Philadelphia: Eastern National Park & Monument Association.

[52]Garrison, L. A. (1983). *The Making of a Ranger* (p. 216). Salt Lake City: Howe Brothers.

[53]Annual visitation—1915 to present. From www.nps.gov/grca/facts/yrstat.htm as of March 11, 2002.

[54]*Visitor Use Management Workshop—Findings and Recommendations.* (1992). Denver: Denver Service Center, National Park Service.

[55]Annual visitation—1915 to present. From Grand Canyon National Park, www.nps.gov/grca/facts/yrstat.htm, as of August 27, 2000.

[56]US Department of Interior. (1997). Transportation, Interior Announce New Partnership to Handle Transportation Needs in Parks for 21st Century. News release, November 25; and Carr, E. (2000). Landscape Architecture in National Parks. *Landscape Architecture,* 90(10), 56–63.

[57]Canyon View Information Plaza. From Grand Canyon National Park, www.nps.gov/grca/matherpt/, as of August 27, 2000.

[58]Grand Canyon Greenway. From Grand Canyon National Park, www.nps.gov/grca/greenway/index, as of August 27, 2000. More detail on this excellent team design project is described by Ewan, J., & Ewan, R. F. (2002). The Start of Something Grand. *Landscape Architecture,* 92(2), 40 ff.

[59]Broadbent, R. N. (1996). Letter from Broadbent, Director of Aviation, Las Vegas, to FAA, September 27. In *Hearing, Grand Canyon Overflight,* S. Hrg. 104-656. Washington DC: USGPO.

[60]Dana, S. T., & Fairfax, S. K. (1980). *Forest and Range Policy.* New York: McGraw Hill.

[61]Robinson, G. O. (1975). *The Forest Service.* Baltimore: Johns Hopkins University Press.

[62]Baden, J. A., & Snow, D., eds. (1997). *The Next West: Public Lands, Community, and Economy in the American West* (p. 31). Washington, DC: Island Press.

[63]*Journey Into the 21st Century.* (1998). Phoenix: Arizona Bureau of Land Mangement.

[64]A comprehensive history of involvement of landscape architects in national parks is Carr, E. (1998). *Wilderness by Design*. Lincoln: University of Nebraska Press.

[65]Arizona Highway Department. (1929). *History of the Arizona Highway Department*. Phoenix:Author.

[66]Crosby, W. W., & Goodwin, G. E. (1928). *Highway Location and Surveying* (p. 181). Chicago: Gillette.

[67]Carr, ibid., 59.

[68]Walker,T. D. (Ed.). (1993). *Application Procedures for Designation for Parkways, Historic, and Scenic Roads in Arizona.* Phoenix:Arizona Department of Transportation, Highways Division.

[69]Everhart,W. C. (1972). *The National Park Service* (p. vi). New York: Praeger.

[70]Howe, J., McMahon, E., & Propst, L. (1997). *Balancing Nature and Commerce in Gateway Communities* (p. 89). Washington, DC: Island Press.

[71]Thompson, J. W. (1998). Desert Redux. *Landscape Architecture,* 88(6), 60–67+.

[72]Phillips, F. O. (1998). 'Ahakhav Tribal Reserve. *Restoration and Management Notes,* 16(2), 140–148.

[73]Heffernon, R., Rex, T., & Andereck, K. (2000). *Visiting Page/Lake Powell: An Economic Analysis of the Page Area Tourism Cluster.* Tempe: Morrison Institute for Public Policy, Arizona State University; and correspondence from the program's technical advisor, Associate Professor, Department of Recreation and Tourism Management, Arizona State University West, September 21, 2000.

Chapter 4

1929 Western Tour: Part II

As introduction to the examination of seven decades of tourism change in the northern California destination (Chapter 5), this chapter continues the narration of the author's 1929 autocamping trip in this same region. It begins with crossing the Arizona-California border and continues through coastal California to the Oregon border. This autocamping case offers a comparison with modern tourism, especially the extent to which tourism has impacted the environment and whether it has been planned for sustainability. It must be remembered that this was long before the popularity of radio, television, and the Internet.

•••••••••••••••••

As we continue our journey westward on **July 12, 1929**, the heat of the desert becomes more and more oppressive and we stop at Carty's Camp for ice water. We are told that service stations with gas and water would be scarce from then on. Our canvas water bag, hung in front of our car's radiator, offers a bit of security and does a fair job of cooling by means of evaporation in this dry heat. In Amboy after getting gas and water we give up further travel at 108 degrees and secure a cabin for the night at $1.25. We are told that the justification for this high price is the cost of water that has to be shipped in by tank truck. But we don't rest, and we greet the next morning as fatigued as the night before.

By now, the memories of northern Arizona and its great geographical diversity and beauty are firmly imbedded in our minds. About 2500 miles from home, a distance greater than Madrid to Moscow, we have experienced almost as diverse and interesting settings as across Europe. By now it is evident that we have mastered camping travel. In spite of many flat tires, extreme heat and cold, primitive road conditions, sun and rain, forested mountains, and desert plains, we and our sturdy Model A Ford remain sound and resolute. This, our first major journey, has already given us great pleasure and new understandings of regions previously unknown to us.

On Sunday, **July 13**, we get up early to get a head start against the heat only to discover two flat tires from stone bruises the day before. After finally getting on our way, we are not about to get the camp stove out for breakfast and stop in Ludlow at Oasis Cafe to eat—ham, eggs, toast, coffee—all for $1.80 for all four of us. As we pass the strange Pisgah Crater we are struck by the unusual appearance of the black lava flow and can't resist picking up a sample. After a detour, we see a mirage and the road now improves greatly on the way to Newberry Springs, living up to its name by giving us a lush green landscape, "a pretty place." Near Daggett we are stopped by official-looking people and wonder what we have done wrong. We soon discover that this is a fruit quarantine inspection and they make a thorough search of our car, suitcases, and lunch boxes. Then we move on and get a chuckle when we pass a lodging sign, "bungalettes."

We move upward and upward for many miles of tall yuccas and cactus and on through Helendale, Oro Grande, Victorville, and finally reach El Cajon Pass at 4200 feet elevation. Here the mountain is verdant as we twist and turn in this rugged Angeles National Forest. From here on the entire setting changes as we pass a very long train with four locomotives near San Bernardino airport and observe vineyards, enormous palm and eucalyptus trees, and our first orange groves! Here we stop for a free orange drink and buy ourselves a half-bushel for 50 cents. Lemons are 5 cents a dozen and grapefruit are 2 cents a dozen.

Upon arriving in Los Angeles, dad calls Della Crowfoot Dugal, a young lady his family had befriended in earlier years near Holland, Michigan. It was an exciting reunion. Brother Lauren's face turned red as Della gave him letters that had arrived from his girl friend back home. Sunday, Monday and Tuesday (**July 14, 15, 16**) we spend in local sightseeing—Venice, Santa Monica, Eagle Rock, Glendale, Burbank, Hollywood, and San Pedro Harbor. Much time was devoted to visiting with relatives of Della's—Jeff, Ervin, Ruth Russell, and especially aunt Della and Miss Lillie. But the climax of excitement was reaching our goal of the Pacific Ocean at Hermosa Beach. Although it was a thrill to know we had achieved this rare objective, it was a bit disappointing because it looked exactly like our own Lake Michigan coast!

Wednesday, **July 17**, all washed and refreshed, we start out for our journey to the Mexican border. In contrast to anything we had seen before, we travel through plantings of avocados, apricots, walnuts, and figs, as well as oranges and lemons. This shore drive takes us through Oceanside, Carlsbad, Encinitas, and on into San Diego. Then we cross into Mexico at Tijuana. Lauren and I noticed a gambling hall, a new experience for us, but of course we could not enter. The terse note in mother's log said it all: "Saw enough in a short time, bought some cards and left."

On our return toward Los Angeles, after arriving at the old town of San Diego and having lunch, mother is fascinated by visiting the site of Helen Hunt Jackson's writing, Ramona, even seeing the chair in which she wrote. The Old Mission of 1770 reveals to us a wishing well, cart museum, beautiful flower gardens, Veronica's harp, a painting by Gabriel Max in which the eyes appear to open and close (some local tourist hype?). We buy some beads, rings, and a native Indian dish. Even though atmosphere was quiet we could feel the vicious mistreatment of Indians of an earlier day.

Thursday, **July 18**, was spent again with visiting, cleaning, and shopping. Of course, Lauren and I were more interested in the strange-looking palm trees that we dubbed "telephone poles with fringes on top." As a diversion, Lauren and I visit the fire house where Elmer, Della's husband, works.

Friday, **July 19**, we say goodbye to friends and anticipate our new adventure northward as we pass through Glendale and Burbank (Station KELW) and get on Highway 101. On our entire trip we have gotten many laughs from the silly archi-

As with most tourists then and now, one objective of travel is to meet friends and relatives. Here we lounge in 1929 with a friend on Hermosa Beach, California. We are somewhat disappointed with the Pacific because it looks just like Lake Michigan shore back home.

tectural expressions of tourist businesses scattered along the way. Here we pass a snack shop in the shape of a beer barrel. For roadside scenery, we enjoy the many groves of pepper trees, oranges and lemons, but especially the world's largest walnut grove, the Grand Walnut Farm. Strikingly new to us are the many oil well derricks, even in the ocean. We pass several farms of beans, sugar beets, and corn. Key communities we pass through are Camarillo, Richfield, Summerland, and Santa Barbara. Camarillo is a pleasant town with streets lined with palms and boasts the slogan, "The Poinsettia City." At Summerland we stop for gas and hot dogs and observe a "real tramp," old and ragged.

Our first major stop is Santa Barbara, where we visit the Santa Barbara Mission of 1786 and the Franciscan Church. Never before had we experienced such a monument to the early history of the West. Here we learn about the Mexican period and that by 1833 the Franciscans had built a chain of 21 missions throughout California. Here the friars' objective was to convert the Indians to Christianity. The Santa Barbara Mission is often called the "Queen of the California Missions." The paintings by Rubens and others, the burial crypt that held 4800 Indian bodies, the Babylonian tree, the beautiful garden, Angels Cemetery, crucifix, and huge geranium and fuchsia plants are of great interest to us. We have lunch at Dos Pueblos Ranch and after passing by many oleander and pepper trees we turn inland at Gaviota Pass. After passing a narrow gauge railroad at Arroyo Grande, we camp at Buena Vista Camp in San Luis Obispo, a 252-mile day of scenic and cultural splendor.

Breaking camp by 7:06 am, **July 20**, we are anxious to see what lies ahead. At Atascadero we are impressed by the Spanish and Moorish architecture. Of interest as we drive along is an area of pear orchards, 12 miles long and 7 miles wide, and a new subdivision called Atascadero Estates. We see grape vineyards near Templeton and hot springs, mud baths, and the remains of San Miguel Mission (1797) near Paso Robles. Near Bradley and King City we see great herds of cattle and acres of beans. The roadside is colored by California poppies and nearby are many apricot orchards. As campers, we stop in Soledad for lunch meat and travel on toward Salinas.

At Salinas, named for salt marshes, we arrive in the midst of their local festival with bands playing and a rodeo in process that have brought out the whole town. This rodeo, begun in 1911, claims to be one of the largest in the world. Mother notes seeing two little boys all decked out in cowboy outfits, chaps and all. As we travel on toward Watsonville we run into fog and note seeing a whaling station, oyster beds, Monterey Bay Salt Co., and a heron. Watsonville is known as the Valley of the Apples, where we are attracted to beautiful hedges of Shasta daisies and then stop to buy groceries. At Santa Cruz we are back to the Pacific and travel along Ocean Drive (Beach Street?). Mother and dad yield to us boys to spend a moment or two on the beach.

Here we seem to get on the wrong road but enjoy the mountain and Pacific coast scenery. Coming from Michigan, where most of the roads of that period were at right angles and along section lines, we anticipate a cross road but find none. Finally, at a mountain crest we get a view of San Francisco and believe our road will finally take us there as we travel near Crystal Springs Lakes.

We approach San Francisco along Skyline Drive, giving us a broad vista of the city, San Francisco Bay, and the Pacific. Lack of a good map forces us to inquire at Colma for directions. As we drive along the ocean beach road (maybe Cabrillo Highway) we cannot help but comment on how our Lake Michigan shore back home is so simi-

Long before the Golden Gate Bridge, we ferry from San Francisco to Sausalito in 1929. Already this area had become a travel destination in itself.

lar—you can't see the other side for either one. We stop to buy postcards and, typical young tourists that we are, a pennant. We travel on, noting points of interest such as Ft. Winfield Scott, a dirigible hanger, big guns at the harbor, Cressy Airport, many fortifications and US Army transport, many yachts in harbor, and Ft. Mason. Although our knowledge of San Francisco is then very thin, we cannot help but feel the stamp of early Spanish, Mexican, and Gold Rush days. It becomes clear that this is a major gateway to the Pacific. The cable cars, begun in 1873, are a curiosity and seem to be the right answer to the steep grades.

We find our way down to the dock for the South Pacific Golden Gate Ferries Co. The dock area is filled with cars waiting and the delay gives us a chance again to appreciate the sweeping view of the harbor. Finally we board after paying our fee of $1.20 and join about 80 other cars for the trip to Sausalito. On the way we see a square-rigged merchant ship and a four-mast schooner. We wanted to stay on the open upper deck for the view but the cold wind drove us back down. Upon landing the road takes us to San Anselmo where we inquire for directions and in San Rafael we found, as mother described it, "a good camp in a nice little valley," Greenwood Park and San Rafael Auto Camp. Their business card lists George Wellman, proprietor, and enticing comments such as "skating every afternoon and evening," and "picnicking and dancing at all hours."

After a bitter cold night we finally break camp, **July 21**, and head north on the Redwood Highway (101) through Petaluma, which claimed its place in fame as "The World's Egg Basket," displaying a Big White Hen sign. Then we move on through a valley near Cotati and note that it is dominated by grain and grape agriculture. At Santa Rosa we see an airport and many cherry and apple orchards near the Russeau [sic] River. California poppies dominate the roadsides.

The trip from here to the Oregon border gives us a new kind of thrill—experiencing the mountains of the Coastal Ranges and the unbelievable redwood trees. Along the way, we note some other points of interest such as the Salvation Army's Industrial Home for Boys and Girls at Healdsburg. On this trip we observe the many vineyards around Geyserville, named for geysers nearby, discovered by Clark Foss in 1851.

Apparently needing a break from mountain driving, we stop for ice cream cones. We pass through many vineyards and drive through Cloverdale and then climb around and around. Then we are back on the crooked and winding road down, down, and down. We notice a swollen tire about ready to burst at the last stop and believe we should take care of it soon. It was a real struggle to master this hilly topography in a Model A Ford. We stop at Ukiah for gas and then go on to change the tire in a "nice, cool, shady spot for lunch" at Calpella. In Willits we buy a new tire and get a welcome drink of ice water.

As we approach Cummings beyond Laytonville we cannot believe any trees can be so large around, so tall, and so abundant. What a contrast to the deserts of southern California! We twist and turn along Highway 101, completely enclosed by millions of straight and tall trees and at Cummings we pause in Coolidge Redwood Park. This we believe is the most beautiful sight since leaving San Francisco. Here we take a picture of our car almost completely hidden behind a giant tree. The beautiful site tempts us to stay here overnight but we push on, getting a glimpse of the Benbow Inn.

Our largest maples and elms back in Michigan had not prepared us for such a giant redwood that dwarfs our Model A Ford. Here at Lane's Camp (now called Smithe Redwoods Reserve) along the California coast modern tourists can still enjoy a remnant of this landscape wonder.

As daylight begins to fade we do accept the attractive camp site at Benbow State Park. Here we are told that some of the trees are 325 feet high and 20 feet through. As we walk about a half mile to the camp store, we pass through some trees with red bark and are told that they were manzanitas, foreign to us back in Michigan. Thus, we spend the night of Sunday, **July 21**, amongst the giants of the natural world, conjuring up the tales we would be telling folks back home—honest tales that we were sure nobody would believe. Here we learn that many of these mammoth monoliths of nature were here in the dinosaur era. Here a visitor feels at one with his God, encapsulated in a special quiet, the smell of musty forest duff, and Lilliputian feelings among these Brobdingnagians of the natural world. Ideal climatic and soil conditions were given credit for this special redwood locale of about 35 miles in width and some 450 miles in length along the northern coast of California.

Monday, **July 22**, we hate to leave our idyllic campsite but look forward to whatever drama the day's travel will bring. We pass through many more redwood groves in Humboldt Redwoods State Park along the Eel River valley. We learn that the F. K. Lane grove was dedicated in 1928, just a year before we drive through. This was named in honor of Franklin K. Lane, a former Secretary of Interior under President Wilson. He was a strong conservation advocate.

We stop for gas and oil, and in a camp near Weott Lauren and I count 900 rings on a redwood tree stump. Always looking at car models, we chuckle as we see a small church mounted on an automobile chassis. Here we see a sign on a tree—278 ft. to the first limb. At Scotia, an interesting example of the times appears—a reforestation

As we travel over this Golden Bear Bridge over the Klamath River in 1929 we realize it represents a major engineering development of its time. Since our trip, it was destroyed in 1964 by a major flood. The new bridge is again flanked by golden bear statues.

nursery and a huge Pacific Lumber Co. sawmill with nine smoke stacks and piles of logs and lumber. Soon after Rio Dell and Fortuna we see the ocean again. Even for a muddleheaded teenager, this scenery is compelling. We stop in Eureka for groceries and have our lunch on the beach. Following lunch we notice that the temperature has dropped considerably as we travel over a lagoon bridge 0.8 miles in length. From here we are in and out of timber country as we curve around the changing landscape.

The bear statues on the Klamath River bridge seem to be symbolic not only of the region but also the major engineering feat that makes such a structure possible. We pass workers repairing the devastation recently caused by a landslide. Up and down we go, spiraling about the mountain drive with high cliffs on one side and gulches and redwoods on the other. A road repair truck pilots us around a reconstruction zone. As we approach Crescent City we see the ocean again and are told this is our westernmost point.

Here our highway turns inland and after more miles of compelling scenery of trees and crystal clear streams, we see a snow-capped mountain in the distance. We continue to climb up and up and around and around to an elevation of over 2500 feet, through more redwood trees. As we wait again for 10 minutes for road repair we see Steller's jays with black tufts, Madrone trees, and make many more hair-pin turns as we negotiate the mountain road. Soon we join US 199 at the California-Oregon border. After several miles of marvelous natural landscape around us we find an enchanting camp site on the Illinois River, appropriately called Riverside Camp. Thus ends our 210-mile day of outstanding Pacific coast scenery.

Comment

As with the first leg of this family autocamping trip, many of the appeals of northern California remain today. The slower pace allowed more intimate contact with the natural and cultural features and communities. Without high-speed freeways, the struggle to make our 1928 Model A Ford pull us over the mountains and camp in all kinds of weather made our experience much more thrilling than today's bland and fast-paced travel.

This autocamping journey of 1929 is interrupted by the next chapter to identify and derive meaning from an analysis of the 70-year change of tourism in the Northern California Destination. The log of this family trip is continued in Chapter 6.

Chapter 5

The Northern California Destination

The travel image of northern California may not be as clear or strong as other places of the West, such as the Grand Canyon, Rocky Mountains, and the urban destinations of San Francisco or Las Vegas. However, it has its own distinctive place qualities. Citizens here resent the stereotype for all of California as a liberal, uninhibited, and self-indulgent society. This region adheres to its belief that it is just the opposite: conservative, traditional, and conventional.

Its physical and cultural geography lend validity to this perception. For generations, a major travel appeal worldwide has come from its spectacular forests of towering redwoods. Outstanding coastal scenery with sheltered coves and beautiful sunsets has created powerful magnetism in the past that continues today. The Sierra Nevada Mountain range is without peer. And it was here that the famous gold rush began. Examples of early vernacular architecture of log, rock, and shakes can still be found in this area. No other region of the world can boast this combination of superlative attributes.

These factors have been so dominant that both travelers and local citizens are much aware of its special place characteristics. Throughout its history, travelers have sought and enjoyed its extraordinary attractiveness for relaxation, adventure, scenic beauty, outdoor recreation, and solitude. Wealthy travelers in early history who came by train knew this, but its great appeal burst into prominence by autocampers in the 1920s. For the locals, its assets have been so influential as to cause several attempts toward secession from the rest of California.

Because of the toughness of its resources, it has not shown as much wear and tear as other destinations, but this is changing. There is ample evidence that burgeoning growth, including tourism, is producing scenic erosion, pollution of air and water, and excruciating traffic congestion on highways and in communities, especially at peak seasons. Fortunately, today there are many signs of progress toward environmental sensitivity and sustainability and action toward protection of place qualities that made it such a magnet from the beginning. Lessons from this historical sketch are sufficient to give cause for greater planning and care in future tourism development here.

A Cornucopia of Assets

Few regions of the country have withstood mankind's exploitation over many decades as well as northern California. This speaks well for the physical resistance of the land to change as well as the persistence of its people. Serious scars of wanton development do show, however. Mining, timber harvest, and abuse of water and wildlife resources are evident. Even so, it continues to attract increasing millions of visitors who appear to be pleased with its many natural and developed amenities.

Mountains dominate the region, creating a huge horseshoe shape with the open end facing south—the Sacramento Valley. The sky is pierced with dramatic peaks, particularly Mt. Shasta (14,162 feet) and Lassen Peak (10,457 feet). The eastern arm of the horseshoe is mainly the Sierra Nevada Range extending southward through Yosemite. The western arm reaches toward the south along the Coastal Range. The northern loop is made up of the Cascades, including Klamath Mountains. This special place is in dramatic contrast to southern California and other areas of the Southwest.

Today's appeal of northern California is amply justified by its place qualities, now being touted by promoters. Inviting descriptions include abundant opportunities for year-round outdoor recreation among the forests and mountains. For example, within Siskiyou and Shasta Counties the hiker and photographer can visit a variety of beautiful waterfalls, including Mossbrae, Kings Creek, Mill Creek, Burney, Hatchet Creek, Potem, McCloud, and Sweetbriar. The region is dominated by vast acreages managed by the FS, including Eldorado, Tahoe, Plumas, Lassen, Shasta-Trinity, Modoc, and Klamath.

In addition, the region contains a diversity and abundance of state park areas including 33 state parks; 11 beaches, rivers, and lakes; 16 recreation vehicle areas; 20 wilderness areas; 24 historical areas; and 8 reserves. Among the scenic byways of the region are Route 151 (Redding-Shasta Dam), Route 299 (Redding-Eureka), Route 3 (Weaverville-Yreka), Route 96 (Hornbrook-Willow Creek), and Routes 44, 89, and 36. The NPS also has a very strong presence in the region, such as Lassen Volcanic National Park and Yosemite National Park. Farther south, along the Sierras, are located Sequoia and Kings Canyon National Parks, including Mt. Whitney (14,494 feet). In addition, there are many national monuments, wildlife refuges, natural landmarks, and national recreation areas.

The Search for Sovereignty

This region's rugged terrain is its greatest asset and also its handicap. For generations it lacked good access and many local people blamed state politics. The political issue of roads has been the focus of agitation and incentive among northern residents for many years. Even as early as the gold rush, pleas were made to the California legislature for better roads. In frustration from inaction, a bill to create a separate state of Shasta was introduced in 1852, followed by several more proposals for separate statehood. A further argument was poor state support for protection against hostile Indians who resented white settlement. The region's persistence toward sovereignty helps explain today's animosity toward the south. As late as 1941, this region, together with a portion of southern Oregon, actually seceded as the new state of Jefferson with its capital at Yreka.[1] Even though World War II halted progress on fruition of this plan, the movement did stimulate greater political awareness. In recent years, this has resulted in more paved roads and the trunk line Interstate 5.

The people of northern California continue to advocate splitting the state into northern and southern sections.[2] At one time the county of Mendocino tried to secede. In 1992, 27 out of 33 counties in central and northern California voted for separation of north from south.[3] At issue is the monumental and critical demand in the south for the north's water and a continuing fight to maintain a slower lifestyle and a balanced economy in the north. Even tourism growth is seen as a mixed blessing, providing replacement for fading economies in many towns but also threatening the abundant natural resources. The geographical physical and cultural qualities of this place have been sufficiently distinct to justify today's concern over tourism's sustainability. Many environmental activists in the north see growth and increased development a major threat to resources such as wildlife, fish, and forests. Many lumber mills have shut down in recent years with environmentalism, poor management, and politics cited as causes.

A north-south cleavage is the thrust of blatant tourism promotion of the "north state" by the Redding *Record Searchlight* newspaper and their special section, *Recreation '98*.[4] Without making precise boundaries for the region, their graphics illustrate that it extends to the south along a line from San Francisco to Lake Tahoe, to Oregon on the north, and to Nevada on the east and the Pacific coast on the west. Even beyond the hucksterism of promotion, there are substantial geographic facts that prove the abundant natural and cultural resources of the region. In addition to the scenic and historic features, the region contains magnificent forests, streams, and mountains, largely held in public trust since it was in the public domain.

Travel Genesis

Unlike the eastern seaboard, California was a part of Mexico, resulting in travel trails oriented south-to-north rather than east-to-west. Although the end of the Mexican War of 1848 brought the state into the Union, its orientation was still toward the south. It took the discovery of gold in 1848 to change this forever—both overland and by water. Wagon trains across the Great Plains and ships bore thousands of immigrants hot with gold fever. The image of California as a land of outstanding travel objectives in the 1920s certainly had ample historic precedent.

An important California place, today as in the past, is Sutter's Mill, east of Sacramento, where the gold rush began, but strictly by accident. John Sutter's dream of creating a settlement empire, New Helvetica, in the Sacramento Valley demanded construction timber. He engaged James W. Marshall to build a sawmill but in 1848 Marshall discovered a few flakes of gold in the tail race. This discovery set off an avalanche of prospectors, not only from eastern United States but from many other countries. No place in the world had ever experienced such an outpouring of entrepreneurship. Soon, thousands believed they could gain wealth only by their own initiative. At that time the fastest travel access from the east was approximately 5 months by water, rounding Cape Horn to arrive in San Francisco. Just as fast as river boats could be built, prospectors could travel up the American River to the gold fields, such as Folsom and Placerville. These wild and madcap times are characterized by place names such as Fiddletown, Rough and Ready, and Hangtown.

A San Francisco merchant, William A. Leidesdorff, is said to be the father of riverboats on the American, to reach the gold fields 120 miles inland.[5] The first was the *Sitka*, composed of knocked down pieces in a shipment from Russia and reassembled in 1847. However, a storm put her to the bottom the next year. She was soon followed by many more, finer, and faster stern- and sidewheelers. Riverboats such as the *Rainbow, Senator, Lady Washington, California*, and the *Antelope*, an excursion boat from Long Island Sound, and many others kept river traffic busy. The most ornate and largest was the 530-ton sidewheeler, *New World*. Prospectors of every race, color, and creed came in droves. Such water transportation spawned many thriving communities alongside the American River.

Then disaster hit. Without realizing the consequences, hydraulic mining produced such volumes of silt downstream that soon the river depth was no longer navigable. Thus ended one audacious and colorful chapter in the rush to the West. The first railroad west of the Rocky Mountains ran between goldfields for 22 miles to Sacramento in 1855.[6] Entrepreneur Sam Brannan of San Francisco became exceedingly wealthy by selling mining supplies to the gold prospectors headed for the American River region. Farmers, soldiers, and merchants flooded his shop. The boom towns on the way were wild and egalitarian. Anonymity fostered freedom from inhibitions, resulting in abundant prostitution, gambling, and boozing. Although the gold rush was short-lived, mostly over by 1850, it changed forever the land use and image of the West. Originally conceived as a wild monster, the land proved it was rich in resources and had settlement potential.

The huge modern California wine industry had its beginnings in the early 1800s when Franciscan monks planted some European grape varieties for sacramental purposes. Reasonably large production then began in southern California and soon moved northward. A major setback occurred in the 1880s caused by a disease called phylloxera. More resistant stocks were replanted and, with new hybrids and better viticulture, vineyards expanded tremendously into the Sonoma, Napa, Santa Clara, and Livermore valleys. Vineyards and wine production have become the major economic power as well as extensive land user.

Throughout the next decades, America was caught up in tremendous turmoil of growth. The gold boom had brought the West into focus, resulting in admission of California as the 31st state in 1850. Issues of population growth, women's rights, slavery, Irish immigration due to potato famine, and Thoreau's *Walden, or Life in the Woods* (a plea for man's union with nature) were indicators of the turbulent times. By 1860 the nation's population of 31 million was showing dissention that finally broke out in the devastating Civil War. Then, as western migration renewed, greater clash with Indians prompted the building of a great many frontier forts. The economy took a dive in the panic of 1873, but with new railroads crossing the entire country by 1875, society and economy again began to climb, focusing attention on the promised western paradise. Industrialization was in full swing and a middle class grew in numbers and in wealth. Even involvement in a great war in Europe did not greatly diminish the nation's continuing progress.

Getting There

In the 1880s, travelers from San Francisco to Portland had two choices.[7] Three steamship companies offered ocean access two or three times a week. Overland travel was much more difficult but included striking landscapes on the way. The Central Pacific Railroad gave access to Redding, followed by 275 miles of stage carriage over rugged terrain to Roseburg, Oregon. The well-shaken and exhausted traveler would have traversed rigorous trails through the mountains of Siskiyou and Rogue River en route. Then the traveler would take the Oregon and California Railroad for 200 miles to Portland. Now, Interstate 5 can take a traveler from Sacramento to Portland in about 12 hours but with a decidedly different trip—a much more bland experience.

The autocampers of the 1920s could reach their travel destinations much more rapidly than the train-carriage travelers of the 1800s and gain an experience as rich or even better. Automobile travelers were free from the schedule and route confinement of railroad lines and carriage trails. They moved slowly enough to grasp the many nuances of the landscape, such as ranches and cattle, vineyards, orchards, vegetable crops, and an abundance of California poppies. It is at the cities that change for better and worse has been dramatic. The scenic and cultural assets between towns still include the power and beauty of the ocean and its beaches, rugged cliffs, mountains and forest backdrop, ancient mammoth redwoods, remnants of Spanish and Mexican missions, the historic stamp of settlement, fishing villages, and extensive acreages of vineyards and wineries.

In the autocamping days of the 1920s, the travel from San Francisco across the bay to Sausalito was by ferry with the Mission San Rafael as the first major point of interest on Route 101 northward. Even at that time, the traveler was aware of moving into "the wine country," as locals call this territory.

A major point of interest then and now is Santa Barbara. Here a must-see was (and continues today) the Santa Barbara Mission of 1786 and the Franciscan Church. This place was important among the 21 missions that had been built by Mexico in California by 1833. Labeled "The Queen of the California Missions," it has enlightened visitors for these many decades. The city, in spite of great growth, has retained much of its original charm. The golden beaches still lure visitors. After an earthquake in 1929, the older architectural character of downtown with rounded arcades, adobe-colored stucco exteriors, and red tile roofs was mandated by the city.

Modern travelers interested in cultural history can now visit 21 Mexican and Spanish missions of 1769 to 1823, linked by the former El Camino Real from the Mexican border to the San Francisco area. This "King's Highway" roughly parallels Route 101 for over 500 miles along the coast. Many have been restored and are interpreted for the public.

Road development in the early 1900s was bogged down with political wrangling and pork-barrel projects, resulting in a maze of special interest and disconnected roads.[8] Not until bond issues of 1916 and 1919 was there a semblance of an overall state system. These early roads, even though often paved with 4-inch concrete, were only 15 feet wide. After the federal highway act of 1916 and the introduction of the gasoline tax, highways began to improve. As automobile registrations boomed way beyond the national average, the move toward better roads and roadside tourist services such as campgrounds and cabins gained momentum.

The autocampers of the 1920s were lured greatly to the entire coastal region from the Mexican border northward. Then the main points of interest included slipping over into Tijuana just to say another country had been visited. Further northward were the amenities of San Diego and its Naval port, occasionally stopping at beaches, admiring the extensive citrus groves and getting free samples, and visiting Los Angeles to see if Hollywood was as sinful as reported.

One of the earliest travel organizations in the nation was the Automobile Club of Southern California. Its Map Service Department distributed 4,103,965 maps in 1928 in spite of the fact that there were only 7000 miles of paved road in the entire state.[9] This organization provided unusual service to its members through its fleet of patrol cars that regularly roamed the highways giving aid. This service included towing, emergency gas and oil, minor mechanical repairs, and first aid service.

Environmental Issues

Except for publicly owned park and recreation areas, little environmental planning and design took place in this destination region over the last 70 years. Two major forces precluded tourism planning and design: swelling in-migration and tourist business opportunism.

Because of forest and mining exploitation of the abundant resources, immense volumes of people came from eastern United States and overseas and settled. Motivated by new jobs and a better economy, little attention was given to the consequences. Clear-cutting of forests exposes hill and mountainside areas to severe erosion.[10] The resulting soil and silt are dumped into streams, ruining water quality and water life. Flooding, resulting from recent clear-cutting, was reported to have destroyed seven homes in Stafford following a "tsunami of stumps and trees." This is a continuing issue. The rate of clear-cuts in the Sierra Nevada has increased by 2500% since 1992. Local communities receive approximately 75% of their economy from tourism and less than 3% from forestry, suggesting that forest cutting issues are less important than tourism.

The population explosion has placed considerable stress upon limited water supplies, prompting the building of dams in streams. Although the impoundments have temporarily relieved the shortage, great damage has been done to fish populations, especially salmon. It was reported that the beautiful Navarro Estuary, once a thriving asset, is now endangered, primarily due to severely reduced flows from dams upstream.[11] The coho salmon, once an abundant resource, are nearly extinct and the steelhead are dangerously threatened. Controversial are the state and federal regulations that have allowed so many riparian diversions. Over 130 illegally built reservoirs on the Navarro System have been identified. This case of a threatened resource deserves attention not only by environmentalists but also by tourism leaders and developers.

Another recent environmental issue reported by the Sierra Club that impacts tourism is the great growth of Concentrated Animal Feeding Operations (CAFOs), especially in the Central Valley of California. When thousands of hogs, chickens, or cattle

A hazardous location for buildings in the West is too close to waterfronts of streams, lakes, and the Pacific. Illustrated is an example of extensive flood damage to a vacation home adjacent to the American River, California.

are concentrated in one spot, the waste pollutes streams, kills fish, and contaminates drinking water. Slaughterhouse production of thousands of animals per day also contributes to odor and waste problems. Tourism planners for the future must consider these as part of their agenda.

Although documentation is scarce, there is no doubt that millions more tourists make considerable impact on the environment. Their automobiles and tour buses increase air pollution and their noise and trampling pose a threat to wildlife. As tourist businesses grow, they make demands on infrastructure, such as water supplies, waste disposal systems, police protection, fire control, and road expansion. Huge acreages of land are consumed by new ski areas, resorts, and other physical developments of attractions, lodging, and food services for tourists. Tourist sprawl invades wildlife habitat, not only reducing numbers of animals but also increasing dangerous people-animal conflict. These developments not only exact monetary costs, they also create social and environmental costs. Planning and development of tourism in northern California must consider the tradeoffs from further growth.

This brief sampling of environmental issues in northern California is sufficient to alert tourism planners and developers that the brilliant natural resource assets of the region also have a dark side. If tourism is to thrive, these and many other related environmental issues must be dealt with in the future.

A Tour Critique

For illustration of how tourism has emerged, a recent tour over the same route that was popular in the autocamping 1920s revealed several gains and losses over these seven decades. Touring for sightseeing had an early precedent that has continued to grow over the last many decades even though travel conditions varied greatly. In addition to more efficient and comfortable automobiles, the tent camping of the 1920s has almost disappeared. It has mostly been replaced by the newer generation of recreation vehicles (RVs)—vans, motor homes, trailers—and travelers favoring lodging in motels or hotels. The drama of northern California's geography has not diminished greatly in the minds of modern touring travelers. A cross section tour from Sacramento to the coast and on north to the Cascades and Oregon border offers today's tourists many of the values available to autocampers of the 1920s.

Sacramento to the Coast

West of Sacramento, Route 128 begins its scenic cross section of valleys, mountains, streams, forests, and diverse agriculture. Most of this highway was available to autocampers of the 1920s and still retains its visitor interest. After passing through flat field crop land of the lower Napa Valley, the roadside scenery changes to extensive orchards of nut trees, followed by rocky road cuts on the mountainside near Lake Berryessa. Formed by Monticello Dam, it was built in 1957 for water storage, flood control, and recreation by the BLM. Concession agreements with several resorts and interpretive centers now assist the traveler with needed services.

In California BLM manages over 17 million acres of public land, much of which is used for outdoor recreation, such as for off-road vehicle use, whitewater rafting, camping, hiking, and other activities. Because California has such a high visitor demand, BLM's policy priorities have been declared in a recent strategic plan.[12] It calls for higher management for visitor services, resource protection, and permitting construction. As with other federal resource management agencies, visitor pressure is demanding greater design and management for tourist use.

Moving northward, the next town for early campers as well as modern tourists is St. Helena. This pleasant town is retaining much of its past with restoration of older wineries and historic buildings and yet is adapting to visitors with touristy shops. This vast wine region experienced two major setbacks in past history: a vine louse infestation in the 1880s and a severe drop in market demand during the Prohibition years of the 1920s. Today, wineries are so popular that traffic volume of tourists in this town is becoming a major issue as reported in a study of tourism in 1990, but no major solution was offered.[13] Modern attractions include the new Napa City-County Library and the Silverado Museum containing memorabilia of one-time resident, Robert Louis Stevenson. The Napa Valley Wine Train, an 18-mile special interpretive and fun attraction, runs from Napa City to St. Helena. Environmentalists fear that this is becoming so popular that it adds to already serious traffic congestion, especially at the existing 90 highway crossings.[14]

Passing through many vineyards, this scenic drive brings the visitor to Calistoga, named by combining the name California with another mineral spring, Saratoga, in New York. The town was laid out by the wealthy gold rush entrepreneur, Sam Brannan, in 1859, and today features his ornate residence. Again, threading through masses of vineyards and wineries, the traveler arrives at Healdsburg. It is evident that history buffs and city planners are guiding tourism's growth to protect the charm and functional needs for both residents and visitors. The downtown plaza and the Carnegie Library restored into the Healdsburg Museum in 1989 are evidence of this sustainable policy.

North of Healdsburg, as Route 128 joins 101, the Alexander Valley is entered. This is a special "winery appellation" area that is divided into two regions. The southern area is supportive of Chardonnay and Gewurztraminer whereas the northern part near Geyserville and Cloverdale is best for Zinfandel and Rhone varieties.

After moving through more vineyards and towns of Geyserville, Asti, and Cloverdale, Route 128 takes off westward toward the coast. The entire scenic drive is well maintained and signed, affording the traveler a variety of beautiful landscapes, not unlike those seen by autocampers of the 1920s. With much twisting and turning, many turnouts allow viewing and photographing the hilly countryside that then flattens out in the Anderson Valley, sprinkled with many wineries. Alongside is Hendy Woods State Park, a delightful break in mountain driving that contains huge virgin redwoods, the first major encounter of these giants since leaving Sacramento. After Navarro, the road takes on its own spiraling, demanding full attention by the driver to keep from plunging into the Navarro River. After many sharp turns the traveler bursts upon the Pacific and joins Route 1. In just a few miles, Mendocino appears.

The Scenic Coast

Route 1 continues its important coastal-redwood theme all the way from Mendocino and beyond to Leggett where it joins Route 101. The fact that landscape vistas and cultural restorations have endured over seven decades is testimony to the values held by local residents as well as to design and management policies of the several public land holders along the way. In *California—Official State Visitor's Guide*[15] are cited many place features of interest to tourists, most of which were established many years ago. In towns, shopping, walking in parks, visiting museums and art galleries, and dining in local eateries are now abundantly available. In between the rural and city areas, lands managed by state parks, FS, BLM, county parks, and private camp and resort areas provide the tourist with many natural and cultural attractions, well rooted to special place resources. Especially from Leggett on, ancient redwoods, wilderness areas, wildlife sanctuaries, rocky precipices, and beaches support a diversity of outdoor recreation interest. Fortunately, for modern visitors, many areas of the big trees, *Sequoia sempervirens*, have been protected and opened to visitor use. In these places, the overwhelming magnificence of this rare display of nature is as forceful as before. These forests continue to dwarf the human ego and force even the most jaded observer to reevaluate his role in the universe.

A major point of interest, seen by autocampers of the 1920s as well as today, is the Benbow Inn, opened in 1926. Now its upscale services cater to wealthier tourists from San Francisco and Sacramento. It boasts designation as a National Historic Landmark and carries on the English tradition of tea and scones in the afternoon. Benbow Lake State Recreation Area offers picnicking, hiking, canoeing, swimming, and sailing. Nearby is Richardson Grove State Park, filled with the huge redwoods and includes a museum visitor center as well as facilities for camping, hiking, and picnicking.

Of particular significance is Humboldt Redwoods State Park, now over 50,000 acres of mostly stately redwoods and an occasional mix of oaks and diverse conifers. Observed by autocampers in the 1920s and now identified as a special redwood drive on the old road is the 33-mile Avenue of the Giants. Ample stops provide the visitor opportunity to admire, bask in the overpowering atmosphere, and photograph these monarchs. Public and private campgrounds, food services, and inns offer needed services. But the dominant theme is marred by occasional private holdings with ticky-tacky curio shops, drive-through trees, and nonnative trinkets. These aesthetic intrusions jar the senses and might better be located outside this great scenic drive.

Remnants of the old road used decades ago offer the visitor a more intimate landscape drive through Scotia, Rio Dell, and Loleta, where it again joins the newer Route 101. From Eureka to Crescent City, any description of the scenic appeal seems redun-

Even though modern slow-moving tourists appreciate this scenic mountain drive along the northern California coast, there is great risk from speeding truck traffic. This issue is a challenge before highway and tourism planners for the future.

dant because the same dominance of redwoods, coastal vistas, and kinky mountain roads abound. Much of this drive benefits from controls of public agencies, such as the outstanding Redwoods National Park. It was basic landscape design philosophy of the early 1900s that stimulated the Sempirvirens Club to pressure the California legislature to establish the California Redwood Park Commission in 1902 and proceed to acquire redwood lands.[16] In 1968, state and federal redwood lands were consolidated to form Redwood National and State Parks.

From Crescent City northeasterly on Route 199 one encounters another outstanding scenic drive. It winds around sharp turns and over major hills as it threads through beautiful forests, such as in Six Rivers National Forest.

There are three major differences between travel here in the 1920s and today. Modern automobiles with their increased power, quieter engines, and more comfortable suspension move up and down the mountains with almost effortless ease compared to the clutching, shifting gears, and straining engines to their maximum capacity in the 1920s. Highway engineering changes, such as widening, hard surfacing, and reducing gradients have also made travel much easier.

A third consequence of change over seven decades is the danger and stress now created by the mix of travel purpose. Commercial use, such as by huge semi trucks and large log-haulers, is conflicting with tourist travel. Tourists seek a slower paced movement in order to experience the sightseeing values of the corridor. Truckers view the curves, steep slopes, and tourists as obstacles. Because of their familiarity with the highway and desire to cover distances as quickly as possible, they often overwhelm tourists, even forcing them off the roads with their higher speed. This design dilemma of scenic roads is not easily solved except by alternate routes for different types of traffic.

Although one can be critical of several negative impacts of tourism on this tour, much of the charm of the 1920s and before remains. There are instances of urban sprawl from metropolitan San Francisco in smaller towns farther north. Traffic congestion threatens scenic appreciation and even safety on some kinky mountain roads. Invasion by franchise sameness dulls some of the area's distinctive qualities. Even so, credit must be given to many conservationists, designers, businesses, city management, nonprofit organizations, and a great array of state and federal agencies for their vigilance on environmental stability, valuable to both residents and tourists.

This tour is just one instance of how many areas of northern California have retained much of their original tourist value in spite of seven decades of change.

The Redwoods

Since the beginning and continuing today, the redwood forests have experienced constant wrangling between timber interests and protection advocates. They had been severely logged since the 1850s, creating huge landscape scars from clear-cutting that were not only aesthetically ugly but also resulted in erosion in watershed areas. The thirst for timber caused extensive harvesting and was compounded by the national philosophy of settlement, resulting in much clearing of forested land, including stands of redwoods.[17] The Homestead Act of 1862 viewed all western lands as open for development.

The redwood protection issue has been caught up for decades in the roller coaster ethic of environmentalism.[18] A reasonably strong effort continued until the 1920s, followed by apathy through the 1940s, taking on new energy in the 1960s and beyond. The 1968 and 1978 Redwood National Park acts made progress for protection but aggressive harvesting took place between these two federal efforts. Even today, the tourist view from the road is deceiving because vast acreages are cut over behind the screen of ancient trees. Among the many pleas for the stay of execution of the redwoods was that of the Sierra Club's, "Epilogue or Epitaph?" of 1963.[19] The timber interests are labeled vandals, barbarians, and immoral abusers of a rare resource. A parallel is made with the extinction of animals to satisfy market demand for furs.

The road to sustainability has been and continues to be very rocky. In the 1960s, environmental groups such as Save-The-Redwoods League and the Sierra Club believed that enough damage had been done and demanded a halt. By consolidating several federal, state, and private forest lands in the redwood region, a total of 58,000 acres became the Redwood National Park in 1968, still a fraction of the total redwood forest. A compromise gave NPS some authority over harvesting in a 30,000 acre Park Protection Zone beyond the park boundary. Park policy includes a great amount of rehabilitation on heavily cut and eroding lands. The unique qualities of this place may now be perpetuated for future generations and long-term conservation. Nature trails and interpretive centers and programs may gradually educate the public on the wisdom of balancing protection with development.

The local social and economic pressure from timber-dependent communities has made it extremely difficult for environmentalists and politicians to defend redwood protection, especially when based only on emotion. Certainly a backlash of public opinion takes place when open discussion between factions that might lead to mitigation is replaced by extreme measures, bordering on terrorism. Tactics such as driving nails in trees so that sawmill operators are injured or burning buildings such as at Vail, Colorado,[20] make news but offer little constructive solution and instead exacerbate the continuing conflict.

Redwood National Park, declared a World Heritage Site by UNESCO in 1980, now enjoyed by millions of tourists, would not exist today if it hadn't been stimulated by many environmental constituencies and a public investment of billions of dollars.[21] Even today resentment among timber companies continues.

Of course, today's protected areas have come at a price and remain controversial. Localities that anticipated a continued high-volume timber harvest, providing their basic economic support, have difficulty accepting another value for these forests—habitat for rare wildlife and revenues from thousands of outdoor recreational and scenery-loving tourists. It is clear in this region of northern California that travel service businesses—motels, restaurants, shops, commercial attractions—are now not only more plentiful than seven decades ago but also are replacing much of the loss in the timber economy.

Several interpretive visitor centers in the Redwood National and State Parks are already in place and others are planned.[22] Most of these provide visitor guidance, but the NPS recognized the need for larger and more in-depth museums, exhibits, book sales, and lecture halls that can provide educational material on sustainability of natural resources. The General Management Plan of 1998 includes plans for such a

An example of long-time land use sustainability is the original F. K. Lane Grove, dedicated in 1928 and now the Smithe Redwoods Reserve, northern California. Decades later it is a beautiful and restful natural resource area for modern tourists.

major interpretive center, located on a "hardened site" and designed to fit into the coastal redwood forest landscape.

Today federal and state agencies jointly administer the Redwood National and State Parks, a combined area of 110,232 acres, visited annually by over 1,250,000 tourists.[23] The area offers 40 miles of beautiful scenic coastline. Visitors can enjoy driving, hiking, shoreline walks, photography, fishing, picnicking, bird watching, wild flower appreciation, and camping. Management programs emphasize changes such as greater public education to cope with increased visitor use. Interpretation/education focuses on stream and wildlife ecology, Native American culture, and special characteristics of the unique tide pools and redwood forests.

The special tourist significance of these Redwood parks are cited here because of their unusual landscape characteristics like no other place in the world.

Toward Sustainability

To reduce the ambiguity of the term sustainable tourism, several authors have attempted definitions.[24] The range includes many different meanings: social, managerial, political, economic, cultural, and environmental. Although all are important for tourism in the West and northern California, the emphasis in this book is on cultural and environmental sustainability.

Throughout the region today many notable examples of sustainable design can be cited. Some had precedents several years ago but few were available to autocamping tourists in the 1920s. Included here is a diversity of cases that illustrate today's trend toward sustainable development of tourism in northern California.

Historic Protection

In spite of California's propensity for growth and newness, historic preservation in the state began early and continues to expand as a major movement, a great aid to tourism planning and development. The Landmarks Club of Southern California was active in mission restoration and preservation as early as 1899.[25] John Russell Knowland is credited with being a major activist in 1902 for historic preservation. By 1925 many of the first European settlements in California were being protected. In 1961, the California legislature authorized the then Division of Beaches and Parks (later Department of Parks and Recreation) to work with historical societies to make a study of the status of historic preservation in the state. After landscape architect William Penn Mott, Jr. became director in 1967, he made many departmental innovations including programs for historic redevelopment.

A major step was taken in 1968 when the department worked with the NPS on the National Historic Preservation Act at Asilomar at the Pacific Coast Regional Conference. This and other events stimulated many citizen volunteers to provide help on acquisition of historic sites. California has had not only strong natural resource preservation advocates but also a long history of many constituencies supporting historic protection and restoration. Evidence of the modern significance of cultural sites to tourists was the creation of the California Cultural Tourism Coalition that produced a 120-page booklet describing 13 cultural site tours.

An example of planning for historic sustainability is the work by landscape architect James Quale for Marconi Conference Center State Historic Park, located in West Marin County near Marshall.[26] This was the site of the high-power Trans-Pacific radio station of the American Marconi Wireless Telegraph Company, established in 1912. The design and development purposes are:

- Preserve and restore the historic buildings and site.
- Interpret the history associated with the Marconi period.
- Preserve the unique natural resources of the area.
- Promote small and medium size conferences in a rural setting.

For these purposes, this 62-acre site combines tourist use with resource protection. Major facilities include lodging, exercise rooms, food service, and conference and meeting facilities. Site development includes a loop trail, sports courts, recreation area, vistas across Tomales Bay, and protection of grassland, forest, and coastal scrub. Major circulation is restricted to pedestrian use of a pathway system. A special element of the site plan is protection of open space where further construction is prohibited. This case demonstrates the resource sustainable and public use policy of the state park system of California.

In spite of the sameness of city expansions everywhere across America, many communities of this region have made substantial efforts toward historic renewal, interpretation, and adaptation to tourism in recent decades. A remarkable change for the better over these many years has been a new generation of museums depicting natural and cultural histories of localities. The uniqueness of place that was nearly obliterated with "progress" is again being recovered. Millions of private and volunteer dollars have been invested in new sites, buildings, and exhibits that offer visitors interesting and informative insight into the past. For many years, local museum advocates accepted virtually any and all artifacts given to them, resulting in what often appeared as a junk yard. Today's philosophy focuses on narrowing interpretation to specific themes, supported by artifacts and descriptive information. New also are audio and visual technologies that instantly give the visitor powerful images and sounds of virtual reality.

Among the many who are providing professional design input for such centers is the firm of Exhibits, Inc.[27] Hannah M. Clayborn, historian and curation consultant, and John C. Howland, architect and designer, are the principals. To their credit are many western works including Sonoma County Museum, Healdsburg Museum, Petaluma Museum, Treasure Island Museum, and work for the Alexander Valley Association.

Closely related to museums, often overlapping in function, are the new visitor interpretive centers. Begun many years ago by the NPS, these new facilities offer visitors a vicarious experience so satisfying that further penetration into wild and fragile landscapes is not needed. The complete visitor interpretive center is very effective to reducing environmental impact of growing visitor pressure. Active in the field of designing these centers are many landscape and design firms throughout the West. For example, the firm of Inside-Outside, Inc.,[28] was founded by John Hanna, now supported by talented staff: Chad DeVore, interpretive planner; Gary Mullins, ecological specialist; Mary Mullins, multimedia designer; Deborah Duke, graphic designer; Mickey Schilling, illustrator; and Lisa Brochu, writer. To their credit in recent years are many public and private interpretive centers throughout the West.

Perhaps the most significant community in northern California to have preserved its cultural and land integrity is Mendocino, the little New England-style community on the coast. It is a gem of historic preservation but now feeling the pressure of too much tourism success. The setting for the TV series, *Murder She Wrote*, and films such as *East of Eden*, this community is frozen in a turn-of-the century time. Back in the 1930s, the Mendocino Woodlands site was one of many Recreation Demonstration Areas that received federal funding for protection and development.[29] The town has been named a National Historic Preservation District and the surrounding area is

The Pacific coastal town of Mendocino has retained its rich historic patina by means of strong preservation policies. However, it is now being threatened by too many tourists. A clue to sustainable concern is the local environmental office, shown by the sign in the foreground.

free from shopping malls and commercial development because it is surrounded by the Mendocino Headlands State Park. The politically savvy landscape architect, William Penn Mott, as director of California park department, envisioned the need for stabilizing this landscape setting and gradually traded timberlands elsewhere to Boise Cascade for the establishment of the park. Now the trails and scenic areas of the park not only protect the community from encroachment but also enhance visitors' experiences with compatible features. Rapidly facing local planners is the growing issue of automobile and visitor capacity. At the moment, it is a fine example of sustainable development. Local museums, interpretive centers, and arts continue to enrich the quality of every visit. The amenities of the Hill House, Ford House, Kelley House, MacCallum House, the Presbyterian Church, and the Mendocino Hotel take one back to the atmosphere of the late 1800s, reminiscent of this town's early logging and port history. Mendocino has no franchise lodging or food services. Artists of the coast display their creations at a popular Mendocino Art Center, and the Mendocino Theatre Company entertains visitors and locals with performing arts. Featured on Lansing Street is a folk sculpture, Father Time and the Maiden, carved from a redwood block by a mill worker, Erick Albertson, in the late 1800s.

Eureka's Old Town redevelopment is not only economically viable with historic reuse by offices but also is aesthetically appealing to visitors. At the end of Second Street is The Carson Mansion, an excellent restoration of Victoriana.

Also up the California coast lies Eureka with its Old Town redevelopment. Preservationists and designers have created a fascinating target for visitors as well as reclaiming a decadent area for local use. The past rocky economy of timber and fishing activities is now being surpassed by tourism. An abundance of quality lodging and food service establishments and museums add to the appeal of Old Town. Once the skid row of the city, it has now been upgraded with restored buildings and new streetscapes that are colorful and functional for both visitors and residents. At the end of 2nd Street is the magnificently restored Gothic-Victorian home with superb craftsmanship in wood and stained glass, once owned by the lumber king, William Carson. However, today in Eureka there are threats of toxic waste from paper mills and a decommissioned nuclear power plant, major concerns of environmentalists. Measures are under way to correct these problems.

Community Tourism Sustainability

Communities are beginning to make plans for solving tourist transportation pressures. For example, around Lake Tahoe tourism has grown so extensively that local people and visitors are now observing major negative impacts, especially traffic congestion. The heaviest use of the area is from Sacramento and San Francisco tourists.

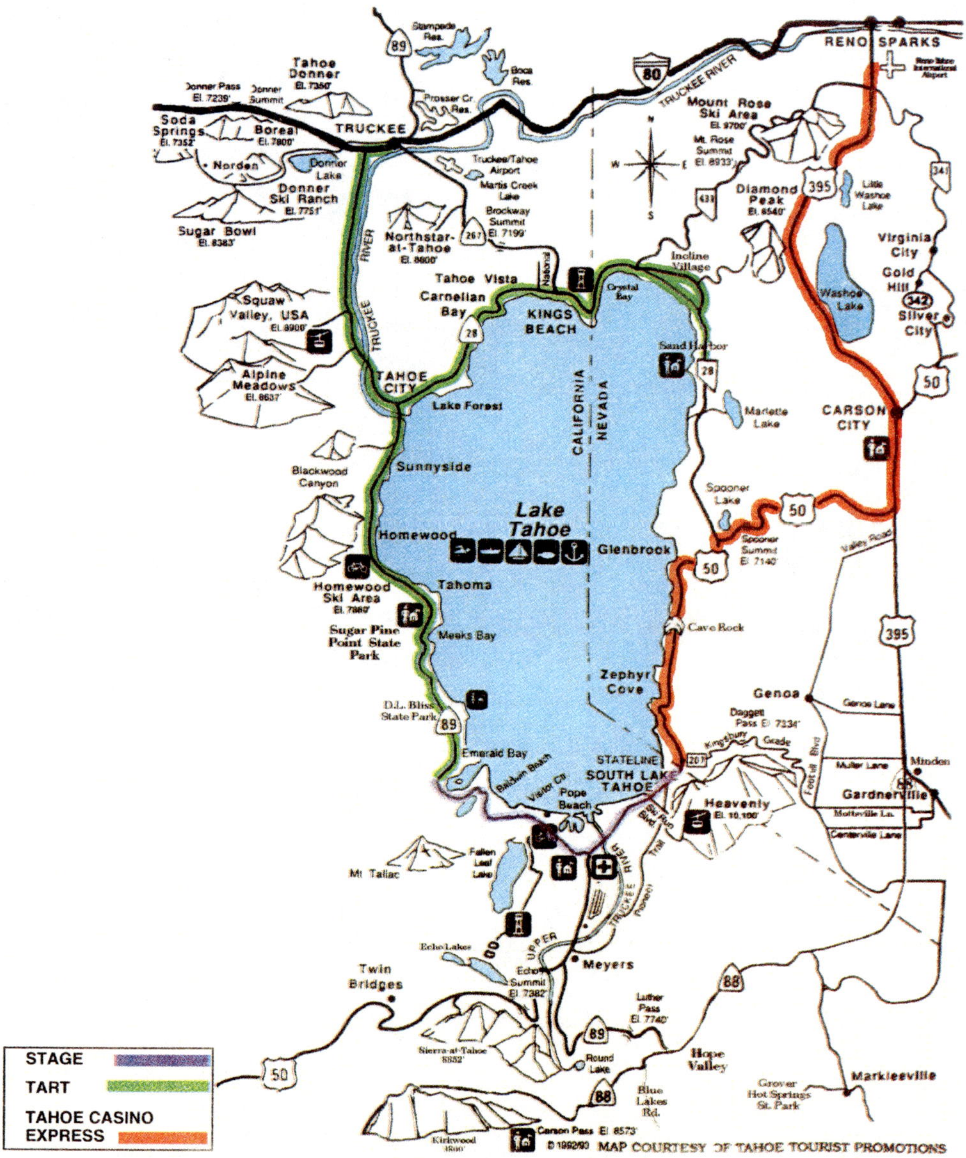

Businesses around Lake Tahoe have greatly relieved peak traffic congestion with the establishment of three new transit systems: Tahoe Regional Area Transit, South Tahoe Area Ground Express, and Tahoe Casino Express. This action represents a constructive private sector effort toward sustainability. (Source: Tahoe Tourist Promotions)

Businesses in several communities of North Tahoe began to share their concerns and initiated a process of solving major problems. For guidance, they engaged the landscape architectural firm of Design Workshop.[30] The first step, led by designer Richard Shaw, was the creation of a quasi-governmental tourist association. This organization has been effective in creating cohesion among the many segments of business, government, and residents that never existed before.

Positive results have already emerged: dissention has been smoothed over, priorities for changes needed have been identified, attractions have been integrated, and a trolley system has been installed to reduce traffic congestion at peak periods. The firm cites this case as an example of the great potential of a catalytic role for landscape architects to build consensus for tourism sustainability.

American transportation ills were brought into vivid focus when several delegates from states and local communities visited systems in Netherlands, Germany, and Switzerland. The conclusions showed how superior people-movement was in these countries and how the US had created its own problems by poor planning of its cities. The delegate from California identified urban sprawl as a major problem here.[31] The higher urban densities in Europe had fostered a balance between modes—automobile, bus, rail, and sometimes air—not done very well here. European planning and land use regulations favored mass transit systems, greatly reducing the volume of automobile traffic and congestion. A significant part of transportation policy is pedestrianism, generally lacking in the US. These lessons from the European experience apply equally well to major tourist attractions in northern California, especially for parks and other resource areas. Both private and public tourism sectors must admit that traffic congestion is bound to exacerbate the problem in the future as tourism expands.

Another instance of such catalytic action by designers is the plan proposal for Crissey Field on San Francisco Bay.[32] The process is resulting in increased environmental sustainability. The site is a National Historic Landmark managed by NPS. It includes a long stretch of beach and tidal marsh that once was the locale of pioneer aviation in the early 1900s. The first challenge was to gain some semblance of harmony among the many constituencies who held their own contrasting agendas for the place, ranging from historic and wetland preservation to local use for windsurfing, walking dogs, enjoying vistas, and getting to the beach. A team of landscape architects was engaged and spent many hours of discussion to reduce conflicts and reach toward consensus for a solution. Those involved included Kirt Rieder, George Hargreaves, Mary Margaret Jones, and Michael Boland. After producing many alternative design schemes, a final plan has evolved that is physically sound and aesthetically pleasing and resolves the majority of concerns that the separate groups had in the beginning.

Because most cities of the nation were established on rivers or coasts, these sites have endured a long history of use and abuse. Originally, these waters were the major arteries of commerce and transport so industrial building was oriented to them. Then as cities grew and new rail and highway access shifted emphasis away from the waterfront, the sites accumulated the worst blight: liquid and solid waste, delinquent and decaying structures, and focus for the worst crime. But in the 1970s a turning point toward reclamation of urban waterfronts took place. A leader in this movement was San Antonio with its Paseo del Rio in the center of town.[33] Within the decade of 1967-1977, the decaying and crime-ridden horseshoe bend of the river had been converted into a major amenity, visited by millions of people and supported by local residents.

This park-entertainment center turned the downtown around—reduced crime, and saved many of the businesses that in most cities were escaping to suburbia.

More recently, a similar revitalization has taken place with the sustainable design of the urban water core of San Jose, California, the Guadalupe Riverfront Park.[34] Landscape architect George Hargreaves has created not only a beautiful and delightful parklike setting for visitors and townspeople, but also important flood control. For many years the US Corps of Engineers has attempted to solve flood control with straight-line concrete channelization. These solutions have proven inadequate and ugly. Hargreaves' astute design, based on fluid dynamics and revegetation with native plants, was accepted as superior to the rip-rap design of the Corps. A riverwalk links several other amenities such as the Confluence Park, Center for Performing Arts, the Children's Discovery Museum, and sites for major festivals. Acting as a designer and catalyst, many political, engineering, and environmental groups were brought together for a final and acceptable solution.

"Highway 89: California's Scenic Mountain Route"[35] is a noteworthy environmental accomplishment. By means of the catalytic role of specialists from California State University at Chico, progress was made on a regional scale. Partly stimulated from travel business loss following construction of I-5 and also from a desire for new marketing, several steps were taken toward integrating tourism development in 12 northern counties, generally surrounding the Route 89 corridor. Using an anthropological approach, the first step was to increase awareness and understanding of tourism in the region. This was followed by workshop meetings of public and private representatives directed toward tourism concerns and planning for the future. A major outcome was the formation of the Northeastern California Tourism Council. Although the focus was mostly marketing, it became clear that there was value in striving toward a regional rather than a fragmented approach. Some obstacles continue, such as turf protection, provincialism, ingrained community rivalries, and lack of cooperation on financial support. Political and institutional sustainability were yet to be achieved.

Important for environmental sustainability and of great assistance to tourism development is the Flood Protection Project of Napa.[36] The design and planning firm of Moore Iacofano Goltsman acted as consultant and catalyst to derive a concept solution to a serious flooding problem. In addition to design, their role was to coordinate the many action groups including the US Army Corps of Engineers, the County of Napa, Napa Valley Economic Development Corporation, and the Napa County Flood Control District. For 36 years residents had experienced devastating losses due to flooding of the Napa River. After many proposals that were aborted, a final acceptable project report was produced, *Supplemental Impact Statement/Environmental Impact Report*, issued by the Corps. Principles of geomorphology influenced the design: slope of natural river kept, not dredged or straightened; natural width and depth remains, river to be connected to floodplain; maintain meander, mud flats, and riparian corridor. The engineering components included: lowering dikes, terraces, oxbow dry bypass, new dikes (only where needed), bank stabilization, pump stations, and bridge replacements. The concept is referred to as "A Living Napa River" because it provides not only engineering solutions for flood protection but also an enhanced river corridor for visitor and resident use.

Scenic Trails, Roads

A modern attempt toward sustainability is the Pacific Crest Trail, extending 2600 miles from Mexico to Canada along the backs of the Sierra Nevada and Cascade mountains. Except for some places of intensive use, the basic natural resources along the trail retain scenic and wonderland values.This trail is seldom visited in its entire length but rather in short runs through forests, waterfalls, streams, and wildlife habitat.

With more modern highway development since the 1920s, especially the Interstate freeways, one would expect drastic reduction of all scenic highway values in this region, but this is not the case. Today, many roads carry outstanding scenic and cultural values, as popularized by William Least Heat Moon in *Blue Highways*. California passed enabling legislation in 1963 for establishing scenic byways and, by 1990, 1022 miles were so designated. These resulted from cooperative action by local governments and the State Transportation Department.[37] The criteria for designation include: land use regulations, land and site planning, outdoor advertising controls, and control of land form changes and structures. The fate of such highways depends greatly on continuity of policies and management over the years.

A recent example of a scenic road is the establishment of the 130-mile Feather River National Scenic Byway, designated by the FS in 1990 and dedicated on October 3, 1998.[38] It runs from Oroville to Hallelujah Junction and is identified as Route 70. This is one application of the Scenic Byways Program of the FS. It is an attempt toward sustainability by protecting and providing scenic access in northern California. Interpretation for visitors includes the historic background starting with the discovery by James Beckwith in 1850 of the most accessible pass through the Sierra Nevada in this region. This led to the establishment of a wagon road surveyed by Arthur W. Keddie in 1867. Following the Western Pacific Railroad construction, Governor Frank Merriam dedicated a new Feather River Highway in 1937, a major engineering feat of the times, creating a serviceable travelway and yet a scenic drive, including three tunnels and seven bridges. The road traverses a region with a long history of gold mining, forestry, and resorting.

Linked to the Feather River National Scenic Byway, over the bucolic Indian Valley, is another outstanding scenic route, Lassen National Scenic Byway, threading through Lassen Volcanic National Park.[39] Throughout are outstanding vistas of forest and mountain and several miles of lava flows of 1914 to 1921, reminiscent of volcanic action on Hawaii. Along the way of about 38 miles there are many opportunities to stop and photograph the views, especially of Lake Almanor and Lassen Peak. Included in the park are 150 miles of hiking trails. The park offers eight campgrounds. California Guest Services, Inc. manages the only commercial services within the park: Drakesbad Guest Ranch, Lassen Chalet, and Manzanita Lake Camper Store. The NPS planners and managers are striving toward accepting tourists and giving them opportunities to be enriched by this unusual setting of 106,000 acres and yet protecting the basic natural and cultural assets at the same time. Recently, a draft of a newly modified general management plan was available for public review.

There are a few other roads in this region that are now shown on maps as scenic roads: Route 50—Placerville-South Lake Tahoe; Route 80—Colfax-Reno; and Route 5—Redding-Medford, Oregon.

This view near Belden in northern California illustrates the scenic drama along the Feather River National Scenic Byway, a prime example of environmental sustainability for tourism. (Source: Scott Lawson, Plumas County Visitors Bureau)

Today's highway maps identify several other roads as scenic even though they have not been officially designated by the highway department. This raises a question of how the scenic qualities will be extended over the years if no program of control and management exists. Experience has demonstrated that without the application of specific scenic road criteria for surrounding vistas, there is no assurance that the scenic values will continue.

An innovative sustainable environmental project is the Sacramento River Trail in the vicinity of Redding.[40] This scenic loop of about 6 miles traverses wooded, historic, and open spaces along the key landscape feature of the city. It was conceived by the city and built with cooperation from BLM and Bureau of Reclamation. It is about 12 feet wide and is limited to pedestrians and bicycle traffic (no motorized vehicles allowed). It offers relaxing hiking for all ages, scenic photography, historic markers about pioneers, and touches several parks and the Redding Arboretum. It has received a national award from the Portland Cement Association and a special environmental award from the California Parks and Recreation Society. Recently planned is a new "Museum of the River" including a dramatic cave experience to the "Visible River" site with dripping water and bats.[41] This case demonstrates even on a small scale that communities are increasing their awareness of environments and the need for their sustainability, for visitors as well as residents.

The Benziger Family Winery near Glen Ellen, California, demonstrates environmental sustainability in its land design, organic horticulture, visitor interpretation, and landscape vistas. Research has proven that visitors enjoy landscape amenities of the setting as much as wine tasting. (Source: Benziger Winery)

An application of the scenic highway opportunities in California is being applied in District 1 along a 121-mile segment of Route 101 in Del Norte Redwoods State Park.[42] Others have been requested, such as from Eureka to the California-Oregon state line, but are held up because of the threat to local property rights. South of Crescent City a segment of Route 101 has been redesigned to improve traffic flow and yet retain its scenic appeal. Where originally proposed, the project would have required removal of about 200 ancient redwood trees. Instead, a reasonably sustainable solution resulted from collaboration among representatives of state and national parks and Department of Transportation of California. The original four-lane proposal was replaced by a two-lane design that included frequent uphill passing lanes. Curves were improved, a 6-foot median separated lanes, and shoulders were paved. Wherever retaining walls were required, their design was compatible with the viewshed. To improve safety, rainwater drains through a specially designed paving rather than across it. Warning signs, linked to pavement sensors, give motorists warnings whenever hazardous conditions occur. Even though this solution enhances traffic flow and is a major improvement over the original design, it may compromise the ability of tourists to enjoy the dramatic scenery nearby if volume increases in the future.

Private Tourism Initiatives

An environmentally sensitive and commercially successful winery attraction is the Benziger Winery complex, in three western locations: two in Sonoma Valley in Cali-

A pleasant travel surprise along the northern Pacific is Mendocino Coast Botanical Gardens, Fort Bragg. This nonprofit attraction includes many colorful plant exhibit areas and a trail to the rocky oceanside cliff where one can view the surf and ocean wildlife.

fornia and one in Oregon.[43] State-of-the-art farming techniques and major production from 63 growers are coupled with an informative and scenic visitor experience for touring families.

Especially significant is the Benziger Family Winery, Sonoma Mountain Estate Vineyards, located near Glen Ellen, California. The Benziger family is responsible for planning the 85-acre ranch for both visitor enjoyment and careful land use. Visitors gain outstanding landscape scenes of the slopes of terraced vineyards and diverse vine-growing blocks for high-quality wine production. Literally favoring family groups, the Vineyard Discovery Center provides in-depth educational material in a well-illustrated and interesting manner. Topics include rootstock selection, grafting, phylloxera disease problems, vine development, trellis styles, and flavor control. The climate and elevation of 1100 feet above sea level favor stable vine growth.

Environmental sustainability of this attraction is fostered by careful farming methods that eliminate use of chemicals, provide compost recycling and equilibrium among vineyards, control of nutrient sources and beneficial insects, use of cover crops, and the newest mechanical management equipment.

From the visitor's perspective, their image of wineries is a complete attraction complex, much more than merely places to sample and purchase wine, according to

Dining enjoyment is enhanced greatly by this relaxing landscape setting for Patrick Creek Lodge in northern California. This example demonstrates the value of long-time resource sustainability as an essential element of a tourist business.

research by Williams.[44] The ambience, atmosphere, and especially the special qualities of the landscape setting were of great significance to the winery-visiting travel segment. Environmental sustainability was exemplified in such findings as scenic country route access, nostalgic and environmentally friendly vineyards, picturesque (noncommercial) stores and facilities, and quaint village setting nearby. The past emphasis on production techniques is being overshadowed by attractive and bucolic landscapes in social and environmental harmony with a distinctive rural setting. These travel market findings are a challenge to winery developers and landscape architects for future tourism success. This case demonstrates the viability of a complete landscape development complex rather than an isolated attraction. It shows excellent adaptation to the land—true sustainability.

Near Fort Bragg is the fascinating Mendocino Coast Botanical Gardens, reaching from Highway 1 to bluffs of the Pacific Ocean. Founded by Ernest Schoefer, a retired nurseryman in 1961, this 47-acre beauty spot is now operated by a nonprofit organization. Sheltered by a native pine forest, the rainy winters and cool foggy summers provide perfect weather conditions for lush growth of 20 plant areas. Visitors can enjoy and photograph rhododendrons, heather, roses, fuchsias, camellias, dahlias, begonias, and an abundance of other plant clusters. In season, gray whales and seals can be seen from a trail along the coast. This outstanding attraction is quite a pleasant surprise in this region, providing lessons in plant education as well as impressive beauty.

Over on the coast, about 80 miles north of San Francisco on Route 1, lies the innovative Sea Ranch resort complex conceived by architect Al Boeke in the 1960s. His idea was to create a development that would retain the charm of the landscape setting, carried out by landscape architect Lawrence Halprin and architect Charles Moore. These designers dedicated themselves to the protection of the natural resource assets at the same time locating structures in a profit-making arrangement. It has demonstrated that sustainability is not only reachable but also profitable. By means of strict regulations, the original landscape quality is being retained. Landscape architect Francis Dean's reaction to this kind of sustainable development: "My own belief is that, in time, we will begin to understand the necessity of learning the role of Nature, even sometimes in concert with science and technology. This I hope will be our destination if we can stall off our own destructive nature."[45]

An illustration of sustainability of planning and design of a commercial food and lodging establishment is the durable Patrick Creek Lodge and Historical Inn, located on Route 199 near Gasquet.[46] Today, the setting along a rippling stream backed by forest has retained its verdant aesthetic appeal. It began in the 1800s as the Patrick Creek Stage Station and was managed by the Raymond family through 1925 when it was replaced by the present lodge. The reputation of family service and atmosphere for food and lodging has continued over many decades. After the purchase by owners Fletcher and Tuttle in 1947 it became known as a socialite destination. Present owners, Bill and Cindy Greer, continue to provide fine service in a sustainable environment. It is surrounded by Six Rivers National Forest with its abundant outdoor recreational opportunities.

Governmental Planning and Design

Sporadically, over these seven decades, landscape architects have demonstrated sustainability in their public and private projects. Landscape architectural historian, Ethan Carr, draws a parallel between the urban park movement in early American history, such as with Central Park, New York City, and major scenic parks of the West, such as Yosemite National Park.[47] Tourism, painting, and literature by the 1820s had created desirable imagery of natural and cultural landscapes. In creating Yosemite, California governor, Frederick F. Low, named Olmsted as chairman of the first Yosemite Commission because of his major role in the establishment of Central Park. Olmsted's original plan of Yosemite cited concern over potential environmental damage by too many visitors and noncompatible uses, such as hydroelectric power and logging, as advocated by Pinchot. By 1944, it was seen that automobile traffic in Yosemite was already creating environmental stress, stimulating the Secretary of Interior to establish the position of landscape engineer for national parks and appointing Mark Daniels to the position. Later, landscape architect Thomas Vint was influential in introducing a rustic style of development to harmonize with the natural setting. Throughout its history, Yosemite National Park development has been under the guidance of landscape architects.

For many years, these designers have made many attempts to retain the basic values of the park as visitor volumes increased phenomenally. A case of current redesign is Glacier Point, originally influenced by Frederick Law Olmsted in 1866 and John Muir and President Theodore Roosevelt in 1903.[48] Glacier Point Road resulted from the design of Frederick Olmsted, Jr. in 1929 and 1930, who preferred to terminate the road far back from the point. However, park superintendent Charles Thompson decided that the road should come closer to defeat the argument for an aerial tramway. From then on, visitors have increasingly eroded this spectacular and popular vista point. In the 1930s, landscape architects created a bold plan that called for demolition of the Glacier Point Hotel because it intruded upon the beauty of the site. Implementation of the plan was aborted due to political issues between developers and protectionists. The hotel remained until it burned in 1969. At one time, a huge contemporary design hotel was proposed directly on the brink but was denied because views of the scenery below would be restricted to guests only.

A more recent plan for rehabilitation of this site was completed in 1997. After many discussions and arguments regarding details of the site and building design, the landscape architectural firm of Royston Hanamoto Alley & Abey developed a final solution. Key design elements are a promenade to control visitors, allowing restoration of surrounding landscapes with native plant materials. A new concession building with restroom facilities is set back unobtrusively against the forest edge. An outdoor amphitheater provides the setting for interpretive programs and yet keeps vistas open. Glacier Point now provides a beautiful and environmentally sound site for the nearly 1 million visitors annually. The role of landscape architects has been strong for over a century and promises to continue a philosophy of sustainability into the future.

Future Challenges

Remarkably, this northern landscape of California has retained much of the rich and appealing travel character it had many years ago. The ghosts of past Wild West remain. If the autocampers of the 1920s were still around today, they could experience many of the same thrills and enrichments they did then. However, the greatest change has taken place at the cities. Seventy years ago, communities such as Sacramento, Redding, Petaluma, and Santa Rosa exhibited their own special place characteristics. Over several decades, they have retained a few qualities of the past but generally have become like every other city in the nation. Although many travel markets may have accepted this change in the name of better tourist services, other travel segments welcome efforts toward historic restoration and protection of place qualities.

Fortunately, between towns, the scenic, wild land, and cultural assets still have great appeal. Important today, as in the past, are key assets of the coast, mountains, lakes, rivers, forests, ancient mammoth redwoods, remnants of Spanish and Mexican artifacts, historic settlement, fishing villages, and extensive vineyards and wineries.

Tourism's future in this region has great promise but only if several challenges are resolved. The positive factors of the past can no longer be assumed to continue in the future. Accompanying the tremendous growth from settlement and tourism is a great amount of wear and tear on the natural resources. No longer can the social and environmental impact of myopic business development be ignored. These and many other concerns face those who hope for tourism growth in this region: community tourism leaders, government agencies, promoters, designers/planners, and investors.

Following are key challenges that resulted from this historic and analytical review of tourism in northern California.

Development versus conservation here has precipitated a lot of bitterness but it is not merely an emotional issue. With projected increases of population of over 50% in the next few years, there is little question about monumental stress on the environment from settlement as well as tourism. Even though northern California's resources as yet have not been depleted as severely as elsewhere, there is increasing drain on them from outside as well as within. The decline in the mining and forestry economies now encourages communities to turn to the seductive lure of tourism. Touted are the positive results, seldom considering that resource protection is the first step toward a tourism economy, especially in this region.

The business sector that hopes to gain new jobs, incomes, and tax returns cannot succeed unless visitor activities can be assured. And most of this business depends on protection of the resources that allow a great many tourist activities. Scenic touring, river rafting, snowmobiling, skiing, mountain climbing, mountain biking, hunting, wildlife watching, aesthetic appreciation of redwood forests, fishing, boating, camping, swimming, and hiking are enjoyed by huge and growing numbers of travel markets. Customers for service businesses will not come if the foundation resources are eroded. Equally significant is satisfying cultural interests such as historic sites, cultural pageantry, festivals, events, ethnic crafts, and "old town" shops and restaurants. Tourism developers here must be supportive of protection of the basic foundations of a tourism economy. Incidentally, such a principle is equally supportive of resident values.

Not only must tourism leaders and the business sector foster resource protection in principle but also in practice. This is a major change in policy, demanding a new business ethic. Theirs is the obligation to guide land use in northern California so that tourist businesses are located where they cause least environmental impact and also the best sites for success. As a general rule it is in communities, not in rural areas, that most tourist business should expand. Here it is most efficient, economically productive, and less environmentally erosive of resources. Yet, each increment of tourism expansion must be tested against the capacity of water supply, waste disposal, police and fire protection, and transportation systems to permit more tourism.

As new generations of visitors and migrants keep coming, many are becoming much more environmentally sensitive. A new awareness of tourism's maximum capacity is taking place. As promoters continue to hawk their travel destination wares, leaders of both public and private sectors of tourism are beginning to show concern over negative impacts. More discussions are taking place regarding traffic congestion, erosion of timber lands, loss of heritage, and the potential need for demarketing.

Future tourism developers can benefit from Native American land use beliefs—that all land features contain spirits that should be respected. The mountains, plains, forests, rivers, and wildlife are perceived not only as physical entities but also as having spiritual influences on mankind's decision making. These mythical beliefs in the supernatural qualities of natural resources gave these early populations a land ethic similar to what is now called environmental sustainability. Tourism planners and developers of northern California can benefit from such an ethic that balances resource protection with use. This principle is similar to Feng Shui, an ancient Chinese philosophy now being practiced with new building development in Asia.

An encouraging trend in this region are the attempts by communities to restore parts of their heritage. Efforts by historic preservation groups are equally supportive of tourism, providing new attractions of interest to growing markets. But to meet needs of tourism it is insufficient to only preserve and restore. Consideration must be given to automobile, RV, and bus access and details of landscape and building design that can withstand mass visitors. Interpretive techniques are available today that can give the visitor a rich and entertaining experience and yet protect the site. However, these are of no avail if not planned and managed.

Another issue in northern California is the perceived threat of increased federalism. Public forest, park, and wildlife agencies have their official mandates, regulations, and policies emanating from Washington, DC. When local residents are not included in the creation and implementation of these policies, they believe their land sovereignty is being threatened. Frequently a public hearing is scheduled only after many public agency decisions have been made.

Fortunately, in recent years the FS, NPS, and BLM, very large land holders in the region, have begun procedures for more effective public involvement. Both nontourism and tourism activities are the beneficiaries. New public-private cooperation in the West has been stimulated by the establishment of the Western States Tourism Policy Council. Through their memorandum of understanding a new mechanism has been created to resolve the many negative issues facing tourism in the future. It must be emphasized that the commercial sector of tourism in northern California, the producer of jobs, incomes, and tax revenues, would almost disappear if it were not for the tremendous number and diversity of attractions provided by federal resource agencies. In spite of some conflict with local residents, these agencies must be credited with protection and management of these natural and cultural resources that support tourist activities for millions of visitors.

Even if northern California does not become a politically separate entity, there is ample support for fostering it as a distinctive travel destination. This historical review has demonstrated the importance of the natural and cultural resource foundation over several decades. These resources continue to weave a unifying fabric for tourism. But if the present lack of political, planned, and developmental unity continues, both the environment and tourism will suffer. Environmentalists and resource extractors such as timber and mining interests will need to move toward a new plateau of compromise and cooperation rather than confrontation. Local governments, federal and state agencies, and the private sector throughout the region will need to work continually with highway planners to resolve mounting traffic congestion, especially at city bottlenecks such as the restriction at Placerville. Innovative programs will need to be initiated to control urban sprawl, particularly from population in-migration from the south. These and other actions are essential if the region is to retain its integrity and cope with mounting pressures from tourism and settlement growth. It is possible to restore many of the tourist values enjoyed by the autocampers of the 1920s but only with greater understanding of the many interdependencies within the tourism functioning system, demanding new cooperation and accommodation among all the actors.

Although residents would prefer to maintain the status quo, the region's tourism success is part of its problem, destined to increase in the future. Visitors, especially from down state, have learned how desirable the area is for vacation and permanent homes. This new market for land development not only threatens local quality of life and escalates land values and taxation, it also tends to force residents to move away. It is difficult to alter this trend.

Because scenic touring is so important to travel markets in northern California, planners need to devise new and better criteria for establishment and control of scenic routes. Two major issues must be dealt with. First, if a road is to be designated scenic, the viewshed must be protected. This becomes difficult because adjacent property owners believe they have the right of land ownership to do as they please. Only when control mechanisms, such as visual easements and sale-leaseback, are in place can scenic qualities nearby be perpetuated. This is often fostered by intervention by landscape architects for creative solutions to planning of roads and landscape corridors. Second, until a parallel route is provided for high-speed and high-volume through traffic, a route cannot be designated as scenic. Competition between tourists and other travelers must be resolved, not only for scenic purposes but also for safety. If no other route can be built, some control measures such as time zoning or tolls must be implemented. Until local residents, tourism developers, planners, and highway officials collaborate on solutions, the issue will not go away.

One of the greatest opportunities for future sustainable tourism in northern California is greater involvement by the numerous landscape architectural practitioners. California has a great number of licensed landscape architects and members of the ASLA. Needed is greater opportunity for communication between developers of tourism projects, public and private, and these specialists of land use planning. They have the training, talent, and experience in balancing development with resource protection and stand ready to assist in several ways. They can provide consultation on site selection. More frequently today they can act as a catalyst between proponents and opponents of tourism projects and create concepts and proposals acceptable to both sides. Of course, they can develop sketch plans, conceptual proposals, and final detailed working plans for complete projects such as resort complexes, parks, recreation areas, scenic drives, and others related to tourism. Most tourism projects today are designed by a team, often led by landscape architects. The many design facets of any tourism project require the input from many specialists.

Finally, a major influence on future tourism in this region is its staunch support of individualism and entrepreneurship. Ever since the coming of autocampers in the 1920s, individuals have continued to respond to tourist market needs and interests. In spite of a sometimes heavy hand by governmental resource managers, tourists today are offered many new independent attractions, lodging, food services, entertainment, crafts, and events. When these developments are located, designed, and managed with indigenous sustainability in mind, they succeed in spite of the pressure from look-alike franchise operations, sponsored by investors outside the region. A great challenge before the tourism establishment in northern California is to maintain and stimulate even more environmentally sustainable businesses appropriate to the natural/cultural theme of this special region.

Endnotes

[1]Weir, K. (1994). *Northern California Handbook* (2nd ed., p. 359). Chico: Moon Publications.

[2]Yeadon, D. (1993). California's North Face. *National Geographic,* 184(1), 48–79.

[3]Weir, op. cit., 21.

[4]Recreation '98. (1998, May). 36-page "Special Section," issued by *Record Searchlight*, Redding, CA.

[5]Drago, H. S. (1967). *The Steamboaters.* New York: Bramhall.

[6]Leadabrand, R., Lowenkopf, S., & Patterson, B. (1975). *Yesterday's California* (p. 30). Miami: Seeman Publishing.

[7]Shearer, F. E. (Ed.). (1884). *The Pacific Tourist* (p. 327). New York: Adams & Bishop (reprinted 1970, Crown Publishers).

[8]Bean, W. E. (1968). *California: An Interpretive History* (p. 376). New York: McGraw-Hill.

[9]*Touring Topics.* (1972). Pp. 20, 21, 26. Automobile Club of Southern California.

[10]Maki, K. (2002, March/April). Clearcutting: Serious Trouble in Our Forests. *The Loma Prietan*. From http://lomaprieta.sierraclub.org/lpo203 as of March 16, 2002. Among the many descriptions of resource erosion in northern California is *Farewell, Promised Land* by Robert Dawson and Gray Brechin (1999). Berkeley, CA: University of California Press.

[11]Adams, H. (2000, October). Sierra Club Sues over Navarro Water. *The Redwood Needles*, newsletter of the Sierra Club Reduced Chapter. From http://redwoodsierraclub.org/articles as of March 16, 2002; and Midkiff, K. (2002). Road Trip. *Low Plains Drifter*, Sierra Club. From http:sierraclub.org/roadtrip/lowplaindrifter as of March 16, 2002.

[12]*Recreation 2000: A Strategic Plan for California Recreation.* (1990). Sacramento: California State Office, Bureau of Land Management.

[13]Runyan, D. (1990). *Planning for Travel and Tourism in Napa County.* Portland, OR: Author.

[14]Weir, op. cit., 222.

[15]*California Official State Visitor's Guide.* (1998). Sacramento: California Tourism Publications.

[16]Carr, E. (1998). *Wilderness by Design* (p. 47). Lincoln: University of Nebraska Press.

[17]Hyde, P., & Leydet, F. (1963). *The Last Redwoods* (p. 46). San Francisco: The Sierra Club.

[18]Schrepfer, S. R. (1983). *The Fight to Save the Redwoods.* Madison, WI: University of Wisconsin Press.

[19]Hyde and Leydet, op. cit., 116.

[20]Cloud, J. (1998). Fire on the Mountain—The Posh Town of Vail is Shaken by an Act of Apparent Ecoterrorism. *Time,* 152(18), 77.

[21]Weir, op. cit. 347.

[22]Correspondence from Cathleen Cook, Redwood National and State Parks, November 17, 1998.

[23]Facts About Redwood National and State Parks. From www.nps.gov/redw/redwfact as of September 8, 2000.

[24]Many definitions of sustainability are in: Hall, C. M., & Lew, A. (Eds.) (1998). *Sustainable Tourism: Geographical Perspective.* UK: Longman.

[25]Hata, N. I. (1992). *The Historic Preservation Movement in California 1940–1976.* Sacramento: California Department of Parks and Recreation, Office of Historic Preservation.

[26]*Marconi Conference Center State Historic Park.* (1992). Sacramento, CA: The Resources Agency and Department of Parks and Recreation.

[27]Clayborn, H. M., & Howland, J. C. (n.d.). *Exhibits, Etc.* Brochure. Santa Rosa, California.

[28]Hanna, J. (n.d.) *Inside-Outside.* Brochure. Red Feather Lakes, Colorado.

[29]Carr, op. cit., 294.

[30]Bennett, P. (1998). Tourist-Friendly. *Landscape Architecture,* 88(2), 44–49.

[31]Fleming, D. W. (1998). A California Look at Europe. *Progress Surface Transportation Policy Project,* 8(5), 5.

[32]Thompson, J. W. (1997). Field of Vision. *Landscape Architecture,* 87(7), 36–41.

[33]Gunn, C. A., Reed, D. J., & Couch, R. E. (1972). *Cultural Benefits from Metropolitan Recreation—San Antonio Prototype.* MP-1046. College Station: Texas Water Resources Institute, Texas A&M University.

[34]Gillette, J. B. (1998). River Runs Through It. *Landscape Architecture,* 88(4), 74–81.

[35]Smith, V. L. et al. (1986). California's Highway 89: A Regional Tourism Model. *Annals of Tourism Research,* 13, 415–433.

[36]Iacofano, D. (n.d.). *A Citizen's Guide to the City of Napa, Napa River & Napa Creek Flood Protection Project.* Sacramento: US Army Corps of Engineers.

[37]Federal Highway Administration. (1990). *An Analysis and Summary of the 1990 National Scenic Byways Study Inventory.* Washington, DC: Author.

[38]*Feather River Scenic Byway.* (1998, September 30). Special supplement. Quincy, CA: Feather Publishing.

[39]Lassen Volcanic National Park. From www.nps.gov/lavo/gmppm, as of September 6, 2000.

[40]Sacramento River Trail. (n.d.). Brochure produced by Redding Convention and Visitors Bureau, Redding, CA.

[41]Visit California. (2001). In *California Tourism.* Sacramento, CA: California Division of Tourism. From www.visitcalifornia.com/state/tourism as of March 20, 2002.

[42]Correspondence from Cheryl S. Willis, District Div. Chief, Department of Transportation, Eureka, CA, November 24, 1999.

[43]Barbitta, M. (2000). The Benziger Family Winery. Presentation, Travel and Tourism Research Association Annual Meeting, Burbank, CA. June 16.

[44]Williams, P. W. (2000). The Evolving Image of Wine Tourism Destination Landscapes. Presentation, Travel and Tourism Research Association Annual Meeting, Burbank, CA, June 16.

[45]Correspondence from Francis Dean, FASLA, September 8, 1998.

[46]Patrick Creek Lodge Historical Inn. (n.d.). Descriptive folder. Gasquet, CA.

[47]Carr, op. cit., 11.

[48] Nelson, D. (1998). Glacier Point Rehabilitation, Yosemite National Park—Designing in a Landscape Continuum. In *1998 ASLA Annual Meeting Proceedings* (pp. 154–155). Washington, DC: American Society of Landscape Architects.

Chapter 6

1929 Western Tour: Part III

This chapter is a description of the continuing log of the Gunn autocamping tour of the West in 1929. It begins with entering the Oregon border from California and includes touring the Columbia River. It is offered here as descriptive of travel conditions and rewards seven decades ago as an introduction to Chapter 7, which is an analysis of changes in tourism development in the same destination over the last seven-decade period and their meaning for future tourism development.

●●●●●●●●●●●●●●●●●

After a very cold night in camp, just north of the California-Oregon border, on **July 23** we are on our mountain road again, anticipating another day of enjoyable landscape spectacles along the Redwood Highway. But all of a sudden, after about 20 miles, we are shocked out of our reverie and thought for sure we had met our doom. It was at a sharp curve (probably near Hayes Hill), with the rock mountain wall on the left and sheer drop of a thousand feet on the right, that Lauren nearly collided head-on with a road grader. As he applied the brakes all he got was a chattering response with no brakeage at all. Fortunately, he is skillful in threading the car through the small width between the end of the grader blade and the dropoff on the right or I would not be telling this tale. Soon thereafter, dad finds a garage in Grants Pass and had the brakes relined and bought a new tire—total of $21. We will never forget Grants Pass as a major landmark on our 1929 tour. While waiting for car repair, dad, Lauren, and I get hair cuts, get a permit at the local Chamber of Commerce, mail letters, shop at the local dime store, and eat our lunch in the car in the garage. We also went down to the Rogue River where Lauren found a US highway sign rusting on the river bottom. After the trip he repainted it as a cherished souvenir.

On our way again we are reminded of what we have learned is a "pass"—Sexton Mountain Pass (2046 feet), Stage Coach Pass (1940 feet), Summit Creek Pass (2800 feet). For the roads and cars of the 1920s, these are significant obstacles. Many miles after stopping for gas we discover the gas cap is gone and drive back to find it but with no luck. At Roseburg we buy a new one for 50 cents. Now our road straightens out; what a change. After passing through Cottage Grove we come to Eugene, all decorated for a celebration called "Sunset Trail." Ladies are dressed in old time costumes and men have grown many different shapes of sideburns. We notice good farm-

Modern travelers can still enjoy this peaceful roadside park, now called the Washburn Wayside State Park, as did autocampers of the 1920s. Located along Route 99 in southern Oregon (the early main highway), these stately fir trees have matured greatly over the last seven decades.

ing country north of Eugene and stop for the day at Benton Lane Park and camp in a pleasant grove of fir trees (still available today on the "old" road).

We leave camp at 7:55 am on **July 24** and enjoy a cool morning. In Corvallis we see our first maple trees since leaving Michigan. In fact, the entire town reminds us of home as we drive on, passing Monmouth Oregon State Normal. We now see mountains in the distance. Passing on through Amity we see fields of bachelor button flowers and the first clouds for several days. Farmers are baling oats. At McMinnville we see hop vineyards. Of course, we are always interested in fellow travelers and see another Ford with crocheted butterfly curtains in the back window. At Newberg we see three cars that we have seen three times before, heading our way. They display a homemade sign: "Portland or Bust!"

Our approach to Portland is along Terwilliger Boulevard, which offers us a great view of the city below. Dad stops to inquire at the Post Office. We cross the Ross Island Bridge (9/10 mile) on our way to visit dad's friend, Mr. Brummels. We pass Libby's packing house. Then we are warmly received by Mr. Brummels, who gives us dinner and we leave at 3:30 after a fine visit. On our way again we pass a Sears Roebuck store, School of Flying, Flanders poppies, and Rankin Airport. Just to say we had been in another state, we cross the Columbia River into Vancouver, Washington, pass through a pleasant park, and stop at the Chamber of Commerce to get a sticker

This 1918 brochure, purchased during the Gunn tour of 1929, describes the Columbia River Gorge and the Vista House Center at Crown Point. Recently, this outstanding viewing facility was completely remodeled and remains a tourist focal point.

for the windshield. We learn that this town was established as an original post of the Hudson's Bay Company. Then a significant entry by mother appears in the log, "We found a nice little homey camp with nice green grass—a real treat—and for the first time we are headed toward Michigan!" And we enjoy the view toward Mt. Hood.

In the morning of Thursday, **July 25**, about 15 miles east of Portland, we make breakfast in the camp kitchen and enjoy the warmth from the stoves. The provision of a common kitchen area is typical of campsites and offers sociability as well as cooking utility. Breaking camp, we begin our scenic drive along the mountainside overlooking the Columbia River. Although we had visited and enjoyed several river and cascade settings in Michigan, nothing equaled this view up the river gorge. At Crown Point Vista House we stop and take in the spectacular view and buy a souvenir booklet.

Then we pass a beautiful series of waterfalls on our right. I am fascinated by waterfalls, perhaps because of the ever-changing motion, the sounds, and nature's way of spilling its water. The first stop is at Latourell Falls, a drop of 225 feet we are told, all within a honeycomb rock cleft. Then we come to Shepperds Dell, followed by the zigzag Wahkeena Falls. But the most spectacular is our next stop—Multnomah Falls. We are told the upper segment is a drop of 541 feet, followed by a lower segment that drops 69 feet. After dad takes a picture or two we move on to even more waterfalls—Oneonta and Horsetail. We move on alongside the river, take a picture through a tunnel, and see salmon nets across the river at the Cascade Locks. We don't quite understand why the fish work so hard to go upstream but are told it happens every year. Here we see an old Ford with a sign: "Don't laugh girls. You'd look bad without paint too." As we move along, we get several glimpses of Mt. Hood in the distance and hope we can get closer.

At Hood River, we turn off on a dirt road to climb toward Mt. Hood. We eat our own dust as we switch back and forth to gain altitude. After about 10 miles we come to a

We are fascinated in 1929 by the many waterfalls along the Columbia River Gorge highway. An example is our snapshot of Latourell Falls, cascading over strange rock formations. The beauty of this mountainside is like none other we have experienced on this trip.

camp site at the end of the road where we view Mt. St. Helens, Ranier, and Adams in the distance and have a picnic lunch. Here, my dad and brother begin to hike across the snow and ice but mother and I don't seem to have the courage, mother complaining that she has another sick headache. Upon their return, we hear all about the great adventure where they climbed on a glacier, saw a stream of water in a deep gash in the glacier, and got their shoes full of snow. They do their best to make us jealous with their tales of conquest. Mother and I attempt to cover our chagrin with elaboration of our enjoyment of the beautiful vista toward the Columbia River from this high vantage point.

Back on the scenic highway, we pass by interesting rock strata that is sometimes tilted and other times so regular that it seems man made. Our road twists and turns in and out over ancient lava rock and finally we come to The Dalles, "a pretty valley city" as mother calls it. Here we take on gas and stock up on groceries needed for our evening and morning meals. At The Dalles we see the barge canal and locks. In spite

The most dramatic of these waterfalls is Multnomah Falls, named after a well-known Indian Chief. This roadside experience is enhanced greatly by the trail and lookout points alongside the falls.

of the lateness of the day and fatigue from sightseeing, we see large road cuts, palisades, Celico Falls, an unusual sight of a sand dune along the railroad nearby, and then pass through another rock-wall tunnel. As we cross a big bridge, we see rapids in the river and a large contraption that we are told is a fishwheel, used to harvest salmon. At about 14 miles east of The Dalles we find a pleasant camp site along the Columbia River, called The Poplar Grove Camp. Here we enjoy cooking our own fresh salmon, a dramatic improvement of our normal canned fare.

At 7:30 am on Friday, **July 26**, we have already broken camp and begun our trek eastward along the Columbia, thinking of our next destination, Yellowstone. We pass along lava deposits with immense rock terraces on the right and the great river on the left. These rock formations stir our imaginations into images of castles, cathedrals, and forts. The bright morning sunshine brings out many colors. Seeing a dead porcupine alongside the road, my brother and I must stop to pull out a few souvenir quills. Then our highway leaves the river and the landscape breaks dramatically from

First seen from Portland on our 1929 trip, we enjoy a closer view of the famous landmark, Mt. Hood. Leaving the main highway, we take a narrow trail up the north slope to its end to get a first-hand understanding of this major scenic feature.

Dad and brother Lauren can't resist the appeal of the mountainside and hike over treacherous ice and snow as far as they can. Less adverturesome, mother and I do not attempt it and enjoy the vista toward the Columbia River valley. Today's tourists are given strict instructions on the dangers of such adventures.

what we have been through. The forest cover has disappeared and the desert landscape is a lot like Arizona. However, this seemingly barren soil must have some merit because we begin to see irrigated crops. At Hermiston we buy gas and enjoy the shady town. Irrigation here must be important because soon we pass the US Stanfield Irrigation District headquarters and observe a combine drawn by 16 horses. Dad sees a sign advertising land for sale at $15 an acre. Our route now takes us through Echo, past the Oregon State Hospital and into Pendleton where we see cattle roundup grounds. In this fertile valley covered with grain fields we stop and have a picnic lunch along the roadside, "Emigrant Park, state of Oregon."

At Meachum we climb to the summit of Blue Mountain, an elevation of 4335 feet. As we come along the Union Pacific Railroad we observe a very long train with many carloads of sheep. The fairly large city of La Grande and its airport come into view as we cross the Grande Ronde River. Someone told us that on this route we are traveling is about where the explorers Lewis and Clark went. After passing a hay inspection station at Baker City we see sagebrush and large lime quarries and stop for a drink at Rattle Snake Springs. As we gradually drop down into the Snake River Valley we pass crop lands of potatoes, red clover, and grain. Finally arriving at Ontario after a day of 315 miles we find a good campground and spend a restful night.

We leave camp at 7:50 am on **July 27** after breakfast and cross the Snake River and state boundary into Idaho. Even though Yellowstone National Park, our next major objective, lies directly east from The Dalles, there is no road that way because of the Rocky Mountain Range. So we travel southeasterly along the Old Oregon Trail to Boise, then follow the Snake River across Idaho and then turn north toward the park. After stopping for gas and oil we move on through Caldwell, Meridian, and Nampa to Boise where we see the Capitol building flanked by a beautiful park.

Our travel then takes us from Boise through the towns of Sunnyside and Mountain Home, rejoining the Snake River at Glenns Ferry. Here we buy gas and have a picnic lunch under some poplar trees at nearby King Hill. A roughly lettered sign makes us smile, "Speed Limit 100, Fords do Your Best!" From an irrigation ditch we fill our water bag and radiator. The many cascades and waterfalls on the Snake are a pleasant relief of view from the plains around us. Our reverie is disturbed by bees flying in and out of the car as we pass 1000 Springs Farm and Banbury Natatorium. For many miles we weave back and forth along the Snake River. This seems to be good farm land, especially for beans. We travel on by Indian Massacre Rocks, Twin Falls, and American Falls, and a dam creating a reservoir of some 1,700,000 acre-feet, we are told. In Pocatello, after our day's drive of 300 miles, we spend the night in the city campground.

Sunday, **July 28**, our departure is delayed to get our Ford greased. Soon after we know we are in Indian territory as we travel through Blackfoot and the Fort Hall Indian Reservations. But we move right through because our mind is set on our destination of Yellowstone. After Idaho Falls we encounter some very rough roads and climb to an elevation of 5500 feet. As soon as we cross the Idaho-Montana state line we have another flat tire. Even though we have become proficient at fixing tires, we are frustrated with the delay. Finally, at 3:29 in the afternoon, we cross the Montana-Wyoming state line and enter into Yellowstone National Park. So far we've had 16 flat tires in 28 days.

Comment

Throughout this trip we accepted detours, extreme heat and cold, setting up and breaking camp every day, frequent flat tires, and many stops for gas, oil, and water for the Model A Ford because of the many tradeoffs of personal travel rewards. Especially significant on this leg of the trip was the outstanding scenic drive along the Columbia River. The quality of this experience seven decades later is diminished greatly by the new Interstate highway but many efforts are being made to give visitors bits and pieces of the old drive. Although travel hazards today differ—highway accidents, threat of hijacking air travel like the catastrophe of September 11, 2001—we will never forget our near-disaster as we rounded a narrow mountain road near Grants Pass, Oregon.

Chapter 7 paints a view of travel changes following the autocamping tour with the purpose of providing not only the historic background but also lessons for the future now facing tourism planners and developers in this destination.

Chapter 7

Oregon and Columbia River Destination

Oregon, and especially the Columbia River Gorge, has lured visitors for over two centuries. Sandwiched between Washington and California, Oregon has its own image and unique characteristics. As a travel destination for many decades, particularly since the autocamping explosion of the 1920s, it has been able to maintain the strongest environmental ethic in the West.

It is a land of contrast from the rugged Pacific coast over the mountains of the coastal range and the Cascades to the plateaus and deserts to the east. The moist climate of the mountains supports extensive forest lands of Douglas fir, hemlock, spruce, and other evergreens. Five mountain peaks over 10,000 feet in elevation, including the spectacular Mt. Hood cap, are part of the scenic and recreational appeal of the Cascades. Additional outdoor recreation is supported by the many lakes and streams. The Pacific coastline offers the tourist compelling scenic beauty. But most famous of all is the one and only historic and beautiful Columbia River and its gorge as it cuts through the Cascades. These descriptions of Oregon's tourism foundation are not a promoter's hype but rather the intrinsic qualities upon which considerable tourism has already been built.

It is the diversity of natural resources here, from mountains to plains, from verdant to desert, from streams and waterfalls to lakes, and from snowy winters to pleasant summers that have fostered great growth in tourism in recent decades. Even though its rich resources have shown great durability, tourism's great expansion in this relatively small piece of geography is now creating great stress. The following historical sketch provides many important clues of environmental challenge before present and incoming tourism developers.

A Powerful Landscape

Archeological digs in Oregon have determined occupation as early as 9000 B.C. but today's Native American descendants of many tribes have been grouped together as Rogue River tribes.[1] It was the lure of beaver, sea otter, and whales that attracted explorers to this region as early as the 16th century. It is believed that Juan Cabrillo and Sir Francis Drake may have been here in the 1500s. Before the ephemeral tramping of European explorers, the region was well populated by a great diversity of tribes of native people influenced greatly by differences in food supplies and living conditions. Tribes west of the Cascades depended upon fish and game and required protective shelters against the rains. To the east there were nomadic tribes living on hunting and gathering. Although described in a few museums, this fascinating story of ancient peoples is yet to be told to modern tourists.

Oregon, and especially the Columbia River corridor, has provided the canvas for painting many landscape values based on observations by early explorers. Landscape architect William Mann has documented these based on research of old journals.[2] Many of the scenic values held by today's tourists, environmentalists, and landscape architects can be traced to the documented responses of these early travelers to the Pacific northwest. Especially significant were British explorers who were caught up in the landscape precepts of the times, espoused by designers "Capability" Brown and William Gilpin.

George Vancouver, although intent upon conquest of new land for England, made outstanding landscape observations of his travels around the Columbia River corridor between 1792 and 1794. He was excited about and documented the powerful landscape pictures he saw that included dramatic land forms, clumps of trees, abundance of flowers, and other picturesque attributes. Such descriptors were rooted in the landscape philosophies of the times. Distinctions were often made between the sublime, picturesque, and the beautiful. Philosopher Edmund Burke and others referred to the sublime as grand, emotionally moving, awesome, and even frightening, the same feelings held by urban dwellers today regarding wilderness.

In contrast, the concept of beautiful evokes feelings of pleasure, popular among most early American explorers because they were romantics. The picturesque also held attributes of the sublime and beautiful but added images that looked like castles, ramparts, and ruins.[3] Hubbard and Kimball, in their text for landscape architects,[4] modified these interpretations by describing beautiful as evoking a smooth transition from object to object whereas the picturesque contains great contrasts of forms.

It may seem strange that one such as Vancouver, intent upon claiming land, would be so enamored over landscape aesthetics. Mann explains this as very logical because Vancouver's entire crew was not rough, low-class sailors but rather sons of dukes, barons, and earls, well versed in the status symbols of beautiful landscape paintings of the period. Several were amateur artists. Many of their drawings were included in Vancouver's book, *Voyage of Discovery*, of 1798. Another British explorer, William R. Broughton, arriving in his ship, *The Chatham*, in 1792, also was enraptured over the magnificent landscape along the Columbia including Mt. Hood in the distance as he claimed the land in the name of King George III.

The most insightful and comprehensive observations and documentation of the Columbia River's natural and cultural resources were recorded by the Lewis and Clark expedition of 1804–1806. At no time before or after had the US government initiated such an ambitious and foolhardy exploration as that of President Thomas Jefferson. Modern space exploration does not even compare to it. Northwestern America had not been charted and Jefferson wanted to know what the land of the Louisiana Purchase was really like and especially what lay beyond. As Jefferson and his secretary Capt. Merriweather Lewis first read Alexander Mackenzie's *Voyages from*

Montreal on the River St. Lawrence, Through the Continent of North America, to the Frozen and Pacific Ocean, their curiosity burned within.

This Britisher had hurt Jefferson's pride by making such a voyage first. Jefferson had envisioned a national American empire extending from sea to sea. Reflecting on the importance of the Lewis and Clark trip, it is possible that without their journals all of present northwestern US might now be a part of Russia, Spain, or Great Britain. No other exploration had such profound implications. Historical writers Ambrose and Abell summarize the deep meaning of this voyage as: an unusual discovery team, a wide range of exploratory experiences, so much of the continent traversed, and a heroic national deed.[5] The journals include an astonishingly complete and detailed description of many plants and animals that had not been identified before. Also included were significant anthropological findings such as their relations with the many Indian tribes, most of whom were not hostile but friendly, contrary to the perception that all Native Americans were savages.

These narratives of early explorers of the Columbia River corridor and especially their descriptions of the powerful landscape read like glitzy advertising brochures by modern tourist promoters. It is no coincidence that tourist popularity of this corridor has grown exponentially since the autocamping era of the 1920s. This has been a blessing for tourist businesses and an increasing curse in the minds of resource managers and environmentalists. Even the most jaded of modern tourists must feel some of the same thrills observed by the first explorers. Nowhere else on the continent is there such a diversity of resources within such a short range. However, no planners visualized the coming onslaught of millions of visitors.

The Early Tourists

Historians report that the Columbia River corridor's past was in direct contrast to today's tranquility. Loosely structured Indian interchange between interior and coast peoples was first impacted by the fur trade of northeastern origin. It is hard to imagine the foolhardy determination of the missionaries of the early 1800s who soon followed: river drownings, lack of food, arduous portages, exhaustion, and Indian attack. Then improvement of trails gave access to immigrants from the southwest and California.

But even in this early period there were some tourists willing to take the risk to view the scenic splendor of the Columbia River. One such was the writer, Frances Victor, who arrived by steamer from San Francisco in 1810.[6] She felt she was a leisured tourist compared to her image of what fur traders faced less than a century before. She noted in her diary her fascination over vistas up and down the river and especially with snow-capped Mt. Hood and St. Helen in the distance. Even the rail portages around cascades were thrilling and adventuresome for her. Today, replicas of historic riverboats provide some semblance of that travel era.

Travel through Idaho to Oregon began many thousand years ago with movements by many tribes such as the Nez Perce, Coeur d'Alene, Shoshoni, and others. Because of rugged mountain terrain to the north, the exploration by Lewis and Clark, the first European descendants to experience this region, followed the Snake River in 1805. Idaho was late to become a state—1890—in the midst of bloody violence among miners. Today, ghost towns are the only reminders of this era, now overshadowed by tourism and agriculture, although some mining continues.

This region had been well traversed by the 1830s by explorer expeditions, mountain men, and fur traders, as well as Indians. People like John Bridger, Jedediah Smith, John Fremont (in 1842 for the US Army), and many others had gained knowledge of this region by traveling it.[7] These travels had laid down many trails long before the Lewis and Clark expedition. Their tales and observations were the foundation for all future travel here.

As a major migration route for hundreds of thousands of people from the East seeking a new life in the West, the Oregon Trail contained many tourist elements in spite of the travel hardships in the 1820s. Land and the landscape held such power of appeal that bitter winters, disease, and Indian conflict did not deter their long journey to the frontier. Historians cite many testimonials from journals proving excitement of families in discovering the abundance and quality of natural resources of the West. Their wanderlust, challenge for adventure, and impressions of the landscape beauty and clear skies were a significant part of their motivation in addition to the search for a new livelihood.

But it was the gold rush that created social and development chaos. Travel service by Butterfield stagecoach lines could no longer cope and, after many organizational and political maneuverings, a mail contract of the government established tri-weekly service between Salt Lake City and The Dalles, and then by steamship to Portland.[8] Three major businesses then dominated travel control: Oregon Steam Navigation Company, Pacific Mail Steamship Company, and Wells Fargo and Company. Even so, passenger travel was expensive, slow, and far from comfortable. Maintenance of stock and network stations about every 15 miles added to costs. Today's Hollywood reenactments of holdups, Indian attack, and all the trials of coach travel on rough and muddy roads are no exaggeration of that early era of travel.

With all the hazards before them it is amazing how Lewis and Clark ever made it to the Pacific in 1805. Records show they were held up by the boiling waters, rattlesnakes, and exhaustion. It is interesting to note that the scenic route of the 1920s is not along any of the most prominent trails of early Oregon history. Instead, the first major road, established by Captain Samuel Kimbrough Barlow in 1846, went south from The Dalles to Dufur, westward between Mt. Hood and Mt. Wilson through what is now known as Barlow Pass, westward to Sandy and on to Oregon City following the original Oregon Trail of 1843.

Of course, the coming of railroads was really the first real joining of the East and West—the meeting of the Union and Central Pacific at Promontory Point, Utah, in 1869. In Oregon, in spite of immigration from the East, the past culture and geographic setting resisted complete change and remained northwestern. Even today, as one travels along the scenic highway beside the Columbia River, there is little hint of this tumultuous past.

In the 1880s, a tourist had two choices to visit the Columbia River Gorge from San Francisco.[9] By ocean, three steamship companies provided steamer travel as often as three times a week. By land, the trip was filled with excitement but made much more difficult and time consuming. The Central Pacific Railroad gave access to Redding, California, then 275 miles by stage up the Sacramento Valley to Roseburg, Oregon, after 2 weeks of shaking and bouncing over rough trails. After crossing the Siskyou and Rogue River mountains, the traveler would board the Oregon and California Railroad for a 200-mile trip to Portland.

Governmental Tourist Development

Throughout Oregon, federal land management agencies, such as the FS, have had considerable land development influence. An interesting case focuses on Mt. Hood. In the 1920s the most controversial outdoor recreational issue of the FS countrywide was a private proposal for a tramway on Mt. Hood.[10] This idea sparked the beginning of awareness of the complexity of tourism and recreation development, quite outside the past scope of responsibility for the FS. In 1926, Fred W. Cleator and Francis E. Williamson, Jr., had made several trips up the south slope and prepared plans for a resort lodge, mountain climbing chalets, and a ski lodge. In that same year a Portland firm prepared plans for a major hotel and a tramway to the summit of 11,000 feet. It was the tramway that stirred up the most controversy that dominated a major meeting about it in Portland to discuss environmental conflicts.

The issue, not settled there, was then taken up by the Secretary of Agriculture William M. Jardine, who appointed a committee to study the future of the site and make recommendation, supporting the hotel–tramway project. But, reflecting on the issue, Jardine was not completely satisfied and called in landscape architects Frank Waugh and Frederick Law Olmsted, Jr., together with president of the Carnegie Institute of Washington, John C. Merriam. They in turn did their own site inspection but could not agree. By this time, Arthur M. Hyde was the new secretary of Agriculture and finally issued a permit for the project. However, because of poor financial backing of the company receiving the award, the project was aborted.

All this political maneuvering suggested to the FS that growing outdoor recreation and tourism needed new policies for the agency. At the request of the Service, Frank Waugh was requested to refine such policies and produced his report, "Recreational Uses on the National Forests of the Rocky Mountain Region" in 1931. This resulted in adding three new positions for planning and management of outdoor recreation projects. The significance of this summary is to show the difficult but necessary acceptance by the FS of their role in recreation and tourism and using landscape architects as competent advisors.

The next major phase was the involvement of the CCC, an "army" of unemployed young men authorized for public works by President Franklin Delano Roosevelt in 1933. Part of their assignment, using special government funds, was to enhance recreation development of forest areas: roads, trails, buildings, and site improvement. Other agencies, including the NPS, also employed CCC workers for similar tasks, improving greatly the facilities within many public areas. For these efforts, many landscape architects were employed in the design of projects. This step led to the transfer of landscape architect R. D'Arcy Bonnet from the Eastern Region of the FS to Washington, DC. In 1937, by his memo, six landscape architects were hired for the California Region, one each in a National Forest.

In the following years, a great amount of design and construction took place, much of which is still in place today. The so-called "rustic design" of log and stone initiated by the NPS was used for picnic shelters, bath houses, drinking fountains, pavilions, lodges, and campground facilities. The idea of a major hotel on Mt. Hood had not died down and when the FS discovered a new funding source, the Public Works Administration (PWA), they engaged landscape architect A. D. Taylor in collaboration with Emmett Blandfield and Ward Gano to design a lodge. This became Timberline Lodge, an elaborate five-story hotel built on the flank of Mt. Hood in 1937.

This structure utilized log builders, skilled woodcarvers, blacksmiths, and other artisans to create what became known as an architectural and site development wonder of the Northwest.[11] By the end of this decade the FS was well established for the development of outdoor recreation and tourist services and facilities, only to be diminished greatly in the next decade with the impact of World War II. By now the role of landscape architects for sustainable design was well established even though that term was not yet in popular usage. By 1939, the FS had installed 23,000 overnight family picnic units and by 1941 there were 1381 recreation areas, 254 winter sports areas, 54 organization camps, and 11 resorts.

This historical background proves the importance of Oregon's landscape values that have become a dominant environmental ethic in this region. From explorers to pioneers of settlement, the aesthetic beauty of the area compensated for the hardships encountered. Even after many generations, Oregon's search for sustainability is now an icon of America's West. The important private sector of tourism would not be here today if it weren't for the general public's belief and even pride in the resources that set the region apart from all others.

Environmentalism

The Changing Coast

Unfortunately, the opposite of sustainability has marred the history of coastal Oregon. Tourism, recreation, vacation home development, and urban expansion have done their share of damage to this dynamic oceanfront. It is amazing that the experience of coastal hazards elsewhere has not been sufficient to alert developers to the fragility of this land edge. Ocean waters can do great damage if construction is too close to the shore. Not only have motels, resorts, and permanent residences along the coast created an ugly visible landscape, they have frequently been destroyed by the powerful erosive forces of the ocean.

An example that continues to demonstrate poor coastal planning is Siletz Spit, south of Lincoln.[12] Developers saw a market for vacation homes here and many were built, several of which have been damaged since by erosive wave action from Pacific storms. Another case is Capes Resort at Oceanside.[13] This very costly condominium was built on a high but erodable cliff with only a 10-foot setback from the edge. The powerful force of El Nino in the winter of 1997–1998 destroyed several buildings and damaged others beyond repair. The main lesson from these and other similar cases centers on exploiting a gullible market to build on predictably unstable land.

Efforts toward "stabilization" are often futile. Even though Oregon has established setback lines, they are frequently ignored or accepted if "remedial measures" such as seawalls or riprap are installed. These seldom last very long and degrade the aesthetics of natural and majestic coastal beauty. Too many seawalls force wave action that erodes sand at the base, eventually breaking down, especially in recent years of higher ocean water levels. For future coastal development, another significantly increasing threat is coming from the probability of earthquake and tsunami forces. Although state and county governments in Oregon recognize the need for better coastal management, stronger measures will be needed in the future for quality tourism development there.

Dams and Power

The land development craze of the 1920s and 1930s saw all rivers as fair game for damming. The growth of settlement, industry, and agriculture placed insatiable demands upon water sources, and reservoirs seemed to be best solutions. The engineering axiom that these waters were being "wasted to the sea" captured the interest of politicians and economic developers. At one time the Columbia River was targeted for the building of 10 dams.[14] This proposal resulted from the 1925 River and Harbor Act as part of the federal interest in stimulating greater economic growth in the northwest. Equally vocal was the private sector, which saw dams as the solution to needed electrical power, agricultural irrigation, and flood control. Little consideration was given to issues such as the destruction of salmon spawning, massive silting behind dams, and pollution threats from redistribution of population.

The policies and use of the Columbia River continue to be controversial—environmental protection versus power production and development. Factual foundations for both forces remain indecisive. Supporters of the existing dams cite how dependent the entire region is upon power production. Environmentalists cite serious reduction of salmon, important to the fishing and canning portion of the economy, not even mentioning negative impacts on tourism. But neither side has researched and documented sufficient details to reach studied conclusions regarding this tradeoff. Meanwhile, tourism planners and developers must increasingly take part in the debates because this resource base is so dependent on how the many issues are resolved at the many sites along the river corridor.

Another major environmental issue in Oregon was a one-time public approval in 1968 of a nuclear power plant proposal. It was believed that swelling demand for electricity would soon outpace the existing supply generated from coal, natural gas, petroleum, and seemingly abundant hydropower. In spite of support by the public and the Eugene Water and Electric Board (EWEB), soon questions of feasibility began to surface. Problems of site selection, excessive fog production (already great along the coast), opposition from farmers, and dangers cited by many journalists began to raise doubts over the next 2 years. With rising opposition, the proposal was finally killed forever by approval of a moratorium in May 1970. This case demonstrates the continuing force of environmentalism in this important region.

Indian Adjustment

As in other regions of the West, the story of Indian–white relations is not one of easy adjustment, even today. Among the first waves of white settlers were missionaries who sought to convert Indians to Christianity, a very strange concept for them that incidentally was accompanied by the introduction of liquor and disease. It is unlikely that Indian history anywhere in the nation was as dark as here in Oregon. Following a period of rather peaceful relations with white explorers, the invasion of Indian territory began conflict. By federal decree, tribes with quite disparate customs, languages, and beliefs were dumped together in a reservation because authorities erroneously thought they were all alike. Assimilation has not been easy.

The white philosophy was one of change and conquer, not only the natural features but also the Native American way of life. From a white perspective, this policy did produce many vibrant communities with a so-called high standard of living. The impact forever changed the appearance and quality of the land and drastically eroded the Indian population with epidemic disease and ruination of their livelihood. Tourism, just another form of economic development, was party to this same half-truth that the social and physical environment was there to be taken and used no matter the consequence.

Following the Rogue Indian Wars of the 1850s, many tribes that had never known each other were forced to live in the Siletz Reservation. Gradually, government regulations stripped them of their resources and even refused them the aid given to the white poor. The remaining Indians of this region have not made much adaptation to tourism, but an exception is the modern Siletz Tribal Smokehouse at Depoe Bay on the coast.[15] Here native crafts and Indian fish specialties are available to tourists. Each year in August, the tribe's powwow is held. With this, some semblance of Indian pride is being restored. Perhaps with greater communication and understanding in the future, Indian-white relations will improve, allowing these Native Americans to give travelers new insight into their rich culture—true environmental sustainability.

Toward Sustainability

In spite of the many negative impacts of land development in Oregon, it has perhaps the best record of environmental awareness and protective action of any destination in the West. For example, in spite of errors of coastal land use planning, Route 101 offers the traveler 362 miles of great diversity and beauty. Here the traveler can observe as in the past many natural features such as sand dunes, rain forests, mountain cliffs, sand beaches, migrating flyways, and a sea lion rookery. A major feature is the largest dune accumulation in the US—some 150 miles in length. They continue to migrate inland as they are fed by windblown sand from the beaches.

For those who seek outdoor recreation activities, there is an abundance of state park and national forest sites. The superlatives written into tour guides are based on sound factual foundations. The major change since the autocamping days of the 1920s is the generally nondescript cities along the coast. However, in between, the many scenic turnouts offer the traveler and amateur photographer many memorable vistas.

Cases

Among the several positive efforts toward sustainability is a popular resort on the coast, Salishan Lodge. Landscape architect Barbara Fealey is credited for the outstanding environmental planning many years ago. Environmental sensitivity dominated the placement of all structures to gain the greatest aesthetic impact from coastal

Many years ago, landscape architect Barbara Fealey adapted resort homes to the natural resources of this site for the present Westin Salishan Lodge and Golf Resort, Gleneden Beach, Oregon. This sustainable land design was successful from both an environmental and visitor standpoint with magnificent views to the Pacific. (Source: O. George Forster, Salishan)

vistas. This desirable development was the result of several groups working together—architects, landscape architects, interior designers, and owners. The structures seem married to the land forms and yet provide enjoyment for visitors and efficient operation for the managers. Even the bar, normally without windows, offers a magnificent panorama of surrounding landscape beauty.

Proposed along Oregon's southwestern coast is an ecotourism project by landscape architects, The Portico Group.[16] Planned is a canopy walkway in an old growth rainforest for observing the flora and fauna of this region. This sustainable tourism project promises to restore local landscapes and offer worthwhile experiences for tourists, thereby assisting the local economy.

The coastal city of Newport, through its City Council and Planning Department, has enacted overlay ordinances for sustainability of its heritage in several locations. The Historic Nye Beach Overlay (HNBO) was the first to be implemented and extends along the Pacific for an area approximately five by six blocks in an old "cannery row."[17] The intent is to protect the historic character by permit control of all future changes. A design review process is in place for all new development and changes in existing facilities and is directed toward the following purposes:

- Preserve the beautiful natural setting and the orientation of development and public improvements in order to strengthen their relationship to that setting.
- Enhance new and redeveloping architecture and landscape resources to preserve and strengthen the historic and scenic character and function of each setting.
- Improve the vehicular and pedestrian networks in order to improve safety, efficiency, continuity, and relationships.
- Improve the built environment in order to strengthen the visual appearance and attractiveness of developed areas.

Detailed criteria for control of building height, setback, roof slope, and facades are included in a manual, "Design Guidelines, Nye Beach Historic District." Site design criteria include building orientation, off street parking, pedestrian circulation, lighting, and signs. The permitting process includes review by all residents within 100 feet of the proposed site, any registered neighborhood association, and the Design Review Committee. Both tourists and residents are gaining from this progressive land planning initiative.

Concern of Oregon's many environmental problems became public under the leadership of Governor Tom McCall, 1967–1975. He established the Department of Environmental Quality in 1967, the Land Conservation and Development Commission in 1973, and the Oregon "bottle bill" that required deposit on purchases of soft drinks and beer to reduce waste and stimulate recycling. An example of Oregon's environmental progress was the elimination of serious pollution from the Willamette River.

Another is the case of the town of Bend that should have died following the demise of the Brooks-Scanlon lumber operation. It revived with the development of vacation homes, retirement homes, and tourism. A major element within the Bend vicinity is the landscape restoration project at Sunriver Resort and a new golf course, Crosswater.[18] Overgrazing and excessive logging had degraded the area. Restoration of the Little Deschutes River was the first task by landscape architects Walker and Macy in collaboration with Interfluve, a firm specializing in stream renewal. The innovative design created new waterfowl and fish habitat. The golf course complex, including a limited number of housing units, is adapted to the landscape and enhanced with native plant materials, dramatically improving the setting after cattle were removed. Part of this design by Gage Davis Association prevents runoff nutrients from the golf course entering nearby wetlands by installing a 30- to 50-foot berm, covered with native plants. This project demonstrates the value of team action by several landscape architects and specialists and proves that development can be environmentally constructive.

Portland is exemplary as a community that cares environmentally. In 1973, the state of Oregon passed a comprehensive land use planning initiative, followed by a regional government of 23 municipalities 5 years later.[19] Urban sprawl is less evident here than anywhere else in the country. A significant aid to public understanding of issues and resolving them is the Coalition for a Livable Future, a consortium of 55 organizations. Portland's success for maintaining its amenities makes it a delightful place to visit. For example, "view corridors" protect vistas from downtown to major landscape features such as the Cascade Mountains and Mt. Hood. The geographical setting within mountains and rivers has helped to condense the urban landscape.

Better than most cities, Portland has retained streetscapes that foster pedestrianism. It is not only possible but also desirable for residents and visitors to walk downtown and enjoy the many plazas. Much of Portland's original New England atmosphere has been retained over these 70 years since the explosion of autocampers. Variety restaurants and sidewalk cafes are enjoyed by locals as well as tourists. The light rail transit offers good people movement, especially to the convention center. These amenities have not been forced upon the people, they have been wanted and supported by the population. Some critics express concern over the possible negative impact of displacing lower income people in the city. On balance, administrative mechanisms are in place that continue pressing for future sustainability.

Today, at the Multnomah Falls site, spalling of rock cliffs and frequent flooding require constant repair and often redesign of visitor features. Several landscape architects, such as Michael Abate (foreground), regularly redesign walks and overlooks for this most popular tourist attraction in Oregon.

In the face of the modified environment, many landscape architects have been involved in recent years with projects designed to retain cultural and natural values. The groundswell of renewed interest in the Lewis and Clark expedition for the bicentennial celebration of 2004–2006 is stimulating site design and development projects throughout this travel corridor. Design involvement has been significant and has varied from resource inventories and area-wide planning to specific site and building plans. In all instances, these projects have involved team effort because of the great diversity of historic and site factors. The objective of environmental sustainability is common to all. Watson cites several cases in which landscape architects have played a major role.[20]

Outstanding is the Lewis and Clark National Trail Interpretive Center at Great Falls, Montana, opened in May, 1998. Keith Thurlkill, interpreter for the FS, served as coordinator for the planning using the landscape, planning, and architectural services of the Portico Group led by landscape architect Becca Hanson.[21] The entire history of the Corps of Discovery's trip from St. Louis to the Pacific coast and return is interpreted in this $6 million facility that was 10 years in the making. Especially important for sustainability was the coordination of many parties throughout the design process. Local community representatives, historians, Indians, archeologists, interpreters, and highway officials were integrated with design specialists from the beginning through construction. At the start, much time and many discussions were involved in the creation of a vision statement, a declaration of the theme, and specific objectives. Because no physical artifacts of the Lewis and Clark trip remained, historical records, the L & C journals, and amenities of the site provided the foundation for design. The buildings are subordinate to the land and all design decisions were directed toward the best quality of visitor experience, not just the whims of the designers and developers.

Exemplary is another Lewis and Clark site project. It includes linkage between a pedestrian plaza at a college and a monument to L & C on the Snake River. Special interpretation has been designed by landscape architect Don Brigham to encompass six sites at the Lewis-Clark State College, Lewiston, Idaho: Centennial Mall Statue Courtyard, History Wall, amphitheater, Historic Tree Grove, International Flag Plaza, and the Centennial Arch.[22] Important collaboration on this project were members of the Nez Perce tribe, the college staff, the sculptor, and landscape architects. The first phase to be completed was the Courtyard with life-size statues depicting the first meeting between Lewis and Clark and the Nez Perce tribal leader Twisted Hair and his son Lawyer. The statues, situated among trickling water cascades over indigenous rocks, also include a young Nez Perce girl digging camas roots under the watchful eye of her elder and a woman picking huckleberries. The sculptor was Doug Hyde of Santa Fe. This educational project is of great value to tourists as well as students and townspeople, a case of sustaining both natural and historical values at one site.

At another location, The Gorge Discovery Center near The Dalles, a demonstration of remarkable collaboration appears. Descriptive exhibits and displays recount the geological history of millions of years of the gorge's formation. Perhaps most impressive for visitors is the lucid description of the Lewis and Clark expedition's stressful and yet successful mission to the Pacific. Its educational value is heightened by its many lessons on the need for environmental stewardship. The organizers cite the

The recently developed Gorge Discovery Center located near The Dalles is an outstanding interpretive facility. Landscape architects and many other planners were involved in converting an eroded site into an interesting and functional attraction that explains the rich cultural and natural history of the area. The central theme of the Columbia River is worked into the floor design.

success of completion in 1997 as due to intensive study, open discussion, conflict resolution, and design concepts from the beginning in 1986 when the Columbia River Gorge Commission was formed. Following competition between three counties for site selection, an old denuded cement plant location was chosen because of its proximity to I-80 and The Dalles as well as the spectacular vistas across the river.

Design challenges included integrating the desires of five constituencies with differing agenda, restoration of an abused site using native plant materials, meeting the standards of the Columbia River Gorge National Scenic Area (CRGNSA), and especially creating facilities best suited to interpretation of this important historic and natural resource phenomenon. Throughout the process, many landscape architects were involved including Richard Shaffer (FS), Virginia Kelly (CRGNSA), Jurgen Hess (CRGNSA), and G. Michael Abbate (Green Works Landscape Architects). Abbate made several important conclusions from this experience, lessons on pitfalls to avoid in the development of such interpretive centers: even the best design concepts can be distorted by contractors; dangerous to consider the effort as only a project with an end—must consider never-ending values and changing objectives; need to focus on how visitor experience can be stimulated, not just what the planners wish for visitors; and without passion for the major goal and a full team approach the project is likely to fail.

An example of sustainable design just north of Oregon is the award-winning Washington Pass Rest Facility along the heavily traveled scenic North Cascades Highway.[23] It was created by a design team: Kelbaugh Calthorpe Associates, architects, with Einar Jarmund as principle designer, and Richard Haag Associates, landscape architects. The site posed several challenges. Extreme climate conditions of low temperatures, heavy snows, and stormy winds demanded special design. On-site electricity is obtained from photovoltaic cells and low-flush toilets conserve limited water supply. The design is reminiscent of rustic national park themes and the site captures the outstanding scenic beauty of the area.

The Pacific northwest tourism has benefited substantially from the design work of the several landscape architects of the firm of Jones & Jones of Seattle, Washington.[24] Their work has thoroughly analyzed the special attributes of place and conceptualized development that fosters visitor use in a sustainable environmental setting. Landscape architectural educator, David C. Streatfield states, "Their work is rooted in a profound respect for and celebration of place. Their designs interpret place as biophysical processes, and as intertwined acts of cultural will and transformation."[25] Examples of their tourism-related works include: Sleeping Lady Conference and Retreat Center, Leavenworth, Washington; Mountains to Sound Greenway, Elk Heights to Puget Sound, Washington; and design input on many other projects such as Scenic and Recreational Highway Study, Washington; Oregon Coast Highway Corridor Planning Study; and Washington State Ecotourism Strategy. In addition, the firm has been a catalyst in several planning consortiums that resolved issues of conflict between development and resource protection.

An example of outstanding sustainable design in Oregon is the award-winning site and structure of Broken Top Golf Clubhouse, near Bend and in the shadow of the Cascade Mountains.[26] As with most modern developments it was the result of collaborative design by landscape architect Arthur G. Beggs and architects Wimberly Allison Tong. The design responsibility included a landscape theme and image for the community in harmony with the natural beauty of the native pine-covered site within view of Broken Top, a Cascade peak. All structural development has the appearance of growing out of the native landscape rather than an attachment to it. Much of the success of this project is due to the intimate collaboration among designers and clients as they studied the special place characteristics of the site to create suitable design solutions. All interior design of buildings and features produce continuous flow between short and long exterior vistas and pleasant human use inside. Testimony to these sustainable qualities comes not only from design critics but also from the visitors.

Throughout Oregon, many new examples of tourism-related projects that demonstrate strong environmental sensitivity are appearing. This trend supports the image of the state as one seeking to preserve its natural and cultural resource heritage.

Scenic Roads

As early as 1913 Oregon began to establish a program of scenic roads, one of the first in the nation, as part of its overall highway system. In 1917 the Columbia River

Highway was the first major road in the Northwest that was designed specifically as a scenic highway.[27] This very special road idea had grown out of deliberations by the Seattle-Tacoma Rainier National Park Committee in 1912, a strange coalition of bedfellows—commercial clubs, civic groups, and chambers of commerce. Although the natural beauty of the river corridor was obvious, the motivation at that time was clearly economic—new moneys from sightseeing autocampers.

A highway engineer with an eye for beauty, Samuel C. Lancaster, had long dreamed about creating a major scenic highway and his interest was sharpened when he attended the first international road conference in 1908 where he learned about scenic roads in Europe. His interest became known and he, along with Samuel Hill, John B. Yeon, and Simon Benson, was commissioned to design a scenic road along the Columbia River and construction began in 1913. The alignment and gradient standards were suited to automobiles of the day. Surveys had identified sites of especially outstanding vistas that became turnouts where tourists could stop, enjoy, and photograph the views. Sustainability of scenic values as well as tourist use dominated the design vision. The stonework of bridges and other structures were built by skilled artisans. Many craftsmen were engaged in the building of this unusual scenic highway.

This scenic road foundation had precedent in the 1919–1920 state allocation when the highway commission authorized roadside rest areas, tree planting, and outdoor

An illustration of the fine stone craftsmanship of the original Columbia River Highway builders in 1913. Today, parts of this outstanding scenic road are being restored as the Historic Columbia River Highway and others are available as hiking trails. (Source: US Forest Service)

advertising control along its highways. Further sign control and scenic easements were authorized in 1960. In 1961 a Scenic Area Board was established that prohibited roadside billboards and scrap yards and designated 3500 miles of scenic roads. Added in 1983 and 1985 were historic elements of scenic roads including bridges and other cultural features.

Oregon now has enabling legislation for designation of scenic roads, administered by the Oregon Department of Transportation.[28] The criteria for initial designation include: (1) provides an outstanding view or vista, (2) contains outstanding or unusual historic values illustrating development of the state, (3) provides for historic or scenic values, (4) appears in local or regional promotion literature as having historic or scenic values, (5) contains unique design or construction features, (6) contains view or vistas of unique landforms, (7) contains significant features involving a notable designer or architect, and (8) has significant historic or scenic values recognized by local population. To rate the importance of the above when making designation, the following criteria are used: exceptionally rare and beautiful and/or historically significant, statewide recognition, and use of segment/structure as a destination and/or preferred route of travel.

Over several decades it became clear that traffic of both commercial and tourist use had outgrown the capacity of the Columbia River road. In the 1960s, I-84 was constructed close to the river, leaving only segments of the original scenic highway. The Oregon Department of Transportation has restored many of these portions into the present Historic Columbia River Highway. These older sections now offer the

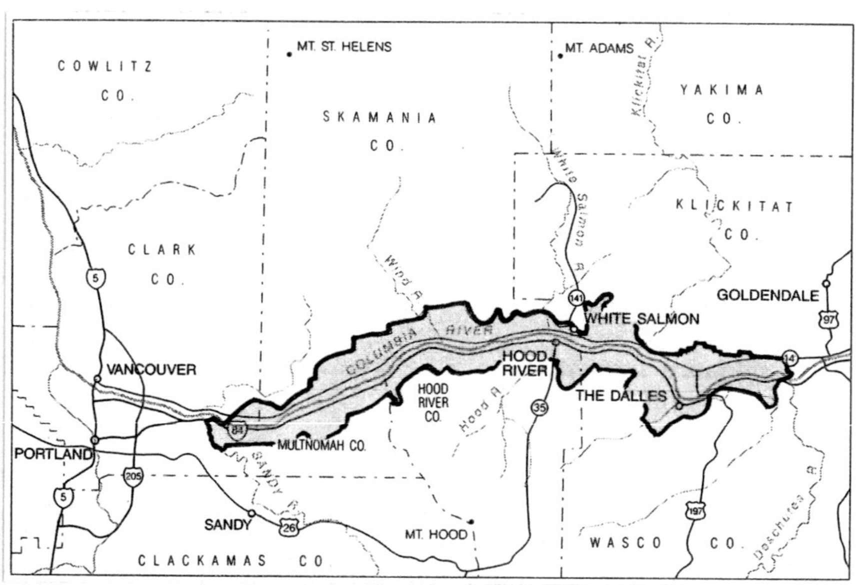

Unprecedented was the establishment of the Columbia River Gorge National Scenic Area (CRGNSA) in 1986, the first in the nation. This 85-mile planned corridor encompasses portions of both Washington and Oregon states. Planning principles include environmental sustainability as well as tourism growth. (Source: CRGNSA)

modern traveler the same outstanding vistas available to the autocampers of the 1920s. The few segments that cannot be restored for automobiles are now redesigned for hike and bike trails. Examples are the sections from Troutdale to Ainsworth State Park and from Mosier to The Dalles.

An Innovative Plan

Today, the traveler along the Columbia River gorge quite likely does not realize he is in the midst of a revolutionary political and environmental planning process that is unique in the annals of tourism development.[29] Now this area has been declared the CRGNSA by Congress and was signed into law by President Ronald Reagan in 1986. It encompasses 292,000 acres along the river for about 83 miles, from the Sandy River on the west to the Deschutes River on the east. The area includes portions of the states of Washington and Oregon, parts of six counties, and 13 key cities. For planning and management purposes, the area is divided into three categories: urban areas, the Special Management Area (SMA), and the General Management Area (GMA). The SMA, about 115,000 acres, has the most stringent regulations: no new land subdivisions, new houses on only 40-acre lots or larger, and forest practices regulated for scenic, cultural, natural, and recreation importance.

The 149,004 acres of the GMA are located primarily in the eastern portion of the region. Here, agriculture and forestry are the main uses with some scattered areas where residential development will remain.

Because the theme of scenery is key to the entire area, an inventory revealed that it could be classified and mapped into 12 predominant "landscape types." In addition, a map of "seen areas" identifies those locations visible from main viewing points. A "landscape diversity" map gauges the variety of visual features founded in visitor

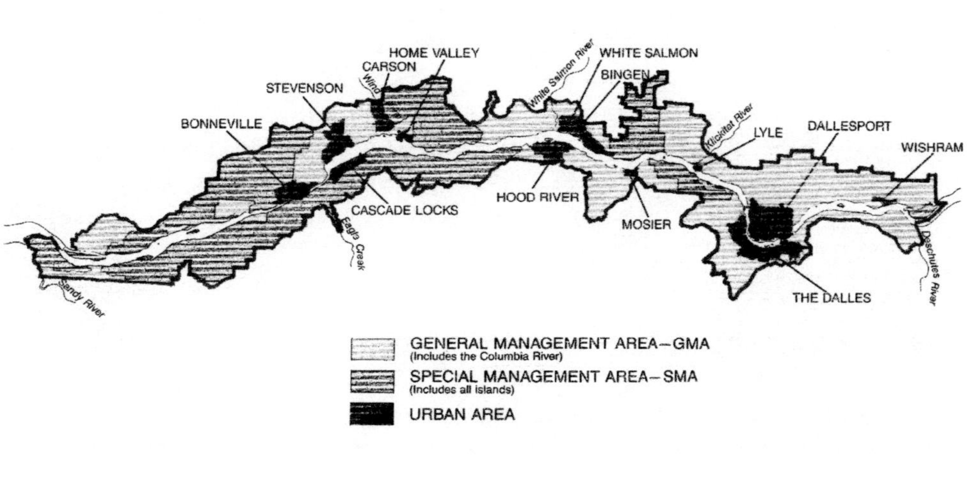

The CRGNSA plan divides the corridor into three major planning areas: Urban, Special Management, and General Management. Resource protection, as well as tourist business, is fostered by planning tourist services primarily in the urban zone. Public and private developers are responsible for implementation. (Source: CRGNSA)

perception of appeal and interest. Then, by combining the maps of "seen areas" and "landscape diversity," a "landscape significance" map is obtained. Because development change is anticipated, these research maps were studied to produce a "visual absorption capability" map—areas that predictably can absorb change. A final map identifies "landscape sensitivity."

This innovative plan encourages private sector development for tourism but is guided into the urban areas and must be compatible with the purposes of the area. The present distinction between urban and rural areas will be perpetuated. New visitor interpretive centers will give visitors opportunity to enjoy, learn about, and experience this special corridor. This public–private cooperative venture represents a departure from the past antagonisms and self-destructivisms of both public agencies and tourist enterprises.

It is easy to understand why environmentalists, recreationists, and politicians fostered the creation of this extraordinary national scenic area. Congressmen, in their support for the needed legislation, used descriptions such as "spectacular canyon," "abundant natural resources," "gorge with sharply raising escarpments," "dramatic waterfalls and geological formations," "fantastic beauty," and "a unique place in the development of this country, and of the early history of the Pacific Northwest." The public–private program and vision for this corridor holds promise to retain many of the values observed by autocampers in the 1920s at the same time that economic growth is allowed to flourish.

Because the creation and administration of this innovative and complicated project required a special organization, Congress called for a two-tiered management approach. Inasmuch as the FS already manages many of the lands here, this agency was given a major role of responsibility. This was balanced by The Columbia River Gorge Commission of 13 members and a six-person staff. This group represents local, state, and national interests and spent 4 years preparing the management plan, including statements of vision, goals, objectives, policies, and strategies for implementation. Although some local residents object to some of the plan's requirements, most of the recommendations are being implemented.

Today tourism here includes much more than sightseeing, such as trail hiking, bicycling, mountain biking, skiing, river running, wind surfing, horseback riding, and cave exploration. Altogether, the Columbia River corridor offers a captivating setting, not only providing a great diversity of modern visitor experiences but also a revolutionary concept of tourism planning. Because the west end of the corridor nearest Portland has reached its tourist capacity, especially at peak seasons, it is now being demarketed by the business sector. The remainder of the scenic region has capacity for greater growth in the planned sites.[30]

Regional projects that impact many jurisdictions and individuals are always confronted by conflict. Because this project involved Washington State and all counties along the Columbia River, cooperation with Skamania County was needed but not readily obtained.[31] After much haggling the county agreed to support the project but only if given ample compensation. The result was a $5 million grant to the county for the establishment of a major hotel–conference facility, the Skamania Lodge. A design team including landscape architect J. Douglas Macy was commissioned to design the project and they selected an abandoned land fill site not far from the end of the

A political tradeoff for sustainable development within the CRGNSA was funding for this Skamania Lodge and Convention Center, located along the Columbia River in Washington. Landscape architects, architects, and local residents cooperated in the planning of this facility that has restored an eroded site and provided an economic boon, replacing the dwindling forest economy.

Bridge of the Gods. Local residents of the surrounding area were brought into the design process from the beginning. On this 140-acre site a 195-room hotel was designed in a contemporary Cascadia style and built against a beautiful forest backdrop, completed in 1994. The community feels this is their facility and have access to the swimming pool as well as other facilities such as tennis courts, jogging runs, and forest trails. The outstanding year-round success has changed the local economy from dwindling forestry to thriving tourism. This project is an excellent illustration of sustainable tourist development, recovering an ugly abandoned site and bolstering the local economy.

The concept of sustainable tourism development of this region must be placed in perspective of the long-term environmental setting. Research by landscape architect Kent Watson reveals that the so-called wilderness of the Lewis and Clark era had already been modified by the hand of man as well as by natural causes.[32] Indians practiced their own fire ecology to sustain food crops. Later on, stock grazing reduced native species of grasses and allowed encroachment by exotic species, such as mullein, cheat grass, Scotch broom, and Russian olive. Animal life, once dominant in this region, had been reduced considerably, especially the condor, grizzlies, wolf, and fish species, such as now endangered steelhead and salmon.

Some local citizens and their county governments fear the loss of tax revenues if too much land is placed in public trust, such as FS inholdings.[33] But the concept of favoring private development only in and around communities where it can be serviced has great merit. More of the surrounding environment of scenic value to tourists increases as business opportunities in the vicinity of cities also increase, assisting in growth of the tax base.

Southern Oregon

From a tourism perspective, southern Oregon refers primarily to the southwestern region adjacent to northern California. It is also dominated by mountains, forests, and rushing rivers. This special place also includes service cities of Grants Pass, Medford, Klamath Falls, Ashland, and Roseburg. A wilderness theme dominates the region. Warm and hospitable are the local hosts of tourists in attractions and services.

From a backwoods atmosphere, many sophisticated developments have been created for traveler enrichment and enjoyment. Several years ago Southern Oregon University started what is now acclaimed Shakespeare Festival in Ashland, held at an authentic outdoor Elizabethan stage.[34] Landscape architect John McLaren is credited with the beauty and extensive plant design of Ashland's scenic Lithia Park along Ashland Creek, now named a National Historic Site. This award is based on its cultural foundation of early Indian encampment and an historic flour mill. The area also gained fame as a mineral springs resort.

Medford, now located on I-5 providing easy access from populous California, dates back to gold rush days. Past economic bases of forestry and agriculture are now assisted greatly by expanding tourism. Picturesque and historically significant are Table Rocks with the 2000-acre Lower Table Rock Preserve nearby. This protected area contains a wide diversity of vegetative, geologic, and cultural resources. Not far to the west of Medford is the small town of Jacksonville, the first National Historic Landmark District to be designated in Oregon in 1966. Featured in the Jackson County Museum are the photographs of prominent artist Peter Britt. The Britt Gardens and Britt Festivals add greatly to the scenic and historic appeals of the area.

The greatest lure of the Grants Pass area is the roaring and challenging Rogue River, now the center for masses of outfitters. The scenic appeal of this area and its growing tourism are helping to make up for a dwindling forest economy. Once a gold mining mecca, some tourists are having fun panning for a few flecks of gold in the streams nearby.

A tourist surprise in this region is evidence of new interest in natural and cultural resource protection and interpretation. An excellent case is the well-designed Douglas County Museum of Natural History in Roseburg. From the time one enters until leaving, the several themes are clearly and interestingly exhibited and interpreted. Latest museum technology is evident with video and audio descriptions that make history live. It is easy for the visitor to project himself back into the several past time frames, making the tour of the region even more meaningful.

Even with many such instances of new adaptation to the changes in society and economy, concerns over employment and quality of life have stimulated the creation

Throughout the West, in spite of much environmental deterioration, new interpretive museums are being established, such as the Douglas County Museum of Natural History at Roseburg, Oregon. These new local facilities become tourist attractions as well as amenities for residents. Of interest to visitors, they interpret the natural and cultural history by means of the latest exhibit technology.

of a grass-roots organization called The Southern Oregon Economic Development Coalition (SOEDC) in 1991.[35] The focus is on sustainable development mainly in Jackson and Josephine counties, including the cities of Medford and Grants Pass. Its innovative scope includes environmental protection as well as jobs and the economy, particularly related to tourism.

This organization really got under way in 1995 with programs to foster new methods of agriculture, forest use and products, cultural heritage tourism, health services, and manufacture of nontraditional building materials. Emphasis is on the basic principle that economic and ecological health go hand in hand.

Among the many organizations brought together in this coalition are: Rogue Valley Oregon Action, Rogue Valley Community Development Corporation, Southern Oregon Growers Association, Convenio de Raices Mexicanas, Community Emergency Resources and Vital Services, Peace Garden Institute, American Indian Cultural Center, Rogue Institute for Ecology and Economy, and the Catholic Community Services of Southern Oregon.

One program especially related to tourism is sponsored by the American Indian Cultural Center. Its purpose is to enhance sales of crafts along I-5 and, with the aid of interpretive centers, provide the visitor with a better understanding of Native culture including legend and lore. A change for the better is new cooperation with major federal land agencies who in the past were adversaries. As a member of the SOEDC, this Native American group is directing its efforts toward only those forms of tourism that enhance rather than deplete the special environmental character of the region.

Also in this region is Crater Lake, deepest in the nation and the only national park in Oregon, established by Congress in 1902. This unusual sight is a major destination feature for many tourists, especially in summer but recently winter has become popular with snowmobiling, cross-country skiing, and snowshoeing. The concession, Crater Lake Lodge, provides lodging and food and tours by boat and bus. Formed from volcanic eruption several thousand years ago, the caldera was created when the core collapsed upon itself.

Native American legends of the collapse of Mt. Mazama parallel the scientific geologic history of this site.[36] The legend offers the story of two chiefs, Llao of the Below World and Skell of the Above World, who fought each other, destroying Llao's house. This battle resulted in the eruption of Mt. Mazama and the formation of Crater Lake. Gold prospectors in 1853 came upon the site and were awe-struck by the view of what they called the bluest lake they had ever seen. Later, William Gladstone Steel was fascinated by this unusual place and promoted its protection, realized on May 22, 1902 when President Theodore Roosevelt signed the bill creating Crater Lake National Park.

Adding to the tranquility of the brilliant blue lake are two major visual features projecting high above the water surface: Wizard Island and Phantom Ship. The only source of water for the lake is rain and snow runoff. Through seepage and evaporation the level remains remarkably stable. Trails offer the visitor access to forest and wildlife scenery. Resource degradation is kept to the minimum because visitor use is limited primarily to viewing and photographing the scenery. From a sustainable perspective, development has remained low due to the encasement by national park and forest land.

Representative of the early policy of national park staff to encourage greater tourist use, the Crater Lake Lodge was opened in 1915.[37] In spite of construction difficulty in this area of harsh winters, a builder from Portland started the project but was surprised by the need for a structure that would withstand 15 feet of snow. The first crude building, even without inside plumbing, was extremely popular because of the magnificent views. After adding more comfortable amenities in the 1920s, the CCC improved the site with indigenous trees and shrubs, adapting the building to the landscape. However, the building deteriorated badly after World War II and NPS took it over as the owner refused to make needed repairs.

Adapting the structure to modern tourist use demanded major reconstruction, completed at a cost of over $15 million in 1994. Because virtually none of the original building could be salvaged and rebuilding demanded new steel structural support, utilities, and safety systems, one may question the decision to rebuild. The original building served a suitable function for its time but today's easier access and tremendous growth of visitors endorse the planning principle of locating major accommodations in nearby communities rather than in the park. In-park facilities of modern standards are less economically feasible due to high investment versus a short season of revenues. When located in communities they benefit from both resident and visitor markets, are supported by local infrastructure, are more economically viable, and eliminate environmentally destructive site preparation and parking facilities within the park. The future sustainability of the park will be enhanced by encouraging commercial tourist services in Klamath Falls and Medford.

A news release of August 1, 2000 from Crater Lake National Park revealed new sonar mapping of the bottom of the lake. Images are produced from 70 million sample points.[38] Shown for the first time are ancient lava landslides and other geologic features. In addition to maps produced from this process, the scientists are developing an interactive display in the interpretive visitor center where visitors will be able to virtually "fly the lake bottom."

The oldest section of the Pacific Crest Trail is the 400-mile walk from Crater Lake to Mt. Hood. The entire trail from Canada to Mexico of 2638 miles was completed in 1972.[39] This scenic and adventuresome trail passes through seven national parks. As of 1995 an alternate spur trail allows access to the thrilling vistas from the rim of Crater Lake. Specially designated camping sites reduce environmental impacts along this spectacular trail. Several portions of the trail are accessible from carparks for day hikers.

A demonstration of important environmental sustainability is the work of NPS staff, Cathy Gilbert, historical landscape architect, and Marsha Tolon, landscape architect. Their project was "Cultural Landscape Recommendations, Park Headquarters at Munson Valley, Crater Lake National Park," 1991.[40] The purpose was to survey existing landscape and development conditions of this significant historic site and to make remedial recommendations. The location is in one of three prominent glacial valleys on Mt. Mazama's south flank.

Although road work had begun in 1918 by the U.S. Army Corps of Engineers, major development of road access, park headquarters, and maintenance structures took place in 1933–1934 by the CCC, directed by NPS landscape architects, Merel Sager, Francis Lange, and Thomas Vint. The dominant design theme was to integrate structures and circulation systems into the natural surroundings, using weathered boulders, masonry, and rustic wood signs. Although these designers preferred a location farther down the slope for these services, the site became fixed. However, after World War II allowed winter use of the park, these facilities were not adapted to snow plow maintenance, demanding changes in details but the overall land use pattern remains. The many drawings, photographs, and reports by Sager, Lange, and Vint represent a wealth of truly sustainable environmental historical documents representing the NPS rustic landscape theme that has continued to this day.

Six categories of recommendations for improvement of this site emerged from this site analysis. A plan for enhancing and screening the maintenance area should be made. All historic buildings should be preserved and no new structures should be built in the historic district. New roads should not be added and pedestrian ways need to be improved to reduce maintenance. Some plant clearing is necessary for better views and any new plantings should replicate the originals. All site furnishings (garbage cans, bike racks, signs) should be redesigned to be most appropriate for the rustic setting. Historic association should prevail for any changes in the administrative complex, superintendent's residence, and other site and building development.

This case is cited here as a typical example of concern over environmental sustainability by NPS specialists.

Commendable are the policies of the Oregon Tourism Commission that slants its advertising strongly toward its natural and cultural resource amenities.[41] Emphasis is on the fresh and clean environment where development is balanced with resource protection. Recently, their survey indicated that this theme should be modified to include tourist opportunities for action, adventure, and enrichment from cultural sites. The intent is to broaden the promotional base to encompass Oregon's special places, people, and stories.

It is clear that Oregon is in the midst of adjusting to changes from the period of autocampers in the 1920s. The several instances of new projects and organizations dedicated to a meld of development and environmental sustainability indicate a desirable trend for tourism in the future.

Future Challenges

Any tourist of today who is old enough to have traveled Oregon in the autocamping days of the 1920s would make three major observations. First, changes in travel modes and services would be striking. Interstate highways, air access, safer and more comfortable automobiles, modern accommodations and food services, and convention facilities in Portland have increased dramatically in quantity and quality. Second, the basic natural wonders, such as striking mountain peaks, forests, the Pacific coast, parks, and the spectacular Columbia River Gorge would still rate high in anyone's sightseeing and photographic desires as well as outdoor recreational lures. Third, the negative aspects of traffic congestion, severe cutting of forests, and erosion of the coast would be more evident than in the early days of travel.

Oregon continues to carry an image of a destination where environmental forces are effective mainly because statewide environmental policies here are stronger than elsewhere in the US. The state once displayed bumper stickers carrying the bawdy message of "Don't Californicate Oregon" (translated: come visit and spend your money but don't stay). In spite of some environmental degradation, the diversity of the natural resource assets of cliffs, sand dunes, and beaches of the coast have retained most of their scenic appeal. The Cascade Mountain range and five mountain peaks including the popular Mt. Hood have endured as scenic and recreational foundations for a great amount of visitor growth. Oregon early on saw the need for retaining the quality of scenic roads and enacted regulations to protect them.

Without doubt, Oregon's most spectacular and enduring appeal is the natural-cultural resource of the Columbia River corridor. Forever changing the history of the US was the Lewis and Clark Discovery Expedition with the Columbia River as a major link. Because of its rare beauty it was the first region of the country to be declared a national scenic area. This historic river cuts through a diversity of landscape character—from forested mountains to desert plains, from wild rural lands to attractive urban settlement, from prehistoric and Indian culture to modern industrialization. Today's retelling and reporting of this historic voyage is stimulating the establishment of new and well-designed museums and interpretive centers.

Very active today are landscape architects who are providing land designs that protect environmental factors as well as producing attractive and enriching development. The new paradigm of using a team of designers, planners, and local constituencies is expediting the creation of sustainable development. But opportunities abound for much greater influence by these professionals in the future, in both public and private projects.

If promoters and developers seek greater tourism growth, past history provides ample support for caution, even limiting growth with tourist demarketing. Enticing more visitors demands expansion of the supply side, mainly new attractions, more services, and better transportation. Regarding new attractions, several issues must be dealt with. The dominant tourist image today is natural resource beauty. A key question centers on the limits of capacity of these resources. Another question focuses on new attractions, such as casinos and theme parks, which may be violating the natural resource image. Coastal attractiveness is already being stressed by poor and excessive development. Coastal roads at peak tourist seasons are choked with traffic congestion. Controversies between forest harvesting and environmental protection spill over into tourism decision making. Those seeking wildland experiences in the future may have no place to go. The old original scenic Columbia River Gorge highway has already been compromised by the new Interstate. Although through traffic is enhanced by this highway, many miles of the old scenic road used by the autocampers of the 1920s are now gone. An indicator of mass tourism pressure is Multnomah Falls, now restricted to the capacity of the parking lot, leaving many visitors dissatisfied with the trip objective, suggesting future demarketing.

Solutions to these and other issues of tourism growth are not easily accomplished, and no simple solution is offered here. The main lesson from historic review of tourism's development is that the entire agglomeration of tourism decision makers must face these issues and work together for future resolution. Today, two mechanisms for greater communication and even cooperation between the public and private sector are now available in the CRGNSA and the Western States Tourism Policy Council. The question in the future is whether Oregon's tourism planners, developers, and promoters, public and private, will commit themselves to implementation of the many positive recommendations. The clamor for more visitors must be balanced by cautious and careful planning with emphasis on potential negative impacts. Each increment of supply side growth impacts all other aspects and especially the environment. Desirable as new tourism incomes may be, they may not be forthcoming if resources are depleted, if access is congested and unsafe, and if the travel experience is disappointing. An equal consideration must be the impact of tourism's growth on the local quality of life. This destination may require demarketing rather than promotion. Called for in Oregon is extension of the strong environmental ethic whenever new tourism development is contemplated.

Endnotes

[1]Warren, S., & Ishikawa, T. L. (1998). *Oregon Handbook* (4th ed., p. 62). Chico, CA: Moon Publications.

[2]Mann, W. A. (1998). Journals of Early Explorers in the Northwest. *1998 ASLA An-*

nual Meeting Proceedings (pp. 168–171). Washington, DC: American Society of Landscape Architects. Also: Unpublished paper by Mann, W. A. (1998). *Capability Brown in the Wilderness: Late Eighteenth Century and Early Nineteenth Century Travelers and Their Writings About the Trans-Mississippi Landscape.* Athens, GA: University of Georgia.

[3]Shepard, P. (1967). *Man in the Landscape* (p. 185). New York: Alfred A. Knopf.

[4]Hubbard, H. V., & Kimball, T. (1935). *An Introduction to the Study of Landscape Design* (p. 77). New York: Macmillan Company.

[5]Ambrose, S., & Abell, S. (1998). *Lewis & Clark: Voyage of Discovery* (p. 21). Washington, DC: National Geographic Society.

[6]Victor, F. F. (1870). *The River of the West* (p. 2). Hartford, CT: R. W. Bliss. (Reproduced in 1958 by Mountain Press, Missoula, MT)

[7]White, R. B. (1991). *It's Your Misfortune and None of My Own* (p. 122). Norman: University of Oklahoma Press.

[8]Winther, O. D. (1950). *The Old Oregon Country* (p. 266). Stanford: Stanford University Press.

[9] Shearer, F. E. (Ed.). (1884). *The Pacific Tourist* (p. 326). New York: Adams and Bishops. (Reprinted 1970 by Crown Publishers, New York).

[10]Tweed, W. C. (1980). *Recreation Site Planning and Improvements in National Forests: 1891–1942* (p. 14). Washington, DC: Forest Service.

[11]Tweed, op. cit., 24.

[12]Komar, P. D. (1997). *The Pacific Northwest Coast.* Durham, NC: Duke University Press.

[13]Komar, P. D. (1999, February 7). Correspondence, College of Oceanic & Atmospheric Sciences, Oregon State University, Corvallis.

[14]Robbins, W. G. (1997). *Landscapes of Promise: The Oregon Story 1800–1940* (p. 272). Seattle: University of Washington Press. Other sources: Baden, J. A., & Snow, D. (Eds.). (1997). *The Next West.* Washington, DC: Island Press. Sherow, J. E. (Ed.). (1998). *A Sense of the American West.* Albuquerque, NM: University of New Mexico Press. Harden, B. (1996). *A River Lost.* New York: W. W. Norton.

[15]Warren and Ishikawa, ibid.

[16]This plan received an "Honor Award" in the 1999 ASLA Awards as reported by J. William Thompson in *Landscape Architecture,* 89(10), 172.

[17]Historic Nye Beach Overlay Zone Handout. (n.d.). Newport, OR: Planning Department, City of Newport.

[18]Strawn, J. (1999). The Laying on of Golf. *Landscape Architecture,* 89(10), 60–65.

[19]Among the key sources are: Kaplan, R. D. (1998). *An Empire Wilderness: Travels into America's Future* (Chap. 29). New York: Random House. Pollack, N. (2000, Spring). American Sprawl. *Enterprise Quarterly*, 12–19.

[20]Watson, K., & Abate, M. (1998, October 2). Panel presentation, Annual Meeting of the American Society of Landscape Architects, Portland, Oregon.

[21]Thurlkill, K. (1998, October 5). Landscape Interpretation Projects of the Historic Pacific Northwest. Panel presentation, Annual Meeting of the American Society of Landscape Architects, Portland, Oregon.

[22]Watson, K., ibid.

[23]Cohan, P. (1998). Washington Pass Rest Facility. *Wood Design and Building*, 16–

18.

[24]Jones, G. R. (1998, September 16). Correspondence and literature from Tom Carlson, marketing, Jones & Jones, Seattle, Washington.

[25]Streatfield, D. C. (1995). Regionalism in Landscape Design. *Process Architecture,* 126, 20–21.

[26]Beggs, A. G. (1998, November 9). Correspondence and supporting literature.

[27]Carr, E. (1998). *Wilderness by Design* (p. 83). Lincoln: University of Nebraska Press.

[28]*An Analysis and Summary of the 1990 National Scenic Byways Study Inventory.* (1990). Washington, DC: Federal Highway Administration.

[29]*Management Plan for the Columbia River Gorge National Scenic Area.* (1992). Washington, DC: Forest Service.

[30]Correspondence from Jurgen Hess, director, CRGNSA, February 18, 2000.

[31]Macy, J. D. (1998, October 1). Oral presentation at site, Annual Meeting of the American Society of Landscape Architects.

[32]Watson, K. (1998). The Way to Oregon: Opening the American Public's Mind on the Historical Landscape of the West. *1998 ASLA Annual Meeting Proceedings* (pp. 165–167). Washington, DC: American Society of Landscape Architects.

[33]Stuebner, S. (1998, February 16). Counties Want to Develop Public Land. *High Country News*, p. 13.

[34]Warren & Ishakawa, op cit., 341.

[35]Legg, J., & Fromherz, F. (1998). Changing Culture and Practice of Development: The Southern Oregon Economic Development Coalition. In M. D. Hoff (Ed.), *Sustainable Community Development* (pp. 193–210). New York: Lewis Publishers.

[36]Park History. From www.nps.gov/crla/crlacr, as of September 8, 2000.

[37]Taylor, K. (2000). Crater Lake Lodge. From www.nps.gov/crla/logehist, as of September 10, 2000.

[38]Images Emerge from the Depths of Crater Lake. From http://165.83.219.72/release/Detail/.cfm?ID=60, as of September 8, 2000.

[39]The Pacific Crest National Scenic Trail at Crater Lake National Park. From www.nps.gov/crla/pct. as of September 8, 2000.

[40]Gilbert, C., & Tolon, M. (1991). Cultural Landscape Recommendations, Park Headquarters at Munson Valley, Crater Lake National Park. From www.nps.gov/crla/munson, as of September 8, 2000.

[41]Curtis, J. (2000, Winter). How Research Shapes a Message. *TTRA Newsletter*, 4.

Chapter 8

1929 Western Tour: Part IV

This leg of the Gunn family autocamping tour of the West in 1929 encompasses the destination of Yellowstone National Park and return travel to Michigan. Although it reveals the many impressions of the unusual features of the Yellowstone region, it shows great anxiety of returning home after 6 weeks of autocamping. In spite of the wearisome tent camping and travel over bad roads and encountering many inconveniences, it was the highlight of the Gunn family experience. It is followed by Chapter 9, an elaboration of changes in tourism in this region over the last seven decades and the key issues this evolution has evolved—challenges to future tourism here.

•••••••••••••••••

We begin our adventure of the many spectacles of Yellowstone on **July 28** by observing the rushing waters of the Firehole River and Cascades and stop to visit the Lower Geyser and the Fountain Paint Pot. This is my introduction to the supernatural, the fantastic, and the bizarre. These steam spouts and mud bubbles are part of a real and yet metaphysical landscape. What a contradiction! What an unearthly setting we think as we see Excelsior Geyser, Grand Prismatic Spring, Turquoise Pool, Biscuit Basin, Mirror Pool, Gem Pool, Morning Glory Pool, and Grotto Geyser. Along with these strange sights we begin to see real bears wandering around, our first such experience outside a zoo. This unusual landscape got its name from the yellow rock edges alongside the Yellowstone River, high bluffs of yellow sandstone, and extensive ridges so yellow they appeared to the early explorers to gleam like gold.

As we found in Grand Canyon National Park, we are again reminded here in Yellowstone that our typical concept of park needs revision. For most of us in 1929 and even earlier our definition of park was that of an urban park—large trees, mowed lawns, "keep off the grass" signs, paved walks, and colorful and well-manicured flower beds. Instead, these are park areas only in the sense that they offer a natural resource setting and contrived development is kept to the minimum. Instead of gazebos and Sunday band concerts, these parks are composed of natural physical phenomena—mountains, forests, rivers, lakes, wildflowers, wildlife, and rare geological spectacles. In Yellowstone, many of the strange natural features appear so demonic that they carry labels such as Devil's Den, Hellroaring Creek, Firehole River, Devil's Slide, and Hell Broth Springs. Nearby we find a campsite and settle into this unfamiliar wonderland.

Purchased in 1929, this Haynes postcard depicts the Old Faithful Inn, a typical rustic design of national park lodges. Built in 1904 for wealthy tourists, it has adapted to a great variety of tourist market segments ever since. Fortunately, it escaped the forest fire of 1988.

The next day, Monday, **July 29**, is catch-up day, rest, and doing a laundry. Somehow mother actually does some ironing. As I recall dad usually wore a white shirt with tie throughout our travels. Mother's log states that dad, Lauren, and I start out on a ranger-guided trail but she notes that I played out and came back. As campers we stand in awe before the imposing three-story Old Faithful Inn built completely of lodgepole pine logs—walls, partitions, posts, braces, beams, and ceiling of log slabs. It is only a short distance away that we wait and witness Old Faithful spouting forth its lofty steamy display. Nearby are campsites where we pitch our tent. At dusk we join other campers on log bench seats and are given an informative and interesting talk by a park ranger. Behind him is the hotel's garbage dump and soon, as if on cue, the black bears come to rummage about, followed by some huge grizzlies as it gets darker.

Evidence of respect for the park custodians of natural and cultural resources is our pleasure upon seeing a park ranger, almost as important as seeing a bear. The flat brim hat and special uniform signify not only authority but a friendly person with dedication to a cause. Even as a lad of 12, I so much enjoy the interpretive stories of bear and other resources I hear that I approach the ranger, Philip Martindale, for an autograph in our souvenir book, *The National Parks Portfolio*.

The next morning, **July 30**, we wake up with frost on the tent and ground around us. We forget that an elevation of over 7000 feet can do this. A few miles from breaking camp we see the beautiful Kepler's Cascades in the Firehole River. As we swing east on the Loop Road we come to Isa Lake and encourage our Ford over Craig Pass. Here we can't resist playing typical tourist by stopping for bear pictures. Not realizing we're at great risk with cubs up a tree and other mature bears about, dad snaps one standing on our running board as I feed it a cookie.

As our road twists and turns and we struggle over the Continental Divide we get a long vista of the snow-capped Tetons and Shoshone Lake in the foreground. As the elevation drops down a bit we come to the small Duck Lake and larger West Thumb of Yellowstone Lake and the low-key development of West Thumb Village. Here we stop to see more bears and observe a fascinating view across Yellowstone Lake to a background of mountains. The drive then skirts the lake as we travel along the West Thumb. Dad is so excited about seeing bears that he uses up his camera film and has to drive 2 miles back to Lake Junction to get more. Mother reports that thus far we have seen 22 bears. She notes that one is lying on the roadside with paws up on the shoulder. But soon we see an unfortunate tourist staring at a bear eating out of the back of his car. We have our picnic dinner (and no bear) at the camp at Lake Junction and hand feed a few woodchucks at the boat landing.

Now the Loop Road leaves the lake and turns northward along the Yellowstone River. We feel we have been transplanted into another world, surrounded by mountains, strange geysers, and wildlife we have never seen before. Along the Yellowstone River valley we stop to watch and photograph outlandish and foul-smelling geysers: Mud Geyser, Mud Volcano, Dragon's Mouth, and Paint Pots colored gray, yellow, white, blue, green. One of these extraordinary mud masses shoots up almost 6 feet. Often we

As the Gunn family visited Yellowstone National Park in 1929 we were as guilty as other tourists of very dangerous acts, such as feeding cookies to a bear from the car window. Recent NPS policies have removed bears from public areas and provided proper wildlife viewing guidance to tourists.

In spite of threats to the Yellowstone Falls, they remain today as powerful a scenic attraction as snapped in this photograph on the Gunn autocamping tour of 1929. Visited by millions of tourists each year, it offers further proof that the travel market for sustainable natural resource features continues.

felt the ground vibrate and rumble under our feet. Mother's comment: "dreadful, ugly, terrible things." Large pestering flies worsen our impressions of the world gone wrong.

Only a few miles further we come to Alum Creek after passing two high conical Crater Hills with hot springs at their base. At Alum Creek the story is told that the horse of mountain man Jim Bridger shrank to the size of a pony after drinking the water. Taking a side road toward the Grand Canyon of the Yellowstone we cross the Chittenden Bridge. We stop for a picture and get back into the car just before a bear did.

We marvel at this great canyon, different in many ways from the Grand Canyon of the Colorado. Dense pine forests reach to the very edge of the canyon walls that are not as harsh but as beautiful with yellows streaked with browns and reds on both slopes. Of course, its centerpiece is the dramatic waterfalls of the Yellowstone (Upper Falls, 109 feet and Lower Falls, 308 feet). At Artist Point we park and the log states, "We could stay and look for hours." This fortunate topographic feature of an overlook, allowing full view of the canyon for a mile to the Lower Falls (and four more bear nearby) seems especially planned for our wonderment. Here, dad, Lauren, and I walk down 495 steps to gain a greater perspective of this stunning vista. Upon our return to the top where mother had remained because of another sick headache we learn she had sat on the bank and fed a bear cub with candy!

Although we hate to leave, we rejoin the Loop Road and push on northward to our next thrill, Mt. Washburn, one mother would just as soon forget. We twist, turn, and climb from our present elevation of about 8000 feet for the next 10 miles and over

Although the excitement of making our Model A Ford gain this apex of Mt. Washburn in 1929 is now gone, it is equaled seven decades later by foot trail access. Although a continuing challenge, National Park Service planners try to foster sustainability in the face of increased pressure from more visitors.

Dunraven Pass (8859 feet elevation), the highest point on the Loop Road, to the side road that would take us to the peak of the mountain. The log shows mother's struggle between the beauty of roadside flowers and the frightening, one-lane, kinky road for 4 miles to the top, 10,243 feet elevation. She admits she is too sick to enjoy it even though she noted the blue, pink, and yellow flowers on the way. Reaching out for comfort, mother quotes Isaiah 49:11, "And I will make all my mountains a way and my highways shall be exalted." At the top we snap a picture of the lookout tower. On the treacherous trip down the brakes on our Model A Ford would not hold sufficiently and Lauren had to turn into the rocky bank to keep from running out of control down the precipitous slope. It is quite a relief to get back on the Loop Road and in another 5 or 6 miles arrive at a fine campground at Tower Fall where we spend the night after an exhausting tourist day. Our intense desire to see it all was much more fatiguing than we had anticipated.

It is here that I have my most excruciating experience of the entire trip. Our tent site is about 100 yards from the camp store where I was sent to buy a loaf of bread. As I approach the store I notice a couple of large brown bears nearby. Then, as I leave, one begins to follow me. As I become more and more terrified, I begin to circle. I soon come to the point of deciding that my best option for this crisis is a meal of bread rather than one of me. After a circuitous route of about 300 yards to the tent, the bear decides I am not worth it and ambles off. For some reason, unknown to me, when dad told and retold this story upon our return home, I was the butt of great guffaws. What was so funny I never understood.

Wandering among trees and bears the next morning, **July 31**, we take the trail to the falls, a very worthwhile sight. A few miles after breaking camp we turn off the main road to see a standing petrified tree (not like those fallen in the Petrified Forest of Arizona) and beaver dams and houses near Lost Lake. The elevation is taking its toll on the Ford and we stop to add water. As we move along now at the top of the park we pass a large rock on the roadside called the Frog and observe more beaver activity nearby.

The Loop Road now takes us westward several miles to our next major attraction, Mammoth Hot Springs, passing by Mt. Everts to the northeast of Gardner Canyon. At Mammoth we see deer, two fawn, a woodchuck, the House of Antlers, go to the Post Office, and have lunch in a campground. Here in this unearthly land we view a great variety of steaming mists and calcareous deposits with algae creating colorful ponds and steps like small waterfalls. It is a huge frozen cascade. Here the more conspicuous springs are Liberty Cap, Minerva Terrace, Mound Terrace, Narrow Gauge Terrace, The Esplanade, Cheops Mound, Jupiter Terrace, Orange Spring Mound, Devil's Kitchen, and Angel Terrace—and we see five more bears today.

Turning southward we are now completing our memorable visit of this wonderland, unlike anything we experienced elsewhere on our trip. We pass by the Hoodoos, Indian Creek Campground, Obsidian Cliff (pick up a souvenir), and see Congress Pool at Norris Junction. We follow the Gibbon River through the Gibbon Canyon and at Madison Junction return to our beginning point of the Loop Road several days before. After crossing the Wyoming-Montana state line where we see our first antelope, we complete our Yellowstone journey by camping in the West Yellowstone campground, weary but very happy for the experience.

From Yellowstone we head back to Pocatello and beyond to Logan on Thursday, **August 1**, starting on our journey to the next objective 180 miles away, Salt Lake City. We make note of some observations on the way: see a horned owl, cross the Continental Divide again, master Targhee Pass (7300 feet elevation), are almost blown off the road by tornado-like winds, cross the Fort Hall Indian Reservation, and see the beautiful mountains beyond Pocatello, "such a purple sight with patches of green," and snow on Mt. Oxford. We made camp at Logan.

Moving on, **August 2**, we enjoy bright sunshine, mountains on the left, and an arm of Great Salt Lake on the right. At Ogden we laugh at the sight of a small building shaped like a beer keg dispensing soft drinks, and enjoy a nearby sign, "Drink Caswell Coffee and Work Like Helen B. Happy." Beyond Bountiful we gain a view of the state capitol and as we stop for gas we learn if we hurry we can catch an organ recital in the Mormon Tabernacle. What a thrilling sight and sound it was, like nothing we had ever experienced before. After lunch in a park we take a sightseeing tour—Brigham Young's Home, Statue of Jim Bridges, Home of the 17 wives, the First Tree, and the State Capital Building. We watch a thrilling derby racer, pass by several salt works, and take the Lincoln Highway to Garfield (radio KDYL). Our log describes Great Salt Lake as a malodorous and horrible place with salt all around. We spend the night in Nelson Camp, Salt Lake City.

On the next day, **August 3**, our travels bring us over the state line into Wyoming. We are now beyond mountains and into barren land but see a bit of agriculture at Wyoming Experimental Farms. We reach Evanston and eat lunch in the car. We travel through a great expanse of desolate and threatening landscape. We had passed Mt. Dell Reservoir, Salt Lake Summit (7035 feet), and Echo Reservoir in the making. Dad stops at Echo Canyon to cash a check. Throughout the day's travel we sing every song we know to relieve the boredom. At Wamsutter we retreat to a cabin rather than pitch a tent in this threatening landscape where you can see forever.

Soon after leaving camp on Sunday, **August 4**, we slop through fresh tar road surfacing for over 2 miles, making a mess of our pretty car. At our first opportunity we stop, get out the emergency gas can and try to wipe off the tar. A strong wind hampers our task by spattering over cleaned areas. This was not our best day.

The desert-like landscape seems to have little appeal and to break the boredom we count 118 cars in a train alongside and find a good road through Rawlins. But soon we encounter another bad detour, pass an airport near Ft. Steele, and at Medicine Bow wait for a train that we estimate is almost a half mile long. Then comes some irrigated land, horses and cattle, a fairly good road that is soon interrupted by another detour. One unusual sight was a long snow shed beside the railroad near Rock River. In Laramie we stop for gas, eat lunch in the car, and remark that it is quite a town. On a winding road for about 5 miles we reach the highest point on the Lincoln Highway, 8835 feet.

Soon we pass Ames Monument and see a large rock that is split in two by a tree growing through it, fenced in as a roadside attraction. As we get closer to Cheyenne, even from a distance of 5 miles, we see the gilded dome of the capital building. Our enthusiasm of visiting the city is dimmed by another flat tire. The delay gives us a chance to buy groceries for the evening and next morning. On our way again the landscape improves as we travel through ranch land and acres of potatoes, quite a relief from the desolation before. After a pouring rain and another detour we get to Pine Bluffs and enter the state of Nebraska. By the time we reach Sidney we are weary from our 326-mile day and find a campsite. By the time we clean some more tar off the car and wash ourselves we are ready for bed.

We don't get on the road, Monday, **August 5**, until 8:45 am due to washing, ironing, cleaning off more tar, and fixing another flat tire. Alongside the road we see good farming land as we pass through Lodgepole and Chappell. We stop at Ogallala for gas and oil and eat our picnic lunch there under a grove of trees. The road gets dusty and rough and the temperature gets hotter as we move on toward McPherson, then another bad detour for 30 miles. After Gothenburg we are on US 30, a much better road and soon pass Experimental Farms. At Lexington, "a nice city," we stop for yet another flat tire. Finally, after a tiring and not very interesting day of 244 miles we pass the car with the Ohio lady we had seen several times before and find a campsite near Kearney.

By 7:06 am, **August 6**, we are on our way again, pass by the Nebraska State Industrial School, the State Hospital for Tuberculosis, and a silly looking building shaped like a mug, called the Root Beer House. Past Shelton we see huge fields of corn that appear to be damaged, perhaps by drought or disease. At the "fine city" of Grand Island we see another Oregon Trail Monument. Columbus is nice and cool but the roads are awful. Then we come to a bit of welcome pavement about 5 miles from Fremont. Here we stock up for supplies and have a picnic lunch in a little park. It is clear that by now we are travel weary. We pass by a Rainbow Camp, Peony Park, and on through Omaha. The toll across the Missouri River is 30 cents, bringing us to

Council Bluffs, Iowa. On a cool and cloudy day, all we can see is corn and wheat, occasionally some threshing. The good pavement quits at Dunlap and we are off on another detour, then pass the Ohio lady for about the seventh time. At Denison we see more corn than ever in our lives and begin to see more Michigan cars, a welcome sight. After a cool and cloudy day over more detours we travel through Manilla, Manning, and Templeton to Coon Rapids. We find our only option is a rather primitive camp site where we have to drive a few miles away to get water. But it was a good touring day of 313 miles.

On Wednesday, **August 7**, for the first time the trusty Ford refuses to start. Guessing that the damp weather may be the culprit, we wipe off the distributor and it starts right up. Passing on through Jefferson, Ogden, and Boone, our only points of interest were a burned car beside the road and a long freight train carrying cattle and logs, probably bound for Chicago. We pass by Iowa State Agricultural College, farm land of corn and wheat, a wrecked Greyhound bus, an Indian reservation, and lose our way at Tama. Then, back on the road we had lunch by the roadside but mother was sick and limited herself to milk, Grape Nuts, and ice cream! At Cedar Rapids we see an encouraging sign that Chicago is only 228 miles away. Again we saw the lady from Ohio on our way through Mt. Vernon and Clinton and then, after crossing the Mississippi, we come to our camp for the night, Elkhorn Lodge, at Fulton.

Thursday, **August 8**, we know we are within reasonable distance of relatives in LaGrange. We go as fast as we dare through Sterling, Dixon, Rochelle, DeKalb ("DeKalb will be lonesome until you come back"), and Geneva. Then we are welcomed by relatives in LaGrange even though there is a whooping cough quarantine sign on the door (we are sure we are immune). It was good to spend a night's sleep in a real house.

Friday, Saturday, and Sunday (**August 9, 10, 11**) we spend touring around Chicago and visiting a great deal. We even went to a Methodist Church on Sunday and enjoyed the service (Donald Gibbs, associate pastor) and a fine baritone soloist.

Monday, **August 12**, after packing for the last time we point our Ford toward home, arriving late afternoon. Our teacher-boarder, Laura Schantz, gives us a great welcome and we are glad to be home, safe and sound, after a glorious adventure. We are very thankful for such a grand travel experience that we know we will never forget.

Comment

Evident even 70 years ago was tourist interest in the special natural and cultural resources of the West and especially on this leg within Yellowstone and on to Salt Lake City. Certainly our travel climax took place in that spectacular wonderland of Yellowstone National Park. As we completed our trip, our interest in roadside views of agricultural land reflected our rural heritage and the fact that approximately one fourth of the employed population in the 1920s was involved in agriculture compared to less than 3% today. When this narrative is compared to the description in Chapter 9 of seven decades of tourism change in this region, many similarities worthy of the attention of future tourism planners are clear. No one can return to the past, but many of the values obtained here by travelers in the past are planning and design challenges for the future.

Chapter 9

Yellowstone National Park Destination

No other destination of the US, and even the world, contains so many natural wonders that have been the source of puzzlement and appeal since the beginning of history as Yellowstone. It certainly was a top attraction for autocamping visitors of the 1920s as well as for millions of tourists today. As the very first national park in the world, it is credited with creating the global movement of resource protection by means of national parks. The criteria for such parks internationally have been influenced greatly by those established for this park.

Yellowstone National Park continues to be a preserve of natural marvels and a tourist attraction at the same time. It is historic as well as spectacular and beautiful. This vast land area of 2.2 million acres of wilderness, mountains, lakes, waterfalls, and 10,000 thermal features was established on March 1, 1872. As an aesthetic, physical, biological wonder it is a special destination place where visitors are offered a smorgasbord of sparkling streams, rushing waterfalls, tranquil lakes, exploding geysers, gurgling thermal pots, serene meadows, spectacular mountains, and a nature-lover's diversity of wildlife. All this and more are available in this place that even the devastating inferno of forest fires in 1988 could not destroy. It is part of an even larger ecosystem that is the ultimate in a natural resource tourism complex. It is reported to be the largest temperate ecosystem in the world under general protection.[1]

Landscape of Unlimited Grandeur and Beauty

Origin

Long before the "discoveries" of Yellowstone by tourists, others had visited and become enthralled by the sublime beauty and oddities of the area.[2] Trappers and mining prospectors had left their mark on the landscape in the 1830s and 1840s. Their descriptions and tales seemed so fanciful to be unbelievable. These rugged, tough, and brawny early visitors could not help but be impressed by a landscape they had never before seen—the freakiness of nature as well as such an abundance of waterfalls, bears, and mountains. What is now called Yellowstone was derived from Mi tsi a-da-zi (Indian for Rock Yellow River), Roche Juane and Pierre Juane (French), and Yellow River (English).[3]

The public health threats in congested cities fostered promotion of not only the urban park movement but also more extensive areas of the West, such as Yosemite and Yellowstone. At the time, most of these regions were influenced by Gifford Pinchot, then director of the federal Division of Forestry. For him and his administrative policies, the economic value of resources, such as forests, was far more important than scenery. As preservationists kept up the pressure for scenic preserves in the West, the Yellowstone National Park Act was passed in 1872. With this precedent, more national parks were added, causing an even greater split between Pinchot and national park advocates. This finally resulted in the establishment of a separate bureau in 1916, the NPS.

A major influence in stimulating the populous eastern America to become interested in Yellowstone in the preautomobile era was the works of writers and artists. *Scribner's Monthly* carried articles and sketches by Thomas Moran in the late 1800s, depicting romanticized versions of the already overstated landscape.[4] Most impressive, though rendered with considerable artist's license, was Moran's painting of the Yellowstone River Falls and Canyon in 1871. Sketches by William Henry Holmes, a prominent "artist-topographer," filled the guidebooks and popular magazines of the day. The many drawings, paintings, photographs, and descriptive accounts were strong influences on stimulating visitor curiosity.

It is hard to believe that this natural wonder would probably not exist in its present form had it not been for the original discoverers' reactions, as described in Nathanial P. Langford's log of campfire comments during the Washburn–Doane Expedition of 1870.[5] It was Cornelius Hedges who objected to the suggestion of a takeover by the expedition party and made the historic statement that the entire area be set aside by the government as a national park, an unheard-of concept at the time. This idea of resource protection and use has now grown to hundreds of areas in the US under NPS jurisdiction. These areas include several classes, such as an international historic site and the following national categories: battlefields, historic parks, lakeshores, memorials, military parks, monuments, parks, parkways, preserves, rivers, recreation areas, seashores, trails, and wild and scenic rivers.

Nathaniel P. Langford in his Diary of September 27, 1870, made the following comments after exploring the Yellowstone region: "amid the canyon and falls, the boiling springs and sulphur mountain, and, above all, the mud volcano and the geysers of the Yellowstone, your memory becomes filled and clogged with objects new in experience, wonderful in extent, and possessing unlimited grandeur and beauty. . . ."[6] "This is probably the most remarkable region of natural attractions in the world and, while we already have our Niagara and Yosemite, this new field of wonders should be at once withdrawn from occupancy, and set apart as a public National Park for the enjoyment of the American people for all time."[7]

Implied in this statement is the dual concept of resource protection and visitor use. This concept has dominated national park philosophy ever since, even provided the foundation for the official mandate of the NPS when it was created in 1916. However, carrying out this mandate has been and continues to be difficult, especially in Yellowstone in recent years.

Because Yellowstone was managed by the military in the beginning, presumably to prevent poaching and attacking tourists by the Indians, the US Army Corps of Engineers were the initiators of roads in the park—16 miles by 1887. By 1906, the Grand Loop Road had been created, a scenic tour of 150 miles that remains today.[8] Designers were Lieutenant Daniel C. Kingman and Hiram M. Chittenden of the Corps. Their design fortunately was influenced greatly by principles already advocated by Olmsted, following contours and touching most of the main points of interest. Aesthetics of the corridor were given prime consideration. Because Chittenden feared a bridge across the Yellowstone River would damage the beauty, he delayed its construction but then finally conceded, creating an artistic span that remained until demolished in 1962.

In a report by Mark Daniels, the "General Superintendent and Landscape Gardener" of national parks in 1915 to the Department of Interior, he states that there are three main functions of national parks: the stimulating of national patriotism, the furthering of knowledge and health, and the diverting of tourist travel to the scenic areas of the United States.[9] He believed that if one actually experienced the natural wonders of the nation that person would have a burning "determination to love and work for, and if necessary to fight for and die for the glorious land which is his." Further, he believed federal aid for national parks is justified in educating the populace to care for their land. Finally, he stressed the need for installation of facilities and services for tourists including accommodations and transportation especially for low-income tourists who are generally priced out of access to the parks. "To foster tourist travel it will be necessary to develop the roads, trails, and other accommodations in the parks to a point where the traveler will not be subjected to serious discomfort."[10] Ever since, such principles of access and visitor service development for low-income tourists have challenged Yellowstone National Park managers.

Not even such leaders in that preautomobile mass travel period envisioned that the day would come when people required no urging to attend national parks and that millions of visitors would eventually pose serious management problems. Automobiles were first admitted to Yellowstone National Park on August 1, 1915, resulting in a total of 958 by the end of the season.[11] By 1999, there were over 3 million visits to Yellowstone.[12] The movement of people without impairing the environment is a perpetual problem. An electric railroad was proposed in 1892 but was rejected by tourists then.[13] Motorcoach tours then and now seem to be a preferred solution.

In spite of some troubles, Yellowstone had gained a worldwide reputation as the supreme national park. Lon (Lemuel) Garrison expressed his feelings this way in 1956 when he became superintendent of the park: "I approached this new job with considerable humility. It was the top field job in the world—the most visible park management position. I was custodian of the world's greatest natural curiosities, the collection of natural resources that had sparked the world-wide park conservation program in the first place."[14]

Class Visitors

Before automobile travel, wealthy visitors came by rail, mostly from the East over the Northern Pacific to Gardiner, Montana, and entered from the north. Then, colorful horse-drawn open-air coaches gave visitors a 5-day tour of the many wonders of the park. This entrance was given greater importance in 1903 by a stone monument called the Roosevelt Memorial Arch.

My uncle, Dr. Joseph Heasley, of Grand Rapids, Michigan, visited Yellowstone in 1910. He wrote about their four-passenger surrey ride of 160 miles drawn by a team of 4-year-old horses after leaving the train. One horse was a gray and the other a sorrel, "with eyes like balls of fire; with bowed neck and standing mane, they looked like demons of the regions we afterward passed through."[15] Further description includes the incident of near fatal crisis over the trail edge as the horses bucked, kicked, and reared as they fought pestering flies. To the rescue came an armed soldier. The capable driver, the soldier, and riders who suppressed their screams finally brought order to the chaos. It should be explained that Yellowstone then was still under military control.

On this trip when Dr. Heasley visited Mammoth Hot Springs, he experienced an activity that many purists today would condemn as incompatible with national park policy. But as revealed in his journal, it was seen as an activity totally appropriate and enjoyable. This experience exemplifies a continuing issue of deciding what land uses are appropriate and compatible with resource protection.

> At Mammoth Springs Hotel, everything was different from the rest of our stopping places. We saw nice green lawns and cultivated flowers. An orchestra furnishes real civilized music in this wilderness, and as the music floated out upon the evening air, it set into action all the musical brain cells we ever possessed.
>
> Soon the reception hall was a whirling mass of dancing beauty. There was the soldier in his blue uniform, the beautiful lass or woman, her cheeks browned from days of exposure to the burning sun, gliding over the floor, beautifully clad in her evening gown, surrounded with mirth and happiness. Little would you think we were in the midst of a field of geysers or the towering mountains and within reach of the stealthy bear, the charge of the buffalo or the wicked claws of the skulking mountain lion. Less do we care . . . our cares and troubles are thousands of miles away.[16]

It is likely that the first tourist camps in national parks were established right here in Yellowstone in the 1890s.[17] Created by W. W. Wylie, they became known as the "Wylie Way." His tours took visitors to the main natural features, made camp each night, put up sleeping tents, a cook tent, and canvas shelters for horses and wagons. A melodian supplied music for campfire singing after Wylie had given a lecture on the park resources. In spite of resistance from railroad-owned hotels, the Wylie Camps, later taken over by the Currys, made a permanent mark on the Yellowstone scene.

It was no coincidence that the Second World Conference on national parks and also the centennial celebration for the founding of Yellowstone was held at the park in 1972. At this conference it was stated that over 1200 national parks or preserves had been established worldwide in response to the original concept of Yellowstone.[18]

The process of getting there today is very bland by comparison because the adventure of travel movement has virtually been eliminated. It can be argued that for this reason the total experience of visiting Yellowstone today has been diminished greatly. Without the expenditure of any effort, is the final achievement as rich and rewarding as it was before?

The Automobile and Environmentalism

The early policies of NPS indicated no conflict, even positive influence, by encouraging more and more visitors to the parks, such as Yellowstone. In fact, it was believed by Director Stephen T. Mather that greater park use would stimulate increased public support for the national park movement. However, as tourist volume increased over the next decades, it appeared that the visitor experience was considerably different from the environmental protection philosophy of national park proponents.

The Yellowstone roadway became king, confining everyone to the vistas of the roadway, buildings, hotels, campgrounds, automobiles, and parking.[19] In the 1920s it seemed that the park managers had staged all these attractions for the tourist—the bears, geysers, and mud pots. It was soon discovered that very few people strayed from the roadway to become fully immersed in the natural resources for which the park was created. The initial "selling" of national parks to the public for this noble use was met with a backlash of touring tourists who were enjoying the new freedom of going places but never stopping to rough it in the wilderness, much to the chagrin of park proponents. In addition, the great masses of campers had already created sanitation problems and polluted streams in Yellowstone by 1913. Perhaps it is unfair to criticize tourists for their shallow experiences in the park because the conditions had been planned this way by well-meaning designers of that period. The increased demand for upgraded accommodations and food services virtually rendered the early posh hotels obsolete.

Today's tourism and the environment here are at a crisis. The tourist experience has been eroded substantially compared with that of the 1920s' autocampers. Mass tourism at Yellowstone has exerted severe degradation of the original resource assets of the area. Because of ecological threats, Yellowstone has been placed by the World Heritage Committee on its list of "World Heritage Sites in Danger."[20]

The millions of visitors today see more vehicles on Yellowstone roads than scenery. Their attention is drawn more to traffic congestion than the spectacular features that prompted the creation of the park in the first place. Dominated by personal automobiles, RVs, and tour buses, the driver's attention is focused on avoiding collision with others as they stop at turnouts, view wildlife, or gain access to services and facilities. The engineering mindset of quantitative solutions has been applied, such as making roads wider, flatter, straighter, and faster. The only four-lane highway in the entire NPS system occurs around Old Faithful Geyser.[21] Missing has been a qualitative solution, giving greater consideration of personal rewards from visiting the park. By increasing volume capacity of roads, the result has been greater congestion, greater deterioration of road surfaces, and poorer opportunity for visitors to view scenery rather than vehicles.

There is a temptation by private tourism developers to give in to base interests of certain travel markets and turn Yellowstone into one big theme park where all key attractions are staged. West Yellowstone already demonstrates this trend with IMAX, a zoo with grizzlies and wolves, T-shirt shops, and outlet stores.[22] Such a pseudo-attraction, an imitation of the real thing, has catapulted this sleepy town of the 1960s into a boom tourist city of 1200 residents who are delighted with tax revenues of almost $2 million a year. Environmentalists, and perhaps a great many tourists, see this entrance to Yellowstone National Park as an ugly carbuncle on the face of a major world-class spectacle of nature. On the one hand, it is meeting all the tenets of the American hallmark, the free enterprise system—give people what they want. On the other hand, this may be a false interpretation of what everyone wants. Gateway cities can provide an essential tourism function of providing needed services, inappropriate within the park. But they need not be ugly, in conflict with national park philosophy, nor catering exclusively to one market segment.

Negative impacts by tourists in Yellowstone National Park over the last seven decades have been substantial. Geysers at the Norris Geyser basin quit erupting because they were plugged with tourist litter.[23] The fascinating colors of Morning Glory Pond are no longer as brilliant because of garbage deposits. Visitor noise, pollution, litter, and erosion of surface soils and vegetation have increased substantially. Elk overpopulation and threats to wildlife have escalated greatly. Aesthetes point to the reduction of scenic appeal of the region because of the building of many more hotels, motels, restaurants, and shops. Approaches to the park are lined with billboards, ugly signs, and cluttered services. As tourist volume has increased, so has the stress on the environment due to expanded infrastructure of water supply, waste removal, police, fire protection, rescue, and traffic control. Winter visitor use, once an opportunity for solitude and tranquility, has now become eroded by roaring noise and exhaust fumes from snowmobiles. Litigation from the Fund for Animals and other environmental organizations has prompted NPS to establish a new policy of phasing out snowmobile use, replacing it with park-managed snowcoach use.[24]

At issue within Yellowstone National Park is the conflict between bears and visitors at Fishing Bridge.[25] This has been a favorite place for both for many years and recently it appeared that the bears were losing and visitors winning in the controversy. More bears have been killed or removed to other parts of the ecosystem as the danger mounted. Of further environmental concern has been the spinoff created by greater visitor demand for more tourist development sprawl: shops, restaurants, lodging.

NPS staff have tried to manage wildlife over these decades but policies have not been consistent. The autocampers of the 1920s came to Yellowstone primarily to see bears, popularizing the terms "roadside bears" and "bear jams," traffic stopped to see bears.[26] As tourists fed and tried to pet bears, injuries increased. Visitors saw Yellowstone as an animal theme park and assumed that management staged these critters for their entertainment. Early legislation for wildlife control was unscientific and directed only to fostering those animals the managers liked. This resulted in removing most of the wolves, coyotes, mountain lions, bobcats, lynx, wolverine, foxes, and hawks.[27] Poaching became an issue. Hunters sought elk, bighorn, and bear for trophies to be mounted in dens and recreation rooms back home. Others killed wildlife to obtain organs for high sale prices because of reputed special medicinal value.

Throughout the history of Yellowstone, NPS personnel have been buffeted about on the issue of visitor use versus resource protection. This vacillation has taken its toll. During World War II the park nearly shut down, facilities began to deteriorate, and postwar appropriations for improvement were not forthcoming. NPS Director Conrad L. Wirth reacted by convincing Congress to support "Mission 66" in 1955, a billion-dollar program to update all facilities in national parks.[28] This effort included major new development within Yellowstone National Park. Landscape architect Bill

Carnes chaired the Mission 66 Committee and Lon Garrison chaired the Mission 66 Steering Committee.They embraced this program as even a conservation measure by channeling motorist use. Garrison, who became Superintendent of Yellowstone in 1956, saw his job as showcasing this new program by planning $70 million worth of roads, bridges, and accommodations, focusing on two new "village" sites, Canyon and Grant Village at Thumb Bay.

Grant Village, because of bad planning, political fluctuation, and even sewage pollution of Yellowstone Lake, was a disaster. It was clearly an aberration that did not function, was unprofitable for concessionaires, and established the wrong precedent for commercial facility location within rather than just outside the park. In the early train-coach access period by wealthy tourists, large and luxurious lodges within the national parks seemed appropriate and adapted to low volume use. Mass automobile tourists demanded such huge physical development that location within the park threatened the integrity of the park's resource base. Even Lon Garrison retreated by admitting that the village was a mistake.

A master plan in 1973 called for removal of overnight accommodations at Old Faithful and West Thumb sites and stronger emphasis on resource protection. But this environmentally oriented plan contradicted its own theme by encouraging new major development at Grant Village to boost tourism.A proposal to place all development of tourist services at entrances to the park and use public transportation within, now known to be a wise plan, was rejected. Over 50 years of mistaken direction, it became clear that even if tourism was a desirable objective, it was destructive of the dominant resources of the park to allow massive development inside the park. Even the location of campgrounds was shown to be an error, especially evident at Fishing Bridge.

Probably the greatest threats to the park's integrity come from outside the boundaries.[29] These include activities such as soil erosion, water and air pollution, logging, mining, oil and gas development, poaching, reduction of wildlife habitat, roads and railroads, noise, housing, off-road vehicle use, and introduction of exotic plants and animals.The wonderland myth has spilled over into the surrounding subdivisions of new houses in Paradise Valley and poisonous byproducts from the New World Mining District.[30] New road building and ski resorts in these areas introduce noxious weeds, encourage poaching, and disturb wildlife habitat. Monoculture agriculture upsets the ecosystem with use of pesticides and fertilizers, and threatens watershed integrity.

An important cultural impact has been imposed upon Native Americans.[31] The takeover of land for the park by the federal government, even for seemingly noble purposes, displaced a great many members of Crow, Shoshone, and Nez Perce tribes. These indigenous people had struck a balance with the Yellowstone land with regular use of fires to enhance game hunting and prevent massive forest fire devastation. Tourism developers promoted Indians only as oddities best suited to museums.The American policy of manifest destiny required that Indians be removed from Yellowstone because of their "savage threat" to tourists.A dominant policy attitude by NPS toward Indians considered them curiosities and producers of tourist artifacts rather than a worthy human culture with its own traditions, beliefs, and affinity for the land.

Recently, a Lakota Sioux leader, Joseph Chasing Horse, staged a dramatic traditional event for the first time in 100 years in protest to the slaughtering of bison that wander out of Yellowstone National Park.[32] To them, the eating of bison is comparable to Holy Communion among Christians. It is consistent with their belief in spiritual attributes of nature. The ceremony began at the north entrance arch. This event was observed by a great many tribes including Algonquin, Apache, Assiniboine, Blackfeet, Crow, Navajo, Nez Perce, Northern Cheyenne, Southern Ute, and Tuscarora. Drawing blood from Lakota activist, Gary Silk, symbolized their historic dependence upon bison, now being denied them by Montana regulation. The lack of communication and understanding between Indians and NPS influences this agency to change personnel frequently. Indian focus is on immediate land and place factors whereas NPS directs its attention to a broad federal mandate.

Revealing consistencies and changes was a study over a 100-year photographic period in Yellowstone.[33] Environmental changes due to geology, climate, and fire are largely beyond management control. Wildlife and plant management criteria designed for hunting preserves are not appropriate for Yellowstone. Within the park, plant and animal changes are so dynamic that new research and management are required on a continuing basis. For example, lake trout have been introduced illegally to Yellowstone Lake, jeopardizing the future of cutthroat trout. The phenomenal increase in visitors has already impacted animal behavior, even those who merely wish to observe and photograph. There is little question that the overall ecosystem will change considerably in the future.

A 32-year veteran of the NPS and Superintendent of Yellowstone National Park for many years, Mike Finley, resigned mid-May, 2001.[34] Having been responsible for planning and management, he was very close to the issues of recent years. To his credit he received many awards for his conservation work: Florida Audubon Conservationist of the Year Award (1989), the Sierra Club Public Service Award for Environmental Protection (1989), the Everglades Coalition Conservation Award (1990), and the American River Distinguished Public Service Award (1996). In spite of his meritorious service, he believed there were several challenges ahead for his successor. Key issues he identified were: energy conservation, population control, water quality maintenance, wildlife management, biodiversity, transportation relief, and urban sprawl. Certainly, these need to be addressed by all the public and private sectors involved in planning and managing the park's tourism and resource protection.

Toward Sustainability

In spite of criticism that people have overrun national parks, generally they have received unusually sensitive design of facilities and services throughout their history. Much of the credit must be given to the father of the profession of landscape architecture, Frederick Law Olmsted. He and other landscape architects had already practiced "naturalistic design" principles in their municipal park designs in the late 1800s for places such as Buffalo, Chicago, Brooklyn, Minneapolis, Boston, and New York. Following the successes of these parks, Olmsted and others traveled West and were especially impressed with the grand scenery of many places.

Throughout the history of national parks, the influence of landscape architects has been substantial. In the early years of the 20th century, the profession had begun to grow and included educators as well as practitioners. Among the luminaries of this period were: Jens Jensen, James Sturgis Pray, Mark Daniels, Charles Punchard, Daniel Hull, Thomas Vint, Henry Hubbard, Frank Waugh, and Frederick Law Olmsted.[35]

The rustic nature-themed jewel of architecture, Old Faithful Inn, was designed by architect Robert C. Reamer and built in 1904 at a cost of $200,000. Its huge size and rugged opulence demonstrate how the national park planners knew their first travel markets were affluent and accustomed to the finest of accommodations. The fireplace is some 16 feet square and the dining room is 50 by 100 feet. Many restorations have maintained its original character.

In the 1930s, landscape architects and foremen of the CCC, a Roosevelt employment innovation during the depression, collaborated on many national park projects including Yellowstone. Much of this design work was performed directly on the sites, allowing maximum protection of existing land forms and plant materials and also the construction of roads, walks, overlooks, and other facilities. Instead of using nursery stocks of exotic plants, native materials were planted wherever grading changes required. Herbert Maier, an architect and also CCC regional officer, had a strong influence on harmonizing development with sites. Perhaps this was the first expression of sustainable park-tourism design. Working with Maier, designer Albert H. Good published a seminal three-volume book in 1935, *Park Structures and Facilities*. This elaborately illustrated report became the standard for state as well as national park development for many decades thereafter. The three volumes were filled with photographs, sketches, and plans, assisted by Thomas Vint, Oliver Taylor, and Norman Newton.

A strong influence on western land design in the 1940s and 1950s was the work of California landscape architect Garrett Eckbo, preceded by Thomas D. Church.[36] Although Church's land design work was primarily for residential projects, it became known as the "California style" and influenced other kinds of landscape architectural projects as well. He viewed his work as an essential blend of site and use. The qualities of the natural place were linked to newly created space. The landscape design philosophy of relating people to the natural world was continued as Eckbo founded the landscape architectural firm of Eckbo, Dean, Austin, and Williams (EDAW). Although their focus was not necessarily on tourism, their design principles were influential on western parks and resorts for many years.

The search for sustainability has not been easy in Yellowstone. For many years the Bureau of Reclamation had pushed for a major dam on the Yellowstone River that would have inundated much of what visitors now enjoy.[37] Horace Albright, then director of the NPS, objected as forcefully as he could. To prevent the Bureau from making initial survey of the region, he ordered his rangers to hide boats. In spite of many threats by the Bureau and the Corps of Engineers, this outstanding scenic marvel still remains.

Of concern by planners and neighboring communities has been adaptation to tourism in response to overwhelming popularity of national parks. Tourism researcher David Snepenger studied tourism's impact on the community of Bozeman, Montana, just 90 miles north of Yellowstone National Park.[38] In the peak of the tourist season, visitors outnumber residents by 10 to 1. The study showed that half of the residents were neutral to the impact of tourists and seemed to tolerate them, still considering downtown as their place for social, commercial, and cultural activities. However, a significant 16% felt that they have been alienated, citing high prices and other favoritism to tourists that tend to shut them out. His study supports similar results by others. Those who perceive tourism as beneficial generally tolerate negative impacts whereby others may see tourism as producing congestion, pollution, and other problems.

Sustainability of tourism places often involves management of nontourist uses. For example, Yellowstone National Park provides important microorganisms for scientific and commercial investigation.[39] The great diversity of thermal and chemical characteristics of pools and geysers represents a laboratory for study of DNA and enzymes. This biotechnology has many practical applications, such as in the papermaking industry, but raises questions of sustainability ethics. Even though royalties for these activities by businesses are welcomed by park managers, critics claim the removal of anything, even microorganisms, violates the park's policy of resource protection.

In recent years, a remarkable change among local residents has taken place in some surrounding communities in response to the phenomenal growth of tourism. In the past, mining, forestry, ranching, and oil/gas were the prime employers. Today the new economic base is tourism, which supports a substantial array of service businesses. But the negative impacts have been recognized in the gateway community of Red Lodge, Montana.[40] In response, a Beartooth Front Community Forum was held. It resulted in establishing several task forces that focused on youth, society, and environmental quality. A Beartooth Front Corporation has been formed whose first task was a citizen-driven master plan for the future. Sustainability was a major objective. With the assistance of planner Lee Nellis, the community made its own inventory of resources and devised a land use plan that ranges from aesthetics to economics that was approved by the Red Lodge City Council in 1995. Sustaining a high quality of life, influenced by nearby Yellowstone National Park, has become a major incentive for new growth controls in Belgrade, Montana, just north of the park.

Another border town, Jackson Hole, Wyoming, has also seen a boom in new permanent homes as well as tourism but now says that enough is enough. This community is nestled in the center of spectacular mountain scenery between Yellowstone and Grand Teton national parks. Beginning in 1914, it grew with tourism's increased popularity because of its natural assets of wildlife, scenery, and other outstanding resources.

Then a major change occurred in 1994 when the citizenry voted to cancel the room tax that had been in effect since 1986. Although it had generated millions of dollars for promotion, the local people finally realized that they were attracting more visitors than the area could support. One measure of this impact was overtaxing their sewage system far beyond its capacity. This decision was very courageous because it flew in the face of the popular trend of promoting more tourism growth, especially because their economy depended mostly on tourism. By 1995, Teton county and Jackson Hole residents and outside environmentalists held workshop meetings leading toward the adoption of a new environmentally sound land use plan.[41] The plan includes financial incentives for resource protection as well as zoning controls.

Among the features is support for clustering rather than dispersal of development over large tracts of land. Open space, scenic areas, wildlife ecosystems, and agricultural lands are protected. This is an example of a new turning point for communities as they reach toward greater tourism sustainability.

A force for greater sustainable tourism development in the area is the Greater Yellowstone Coalition. It is attempting to guide development that can continue to provide economic value but do a better job of resource protection. It has prepared a general plan of recommendations that, if and when implemented, should make major improvements in the region. These are paraphrased as:

- Wildland resources must not be degraded by new recreation and tourism development.
- Tourism projects should be required to make environmental assessment to determine potential natural and cultural resource threats.
- Tourism planning must be integrated into all other area planning.
- All federal and state agencies involved should cooperate on visitor management plans.
- Carrying capacity of sites should be measured and followed up with monitoring change.
- Tourism programs should include environmental education.
- Greater cooperation among resource managers and tourism interests is needed.
- Better research and interpretation on tourism impacts should be made.[42]

A landmark effort by the National Park Service, resulting from two major workshop discussions, has produced *Guiding Principles of Sustainable Design* that includes guidance on interpretation, natural resources, cultural resources, site design, building design, energy management, water supply, waste prevention, and facility maintenance and operations.[43]

The Greater Ecosystem

Although the geological wonders still dominate popular and political considerations of Yellowstone, managers are increasingly concerned about wildlife in the larger ecosystem. If wildlife is to be adequately understood and managed, the scope of land area must be broadened beyond present park boundaries. The greater ecosystem area extends as far north as Bozeman, Montana, east to Cody, Wyoming, south to Montpelier, Idaho, and west to Monida, Montana.[44] In a 1984 conference on the management of biosphere reserves, Robert Barbee and John Varley of NPS emphasized the fact that the Yellowstone ecosystem is many times larger, demanding entirely new collaborative management. They observed that when The Man and the Biosphere Program recognized Yellowstone National Park it failed to consider that the greater Yellowstone region, not just the park, was and remains the largest, essentially intact, wild ecosystem remaining in the temperate zone of the earth.[45] This becomes a major issue considering that grizzly bear, bison, and elk fail to recognize the park boundaries set down by Congress and regularly use surrounding areas under other jurisdictions.

Surrounding Yellowstone National Park are extensive lands under different jurisdictional policies that complicate administration. Included are many national forests such as Gallatin, Custer, Shoshone, Deerlodge, Beaverhead, Targhee, Teton, Bridger, and Caribou. Significant are Grand Teton National Park, Red Rock Lakes National Wildlife Refuge, National Elk Refuge, and Grays Lake National Wildlife Refuge. Also surrounding the park are many privately held lands. A further complication of management is that the park itself lies in three states—Montana, Wyoming, and Idaho—each with its own traditions, legislation, politics, and taxation policies. Fortunately for visitors, the leaders of this maze of jurisdictions strive to work things out so that resources are protected at the same time visitors gain an enriching experience, but it is demanding eternal vigilance and maybe legal changes. The restoration of natural systems, such as for the greater Yellowstone ecosystem, may require changes in the strict interpretation of personal property rights.[46] One recent aspect of this desire for better biological balance for elk and bison is the new policy of reintroducing wolves.[47]

Although most of the campgrounds of the 1920s continue to exist they have been modified. Some have been upgraded to meet the demands of recreation vehicles that need sewage dump stations and one campground even has hookups for water, electricity, and sewage service at sites. This was an era when bears and other wildlife were looked upon as entertainment with little consideration for the welfare of either visitors or the animals. Fortunately, the last several decades have witnessed considerable enlightenment about wildlife, their ecosystems, their behavior, and visitor management in parks. Open garbage pits have been abandoned, most bear populations have been attracted to areas with few visitors, and park management offers many guidelines and warnings to tourists about how to behave in this environment. New technology, a rental interactive compact disc device plugged into the car, can provide today's visitor with enriching information on sites as a car tour of the park is made.

Evidence of increased collaboration among public agencies on the broader Yellowstone region was the creation on December 19, 2000 of a joint bison management plan.[48] Signatories included the NPS, Department of Agriculture's Animal and Health Inspection Service, FS, and the state of Montana. This joint effort resulted from several years of controversy and field mediation regarding the control of brucellosis threat to ranchers' cattle. This represents a major sustainable action of value to not only an objective of improved bison and cattle health but also for wildlife viewing, an important activity of tourists.

Managers today are more aware of potential threats to the environmental integrity of the park than in the past. Commercial development, subdivision of land, surface mining, oil and gas exploration and extraction, and geothermal wells—all outside but near the park—predictably can have an adverse effect upon the park in the future.

Not a major factor in 1920s but increasing today is the need for visitor interpretation of the cultural background of the park. Examination has revealed that human use of the area reaches back over 10,000 years. A new development and management plan recognizes that the park contains over 950 historic structures, many associated with the military management from 1886 to 1918.

Because of the many years of Smoky Bear propaganda, the general public has come to believe all forest fires are destructive and should be suppressed. The extensive fires

Modern visitors to Yellowstone National Park see an abundance of bison, now a herd of 2000, rather than bears. However, travelers are reminded that even bison are wild animals and require extreme care when being approached for photographs. (Source: Patricia Stokowski)

in Yellowstone in 1988 that burned about 793,883 acres raised considerable furor from the press and public, suggesting that greater NPS control should have been exercised. A flood of scientific studies and management declarations have concluded that this was primarily a natural phenomenon and might have happened earlier had all favorable factors been in place. Although some old-growth timber has been reduced, succession species and wildlife habitat have been enhanced. One author-observer quipped that it was easy to get the impression that park wildlife was better adapted to fire than the human beings running around studying it.[49] No adverse reactions against endangered species have been observed. From a tourism perspective, visitor flows within and outside the park actually increased, stimulating even greater tourist business economy in the region. Although the concept of urban fires is destructive, fires in extensive resource areas such as Yellowstone may actually have greater benefits than disadvantages when considered in the context of natural ecosystems over time.

A research study of the visitors to Yellowstone National Park following the major forest fire of 1988 showed that the majority favored natural (lightning caused) fires and that they should be allowed to burn out.[50] They also indicated that they believed fires were necessary and that overall park qualities were not diminished in the long run. This shows that often the travel market is much more sophisticated and knowledgeable than given credit by managers.

Contrary to alarmists, the forest inferno of 1988 did not create permanent damage to the natural resources of Yellowstone. Plant and animal life have returned remarkably well. This experience suggests that fire, when properly controlled, can be an effective management tool. (Source: Patricia Stokowski)

This discussion on sustainability and the broader Yellowstone ecosystem represents what Flores calls a maturation of the sense of place.[51] Former fragmented tourism development here and throughout the West tended to diminish the sense of this being in a very special place, emerging from the changing cultural values as they develop on these unusual landscapes.

Future Challenges

The future solution to the crisis in tourism's relationship to the environment at this destination depends on new and unprecedented planning and management, both within Yellowstone National Park boundaries and in the surrounding area. Neither tourism nor the resource base can stand much more expansion without major change in policy. This conclusion, well founded in the history and background of this region, begs policymaking and action by thousands of public and private entities, a formidable but essential task because all are involved in deciding on their future.

Within the national park, management and staff face many difficult decisions to continue to fulfill their official mandates of resource protection and visitor use. Clearly, this effort is much more complex than in the 1920s, mainly because of exponential growth of visitors. Backcountry use now includes winter, virtually unknown 30 years ago. Total visitors have increased from 260,697 in 1929 to over 3 million today, a staggering growth of almost 12 times the volume with no comparable increase in NPS staff.

The autocampers of the 1920s encountered the natural phenomena at a much slower pace, allowing greater visual absorption of the diverse features. Then, in addition to the major waterfalls, geysers, mountains, valleys, and verdant landscape, the abundance of bears topped the experience. Their entertaining performances at hotel garbage dumps at dusk, interpreted by park rangers, added spice to the Yellowstone experience. And the earlier guidebooks were written as travel flow experiences, not mere descriptions of stops on the way. Today's wildlife management policies have become much more enlightened through research. Tourists are now strictly instructed that animals are wild and that for their personal safety they must respect this important fact. Information supplied by park management, however, suggests locations where best views of wildlife may be obtained and how to do it safely. Visitor interpretive centers provide an excellent sustainable service.

Not knowing how their grandfathers experienced Yellowstone, today's travelers many not be aware nor care about the changes over many decades. A modern highway system with cloverleaf exchange and ramp carries volumes of automobiles, RVs, and tour buses. Even the tour guides have changed. Today there are separate tour guidebooks for different travel segments, such as those seeking wildlife, geology, history, or adventure. In so doing, perhaps the sense of place for Yellowstone as a kaleidoscopic whole may have been lost. The faster pace, not staying long in the park, and seeing more tourists than natural wonders may prohibit full appreciation of the variety of visual impressions, sounds, and smells unique to this special place.

However, the majority of the geysers, mud pots, fumaroles, and hot springs are still active and as unusual and interesting as ever. The escarpments and rivers are as they were, creating spectacular waterfalls as scenic as before. The Grand Loop (formerly Loop Road) is the same as it was except for road improvements. It continues to provide visitor access to the many natural attractions en route. Headquarters remain at Mammoth Hot Springs, established by the US Army for their patrol of the park from 1886 to 1918. The lakes and rivers are located as they were many decades ago.

Today's travelers, in spite of changes in the park for decades, may not feel that their experience has been trivialized. In an age of spectatorism, travelers now depend on others to help them ease through the experience rather than obtain their own serendipitous responses. However, to the credit of planners, designers, and rearrangers of Yellowstone, the basic qualities of this unusual region may not have been eroded seriously, as expressed by Meyer in 1996: "An appreciation for the park's beauty, its uniqueness, its tourism and recreation capabilities, its wilderness, democratic ownership, and educational values have persisted over time."[52]

The major issue imposed on NPS management is burgeoning visitor use. In spite of increased competition from theme parks, sports arenas, and convention centers, Yellowstone continues to attract and satisfy a huge travel market. Greater demands in the future will have to be placed on control of litter, noise, pollution, and erosion of surface soils or the basic character of the region will be lost. Thus far, the unusual resources of the area have endured great elasticity of visitor use but now show great stress.

Well known to the management of Yellowstone is the challenge of how to meet the transportation demand without impairing the environment. One solution, now in place at Yosemite, is shuttle bus linked to perimeter parking.[53] The cost of the system is assisted greatly by the tax returns from sales of souvenirs and other products in nearby shops. New mechanisms of control may not be popular but are necessary options. The public will argue that this is *their* park and therefore resent higher entrance fees, lottery admission, or prohibition of personal automobile access. Distasteful as these may be, these and other means of controlling traffic must be essential items on the future agenda of NPS at Yellowstone.

Future physical stress may be reduced by the installation of major visitor interpretive centers. When located near access and on "hardened sites," such centers can provide masses of visitors with a vicarious experience without damage to the hinterland. Creative design could include exhibits, live presentations, videos, demonstrations, and museum artifacts. Although some new park staff would be needed, most of the operational burden can be assumed by volunteers, especially from nature and conservation organizations. These centers offer opportunities for joint public-private venture. Profit-making elements, such as food service, gift and souvenir sales, and even admissions to performing arts productions, could relieve some of the financial burden of the NPS.

If Yellowstone is to cope with more growth, greater funding must be provided. The seriousness of this need must be brought to the attention of Congress because the park is a responsibility of the federal government. Equally important are other sources

Increasingly, landscape design solutions are solving issues of threats to the environment from too many tourists. Boardwalks eliminate erosion from trampling and yet offer vantage points for viewing and photographing special landscape features. (Source: Patricia Stokowski)

of funding, such as from nonprofit organizations, businesses, and nearby communities that gain economically from the tourist business stimulated by the park.

More complicated but essential will be solution to the many environmental issues surrounding the park. For plant and animal life, the larger ecosystem has already been delineated. To protect the integrity of the park, new organizational structures for the region may be necessary to study, analyze, and recommend improved policies for land use and development, such as was done for the Columbia River in Oregon and Washington. The first step is to increase cooperation between the park and surrounding leaders, followed by initiating stronger legal controls. The more that surrounding communities depend on a growing tourism economy, largely created by the park, they may feel it is their duty to support the park, especially financially. Already in place is a cooperative public-private mechanism for resolving tourism-environmental issues. The Western States Tourism Policy Council with jurisdiction over Yellowstone and surrounding states has pledged its purpose of dealing with visitor growth problems.

Opportunities are abundant in the future for greater professional work by environmental organizations and landscape architects, both within and surrounding Yellowstone National Park. Needed is more aggressive application to tourism land use and site design issues. Individual projects, such as for outdoor recreation, can

Located just west of Yellowstone on Island Park Reservoir, Idaho, is this sustainable solar-powered toilet facility. Included in the complex is an interpretive kiosk that helps visitors understand the area's environment. The master plan for the area provides for perimeter parking that encourages nature appreciation only on foot trails. (Source: Wirth Design)

benefit from plans that demonstrate sustainability of resources. Outside the park, landscape architects could perform stronger and more diverse roles, such as serving on city councils, land use planning boards, making areawide studies of well-planned tourism development, and providing solutions to controversies between environmentalists and developers. Especially important could be their role in improving environmental sustainability for tourism projects, such as housing, resorts, camps, circulation, and signage. Through their design work, significant vistas can be protected, soil erosion can be reduced, and native vegetation can be restored at the same time that visitor enjoyment is enhanced. When they collaborate with other design specialists and local residents, the best environmental solution will be obtained.

An option for more sustainable management of Yellowstone National Park is to perform a detailed task of monitoring change and rely on the results for clues to resolution of negative impacts. There has been a tendency to respond more to political pressures rather than upon scientific facts.[54] For example, changes in the complicated interactions between plant and animal associations can reveal the need for new management practices. Intensive visitor use is confined primarily to travel corridors, leaving the majority of the 2,219,791 acres open for better practices by biologists. The greater ecosystem of Yellowstone, encompassing vast areas outside the park boundary, demands more scientific answers to counter many of the emotionally charged controversies. And certainly more and better research is needed for future planning and management of tourist impact on the environment if sustainability is to be achieved.

It is to be hoped that the tendency to convert Yellowstone into a contrived theme park by replacing native flora and fauna with Disneyesque features popular with some tourists will cease. The park's basic character and spirit of over a century ago is worthy of saving.

Because of the critical design role of landscape architects for tourism and parks in the West, the Chapter 10 is devoted to their great opportunities for sustainable design in the future. The purpose is twofold: to alert developers of tourism to the specialized assistance they can obtain from these professionals, and to stimulate more landscape architects to strive toward better and more frequent tourism design and planning in the West in the future.

Endnotes

[1]Glick, D. (1991). Tourism in Greater Yellowstone: Maximizing the Good, Minimizing the Bad, Eliminating the Ugly. In *Nature Tourism: Managing for the Environment* (pp. 58–74). Washington, DC: Island Press.

[2]Meyer, J. L. (1996). *The Spirit of Yellowstone: The Cultural Evolution of a National Park.* New York: Rowman & Littlefield.

[3]Chittenden, H. M. (1964). *The Yellowstone National Park* (p. 8). Norman: University of Oklahoma Press.

[4]Meyer, op. cit., 70.

[5]Lee, R. F. (1974). *Family Tree of the National Park System.* Philadelphia: Eastern National Park & Monument Association.

[6]James, H. (1939). *Romance of the National Parks* (p. 14). New York: Macmillan.

[7]Chittenden, op. cit., 81.

[8]Carr, E. (1998). *Wilderness by Design* (p. 32). Lincoln: University of Nebraska Press.

[9]Reports to the Department of Interior for the Fiscal Year Ending June 30, 1915. (1916). p. 894. Washington, DC: US Government Printing Office.

[10]Reports to the Department of Interior . . ., op. cit., 846

[11]Reports to the Department of Interior . . ., op. cit., 873.

[12]Yellowstone National Park. From www.nps.gov/yell/index, as of September 18, 2000.

[13]Chittenden, op. cit., 133.

[14]Garrison, L. A. (1983). *The Making of a Ranger* (p. 273). Salt Lake City: Howe Brothers.

[15]Heasley, J. A. (1910). *A Summer Vacation in Yellowstone National Park* (p. 12). Grand Rapids, MI: Author.

[16]Heasley, op. cit., 70.

[17]Albright, H. M., & Taylor, F. J. (1928). *Oh, Ranger* (p. 132). Stanford: Stanford University Press.

[18]Elliot, Sir Hugh (Ed.). (1974). *Second World Conference on National Parks* (p. 15). Morges, Switzerland: International Union for Conservation of Nature and Natural Resources.

[19]Schmitt, P. J. (1969). *Back to Nature* (p. 171). New York: Oxford University Press.

[20]Magoc, C. J. (1999). *Yellowstone: The Creation and Selling of an American Landscape, 1870–1903* (p. 169). Albuquerque: University of New Mexico Press.

[21]O'Brien, B. R. (1999). *Our National Parks and the Search for Sustainability* (p. 42). Austin: University of Texas Press.

[22]Kaplan, R. D. (1998). *An Empire Wilderness* (p. 287). New York: Random.

[23]Glick, op. cit., 65.

[24]Frost, R. (2000, November 22). *Winter Use Decision for Yellowstone and Grand Teton National Parks.* NPS News Release. From www.yellowstone.com/parkinformation as of April 9, 2002.

[25]O'Brien, op. cit., 43.

[26]O'Brien, op. cit., 103.

[27]O'Brien, op. cit., 99

[28]Chase, A. (1987). *Playing God in Yellowstone* (p. 204). New York: Harcourt Brace.

[29]Reese, R. (1984). *Greater Yellowstone* (p. 64). Helena, MT: Montana Magazine.

[30]Magoc, op. cit., 176.

[31]Keller, R. H., & Turek, M. (1998). *American Indians and National Parks* (p. 64). Tucson: University of Arizona Press; and Magoc, ibid.

[32]Iwanski, L. (1999, February 28). Tribes Urge End to Buffalo Killing (AP). *Bryan-College Station Eagle*, p. A7.

[33]Meagher, M., & Houston, D. B. (1998). *Yellowstone and the Biology of Time.* Norman: University of Oklahoma Press.

[34]*Yellowstone Superintendent Announces Retirement from National Park Service.* (2001, February 6). NPS News Release. From www.yellowstone.com/

parkinformation as of April 9, 2002.

[35]Carr, op. cit., 95.

[36]Pregill, P., & Volkman, N. (1993). *Landscapes in History* (p. 690). New York: Van Nostrand Reinhold.

[37]Reisner, M. (1986). *Cadillac Desert: The American West and its Disappearing Water* (p. 213). New York: Viking.

[38]Snepenger, D. J., et al. (1998). Is Downtown Mainly for Tourists? *Journal of Travel Research,* 36, 5-12. Similar results were obtained by Butler, R.W. (1980). The Concept of a Tourist Area Cycle of Evolution: Implications for Management Resource. *Canadian Geographer,* 24(1), 5-12; and Ap, J., & Crompton, J. L. (1993). Residents' Strategies for Responding to Tourism Impacts. *Journal of Travel Research,* 32(1), 47-50.

[39]Rapanshek, K. (1997). Prospecting for Genes. *Wyoming Wildlife,* 61(12), 10-17.

[40]Howe, J., McMahon, E., & Propst, L. (1997). *Balancing Nature and Commerce in Gateway Communities* (p. 115). Washington DC: Island Press.

[41]Howe et al., op. cit., 56.

[42]Glick, op. cit., 68.

[43]*Guiding Principles of Sustainable Design.* (1993). Denver: National Park Service.

[44]Glick, op. cit. 60.

[45]Barbee, R. D., & Varley, J. D. (1984). The Paradox of Repeating Error: Yellowstone National Park from 1872 to Biosphere and Beyond. *Proceedings, Conference on the Management of Biosphere Reserves.* Gatlinburg, Tennessee: National Park Service.

[46]Sax, J. L. (1991). Ecosystems and Property Rights in Greater Yellowstone: The Legal System in Transition. In R. B. Keiter & M. S. Boyce (Eds.), *The Greater Yellowstone Ecosystem: Redefining America's Wilderness Heritage* (pp. 77-84). New Haven: Yale University Press.

[47]*The Reintroduction of Grey Wolves to Yellowstone National Park and Central Idaho.* (1993). Environmental Impact Statement. Washington, DC: US Fish and Wildlife Service.

[48]Karle, M. (2000, December 20). *Federal Agencies Reach Agreement on Management of Yellowstone Bison.* NPS News Release. From www.yellowstone.com/paarkinformation as of April 9, 2002.

[49]Coniff, R. (1989). Yellowstone's 'Rebirth' Among the Ashes is Not Neat Nor Simple But It's Real. *Smithsonian,* 20(6), 36+.

[50]Bath, A. (1990). 1989 Summer Visitor Attitudes Toward Fire and Fire Management Issues in Yellowstone National Park. In J. Gramann (Ed.), *Proceedings, Third Symposium on Social Sciences in Resource Management* (pp. 86-87). College Station: Texas A&M University. See also: Karle, M. (2001). *Changes in Yellowstone Since the 1988 Fires.* NPS News Release. From www.yellowstone.com/parkinformation.html?content, as of April 9, 2002.

[51]Flores, D. (1998). Spirit of Place and the Value of Nature in the American West. In J. E. Sherow (Ed.), *A Sense of the American West* (pp. 31-38). Albuquerque, NM: University of New Mexico Press.

[52]Meyer, op. cit. 25.

[53]O'Brien, op. cit. 127.

[54]Keiter, R. B., & Boyce, M. S. (1991). Greater Yellowstone's Future: Ecosystem Management in a Wilderness Environment. In *The Greater Yellowstone Ecosystem: Rede-*

fining America's Wilderness Heritage (pp. 379-413). New Haven: Yale University Press.

Chapter 10

Sustainability Challenges for Planners and Designers

The future of tourism in the West lies primarily in the minds and hands of three major groups: investors/developers, community leaders/residents, and planners/designers. The planners/designers vary greatly in their understanding of tourism in its full context. No matter the scale of involvement, from small to large projects, knowledge of *tourism as a system* is needed if better tourism is to be developed in the future. It is helpful to think of overall tourism as an interrelated system composed of five major components: attractions, transportation, services, information, and promotion. Any change in one component affects all others. For example, even for a small site planning project, such as for a restaurant, other parts of the system will influence its land design. Decisions by managers of components such as transportation and access, tourist attractions, lodging and other services, tourist information, and promotion have an influence on location and design. The planning of resort complexes depends greatly on similar functional elements within the tourism system. For planners and designers, these understandings are often derived from cooperation with those who control the other parts of the system. In addition, today there are many other sources, such as books, tourism research journals, university tourism specialists, and Web sites on tourism planning. All of the recommendations in the preceding chapters should be reviewed by planners/designers for new opportunities of creating better tourism in the West.

Throughout the preceding chapters, new challenges and expanded roles of planners/designers have been discussed, but because of their specialty of land design, the important input of landscape architects in the future is given emphasis in this chapter.

The organization that sets standards and policies for the profession is the American Society of Landscape Architects (ASLA) with approximately 12,000 members. Worldwide, this field is represented by the International Federation of Landscape Architects. Professionals within the field of landscape architecture include researchers, teachers, writers, and practitioners in both governmental agencies and the private sector.

The *ASLA Declaration on Environment and Development*, adopted on October 2, 1993, includes the following strategies, all applicable to future land design for tourism in the West:

- Accept responsibility for the consequences of our design, planning, management, and policy decisions on the health of natural systems and cultural communities and their harmony, equity, and balance with one another.
- Generate design, planning, and management strategies and policy from the basis of the cultural context and the ecosystem to which each landscape belongs at the local, regional, and global scale.
- Develop, use, and specify products, materials, technologies, and techniques that exemplify the principles of sustainable development and landscape regeneration.
- Seek improvement in knowledge, abilities, and skills; in educational institutions; and professional practices and organizations to more effectively achieve sustainable development.
- Actively engage in shaping decisions, attitudes, and values that support human health, environmental protection, and sustainable development.[1]

Throughout the history of tourism in the West, landscape architects have played a significant role, as cited many times in this work. New and old resorts, parks, roads, and interpretive centers now exhibit the sustainable land design concepts of these professionals. By means of planning healthy natural and cultural systems, their modification for human use and preservation of resources for the future, they provide a key role in planning, decision making, and management.

The profession of landscape architecture in this country dates back over 100 years. This profession encompasses a much broader scope than its main focus of site design. Frederick Law Olmsted is credited as the founder because of his landscape philosophy and works. Because Olmsted had been a farmer he understood the physical features of the landscape—vegetation, soils, drainage, air flow, slope, and geology. Because he was well versed on political, economic, and social issues of his period, he knew how to implement environmentally sound park projects throughout the country, most notably Central Park, New York. Because he was sensitive to natural resource aesthetics and the value of open space, he was instrumental in establishing major western national parks. His is a legacy of protecting landscape character alongside creative modification of land for human use. Generations of landscape architects ever since have aspired to his principles of design.

Needed today in the West are many new "Olmsteds," designers who can accept the altered land as it is today and yet retain landscape character and distinctive place qualities for new tourism design. By their advocacy and creative design, especially for burgeoning tourism, they can bring back the essence of western paradise. Now is the time to follow Olmsted's principles and actions to protect quality landscapes and yet create new developments that demonstrate restoration of past landscape values.[2] These values encompass human enrichment from closer contact with and understanding of the abundant natural and cultural forces of the West. The dynamics of change need not destroy these values if given superior design guidance.

Although landscape architects have already been very active in the West with many public and private works related to tourism, the historical sketch related in earlier chapters suggests many opportunities and responsibilities for restoring older values, enhancing tourism, and resolving major issues. The following discussion offers challenges to landscape architects and their associates for creating a better western tourism. Their leadership, design team efforts, and public involvement hold great promise for major improvement of tourism in the West.

Understand External Factors

Landscape architects traditionally have directed their attention to specific sites. From the early estate design to modern subdivision planning, the design responsibility to the client has been for a specific piece of land, within the ownership of the client. For today's practitioners of landscape architecture, this client-designer relationship still holds but requires an additional dimension for tourism applications. The success of the site design is as dependent upon external factors as those for internal design and management.

For land design of tourist facilities, a major external factor includes the natural resources surrounding a site as well as those within. No site project can be removed from its context. The nearby forest cover, water drainage, threats from flooding and coastal erosion, wildlife habitat, and topographic change are part of the overall design. As landscape architects work with clients to determine the design program (what is to be developed and where), the pros and cons of these external influences impinge upon the form and location of all design elements. Vistas and other relationships with these outside factors are especially critical in America's West.

Among external factors that can enhance design are the cultural and historic influences, dating back to prehistoric settlement of the West. Native American occupation has made a significant imprint on the region. The several European waves of settlement for fur trade, mining, agriculture, and forestry and their great ethnic diversity can support design themes that landscape architect Christopher Dagenhardt has labeled "historic design referencing."[3] This need not be tacky mimicry but rather a carefully thought out design essence of a significant past. Already there is a trend for franchise food shops to abandon their flashy brand labels when locating in historic districts, adapting their businesses to historic reuse. The challenge before landscape architects is to take the time to investigate all external factors at the very start of any tourism project. Not only will the unique character of the site be perpetuated but also the tourist will gain insight into the very special place characteristics, for the enjoyment and enrichment they can obtain nowhere else.

Clustering is a concept that has much merit but has been slow to be accepted. Modern summer home complexes and multiunit resorts still occupy very large lots, cutting deeply into natural resource and ecosystem settings that might better be protected. This practice stems from the market argument that this is what the public wants, even in forest and mountain areas. But they usually are not given a better choice. The concept of clustering concentrates development of structures rather than scattering them over a large area. When markets understand the true conditions of clusters versus dispersal, they are convinced of the practical, environmental, and societal value of clustering. Cultural ecologist William H. Romme supports clustering from an ecological point of view, arguing that tighter patterns of development do much less damage to ecosystems, leaving protected open space devoid of development, especially important in rural mountain regions of the West.[4] These open spaces can be protected, not only by governmental means but also by visual and conservation easements and land trusts.

With a doctorate in landscape and urban planning, Dr. Russell Arthur Smith advocates a modification of the cluster concept, calling it a "comprehensive integrated approach."[5] For a destination of resort hotels, there is merit in involving many neighboring sites (and even multiple owners) into an integrated whole rather than an ad hoc approach with each developer going his own way. Required is not only new cooperation but also land use controls that assure sustainability. A cost-effective argument also can be made. Clustering reduces greatly the length and investment in roads, water lines, sewage lines, power lines, and the costs of their maintenance. A societal argument favors clustering, providing stronger linkage among neighbors and a better feeling of belonging in a community.

Especially in the West, other external factors contribute to both business success and sustainability. A site's relationship to highway access is very important but requires special design for tourism other than capacity. Today's interest in ecotourism and adventure tourism may require new road access to remote sites, often doing great damage to natural resource factors. Some urban attraction sites force visitors through ugly and dilapidated corridors, detracting greatly from the psychological anticipation of the attraction feature.

As landscape architects become more sensitive to external site factors and the market realms of tourists they can assist developer clients in understanding these factors. Resulting development can be even more profitable while a sustainable environment is maintained.

Design for the Dual Client

Typically, the client of a landscape architect as practitioner is the owner–developer of a specific site. For tourism in the West this may be for a motel, resort, park, interpretive center, museum, or other public or private project. Certainly the wishes of this client must be honored, but for tourism an equally important client is the *prospective traveler* who will be using the land development project.

In the past it was sufficient for the landscape architect to add intuition and personal experience to the owner's recommendations to identify the "program" for the project—the functional needs that are to be placed on the property. Today this is insufficient. Added must be travel market information, insight into the characteristics of the potential guest, such as trends in demographics, preferences, lifestyles, habits, and expenditure levels. For example, today's population is aging. Some are very active, others passive. Some are affluent, others are not. Some people prefer a long trip once a year, others more frequent short trips. Many today are mixing pleasure with business in their travel itineraries. These and many other differences mean that potential visitors cannot be generalized. Market specialists now identify a number of market segments with only a few that may be suited to a specific project.

If landscape architects are to create land designs for tourism projects in the West, the needs of the potential tourists must be added to those of the client. Travel market information must be part of the design process. This added dimension requires new knowledge by the designer or the addition of a travel market analyst to the design team. The result will be a more environmentally and economically sound establishment if both the owner and prospective users are considered in the process.

Create a New Kind of Western Community

A relatively new challenge before landscape architects and other designers of the West is a shift from federal power for decision making to that of local communities. Even though vast regions of land are still managed by federal agencies, there is a groundswell of local determination. Tourism, because it is probably the greatest of all local economic generators, will benefit from this new direction. Because the scope of responsibility for most urban planners omits tourism, this void must be filled if communities are to fulfill their role for tourism.

Today's residents of western communities are more sophisticated and desirous of guiding their own destiny. Although they recognize the need for local-federal cooperation, they are accepting greater responsibility for directing their own futures. More than ever before, local residents understand the need for sustainability for both their economy and their quality of life. A new land ethic, local rather than federal, is emerging.[6]

With this new West comes the abundant opportunity for practitioners of landscape architecture to be on the cutting edge of planning and design that radiates from the community outward rather than from the federal government downward. This requires new thinking and action by both civic officials and landscape architects. Designers may need to become more active in local politics, especially on matters of community and tourism land use. It may mean greater memberships in environmental advocacy groups. Landscape architects may need to publicize their capability in adapting tourism to community plans.

Designers and developers can now capitalize on the new trend of local residents to enhance their quality of life that demands greater environmental sensitivity. New land use measures and designs can enhance the aesthetics of entrance drives. Rerouting and traffic control can reduce gridlock downtown. Building and site design in harmony with the neighboring resources can improve the quality of the community. Alignments of streets can frame vistas to distant mountains and forests. Architectural standards can be liberating rather than constrictive, still providing the diversity of business services desired by travelers.

Sites adjacent to parks, forests, and preserves (gateway communities) demand special planning and design that is compatible with these protected areas. The popular epithet of overcommercialization, often expressed by conservationists, is an indictment on design and planning rather than commerce. The traveling public wants and needs a diversity of services but there is no need for the sprawl, ugliness, and congestion of the past.

Entrance communities can be attractive, efficient, economically sound, compact, and desirable for both residents and visitors, but only when the business sector, local leaders, residents, and designers work together. Instead of feelings of antagonism between park management and the community, much can be accomplished by working together, particularly on issues of aesthetics, capacities, infrastructure, and design standards.[7]

Needed today are landscape architects and others who advocate and practice community landscape ecology—for human values as well as stronger protection of and relationship to the given environment. More compact development can lessen the impact of the automobile on surrounding environment. Better water management that utilizes natural forces is not only environmentally sound but also less costly. Principles of landscape ecology foster better human health, especially for reduction of air and water pollution, less traffic congestion, and reduction of threats from toxic wastes. Again, it must be emphasized that the better the quality of communities for residents, the better they are for visitors.

A further complication of tourism projects, especially for all food and lodging businesses in communities, is their dual market objectives. These enterprises must meet both resident and traveler markets for their success. Hotels, often considered exclusively for travelers, frequently include resident services such as dining out, weddings, receptions, reunions, entertainment, events, and meetings of local organizations. Most food services cannot succeed without both resident and visitor markets. Both resident and traveler functions must be part of design considerations regarding location, site selection, and site and building design.

A new community planning challenge is accommodating increased volumes of cruise ship passengers at harbors. The tremendous growth in popularity of cruises exposes the need for redesign and development of waterfronts for visitors, once only serving shipping needs. Harbor areas with existing streets, warehouses, fuel storage, and unloading/loading facilities require major renovation to host visitors. New consideration of aesthetics and tourist functions is in demand.

Landscape architects have great opportunities in the future for guiding western communities toward environmentally sound development for both residential and tourist use.

Create Sustainable Coastal Plans

A challenge before landscape architects today is to foster better western coastal planning, design, and development. There is ample evidence of improper land use around inland shores and along the Pacific coast. Although solution is very complicated, landscape architects have the capability of guiding resolution because of their special training and experience.

Coastal areas of the Northwest and particularly the beaches have a long tradition of public access.[8]. Testimony to this tradition are photographs of beach visitors in the early 1900s and the historic water routes up and down the coast. Over many years, the number of state, federal, and local park and recreation areas has increased public agency presence greatly along the northern California and Oregon coasts.

Private coastal land ownership, however, reflects the principle that property owners can make any use of their land they wish. This practice is somewhat defensible but also foolhardy. It fails to recognize the powerful natural forces from the ocean that can be so destructive. Severe erosion and loss of property have prompted legislation directed toward control of coastal land use to protect investment. It is gradually being recognized that instead of being restrictive and costly, these regulations are more economically sound and foster more stable development farther back from the shore. Landscape architects, as they become involved in coastal projects, could perform a very constructive role by encouraging development only at safe distances from shoreline hazard.

Orientation of large structures close to the waterfront that creates virtually a concrete wall along the shore restricts use to only a few. Frequently, the relationship between buildings and the beach are often cut off by a beach drive, making access to the beach very dangerous and reducing greatly the aesthetic value of backlands. Instead, a concept that keeps the roadway back of buildings and open space between building envelopes adds materially to the resort success as well as guest satisfaction. This concept was put forth as "concentrated dispersal" in 1972.[9] The greatest barrier to implementation of this concept is the existing lot pattern and mix of ownership. However, even this can be solved by joint action for planned unit development.

Related to this is the challenge to landscape architects for greater education, advocacy, and support of coastal regulation and better planning. Even now some developers have fostered the location of schools and hospitals at safe distances from the shore. Landscape architects can engage in more public seminars, news releases, and research reports that identify the many known coastal hazards and problems of waterfront development. Not only is this good wisdom based on past history but also more enduring, based on geologists' predictions that even more violent storms and erosion are likely in the future. Better coastal planning will also foster the retention of water life habitat along the Pacific coast. By restricting human encroachment, endangerment of many waterfront species can be reduced. Certainly there is need for greater enlightenment and advocacy by landscape architects regarding better coastal planning, essential to better tourism development in the West. With greater stimulation and commitment, designers can exercise a strong positive influence on land owners, developers, residents, and governments to learn the facts about coastal issues. Only in this way can the heritage of rare coastal assets be perpetuated.

Become a Catalyst

A major emerging role of landscape architects is that of catalyst for conflict resolution regarding site selection and development. Tourism project proposals often set environmentalists against developers. Acrimony and conflict can become polarized and continue for years. Resolution of differences is difficult and demanding of extreme tact and diplomacy, often taking a great deal of time. Landscape architects often perform this role and create concepts sensitive to environments and also acceptable by developers.

Designers as unbiased facilitators usually follow several key steps. First, it is necessary for opposing sides to replace their anger, emotion, and vindictiveness with rational identification of specific issues. With the landscape architect as mediator, public meetings and focus groups can be used to obtain consensus on the specific issues of contention. Often, this step alone helps each side to understand the others' point of view.

Second, it is necessary to research the issues. Environmental concerns need to be studied in detail. If wildlife and plant life are of concern, specific study of the proposal's impact should be made by competent and respected biologists. When the facts are known, erroneous beliefs are deflated. At the same time, a clear picture of the proposed development is needed. The landscape architect can be instrumental in requiring more factual information on the impacts of the proposal.

Third, with more complete information in hand, the landscape architect can assemble a team of planners and designers to begin the creation of alternative design concepts that reach toward resolution of original conflicts. When this stage is kept loose, conceptual, and open to public input, the alternatives are more likely to meet the acceptance of all parties.

Fourth, tentative design concepts may reveal the need for removal of obsolete policies and regulations. Community ordinances, laid down many years ago, may not have anticipated the kind of development being proposed and may need repeal or amendment. If state or federal properties or regulations are involved, the desired project concept, acceptable by all parties, may require new legislation.

As can be seen, this process is workable only when all parties are willing to put aside animosities and work toward a common goal. With skill and imaginative concepts for development, a landscape architect can be the catalyst for resolving conflict and creating a worthwhile sustainable tourism development.

Become More Assertive Environmentalists

Environmental concern has always been a precept of the profession of landscape architecture. It is part of training and because all design for development is based on land, resource protection is axiomatic.

But for practicing professionals the maintenance of day-to-day office routine and design of projects tend to dominate the designer's time. An important challenge is to break from this routine sufficiently to learn more about environmental issues. Sources are abundant: TV specials, books, and even news items. There is hardly a design project that does not contain elements of environmental concern. The better a designer is informed, the better can be a design concept and solution. Essential is knowledge of trends in use and misuse of resources such as water, land forms and soils, wildlife, and vegetation, not only by tourism but other land uses as well. In every area of the West today, much is being written and discussed about threats to these natural resources. Equally significant are cultural resources: archaeological sites and artifacts, historic sites and communities, and ethnic factors. Virtually every tourism design project involves aspects of both natural and cultural resources. The better informed that a landscape architect is on these topics the better will be the design solutions, especially toward goals of sustainability.

An issue facing landscape architects is their own *environmental advocacy*. How to balance conservation advocacy with client wishes often can be a difficult task. In the past, developers preferred to flatten every site with bulldozers. Such action destroyed any landscape integrity the site may have had. With skill and tact the designer may be able to convince the client that the functional objectives can be reached with minimum change to important landscape features. The first step in this process is to clarify the landscape program objectives with the client. Some landscape architects spend many weeks and even months clarifying the specific land use program. Paralleling this step would have been detailed site analysis, a complete description of land forms, soils, drainage patterns, existing vegetation, weather influences, and overall landscape character. With only cursory testing of program desires against the site factors, critical site or program limitations may be revealed—the site just may not support the intended uses.

A question of integrity centers on the extent to which the landscape architect can stand up for environmental protection even to the possibility of losing the contract. More likely, because resource factors are so critical to tourism, an owner-client may discover how valuable the designer's advice on resource protection is to the success of the project. When this is done, both short- and long-range sustainability can be accomplished.

An important opportunity for landscape architects, especially in the West, is to *write and be published* on environmental issues related to tourism. Many landscape architects have honed their writing skills and discovered how valuable this can be for project publicity as well as professional reputation building. Today's editors of newspapers, magazines, professional journals, and books are eager to obtain substantive writings on solutions to environmental concerns. Landscape architects in the West are qualified to prepare regular newspaper columns on concepts for resource protection in tourism design projects. More tourism projects should appear in the profession's basic journal, *Landscape Architecture*. Other journals related to land use, such as for soil conservation, planning, park and recreation management, tourism research, land development, would benefit from articles on constructive solutions to tourism and the environment. Annual conferences and their proceedings offer landscape architects an excellent outlet for their project descriptions, research results, and advocacy. In recent years, more books, such as Ethan Carr's, *Wilderness by Design*,[10] are describing the philosophy, practices, history, and works of landscape architects. The opportunities are abundant but need greater input by landscape architects.

It is now being recognized that many of the disappointments of tourism project implementation lie at the political level. Often the body politic is unaware of the landscape architectural profession. Some landscape architects have recognized this problem and have become *more active on city councils, advisory boards, and civic organizations* in their own area. Some landscape architectural firms today reward staff members who become involved in community affairs. This action is not just self-serving but rather is directed toward the public weal for a more environmentally sustainable community.

Such public involvement by landscape architects has several advantages. It has great learning value for the designer. It opens up the large sphere of governmental and nonprofit influence on all land development. The designer gains a better understanding of the critical influence of regulations and public opinion on tourism and the environment. Of course, it has great public relations value for the landscape firm. Designers become better known, their work becomes better understood, and their public statements are more frequently quoted. Those who have become more involved in the political arena believe that the extra time involved is well worth it.

An essential element of new environmentalism is fostering *better ethics*. Judgment on the moral value of a decision to develop is important, questioning whether it *should be done*. When designers and developers consider whether the proposed project is best for the physical environment and society, an ethical measure is placed on the decision to develop. For example, new voltaic and wind technology for electrical power tend to encourage ecotourism development in resource areas that should be protected because of their rare or fragile landscape character. Such action requires an ethical decision on the part of designers and developers.

As landscape architects become more proactive in environmentalism everyone benefits, especially as applied to western tourism: investors, developers, communities, and travelers.

Integrate Macro and Micro Tourism Planning

Traditionally, landscape architecture has focused on the site scale. For western tourism, landscape architects have the opportunity to integrate their site projects into two other scale dimensions: destination and region.[11] This concept of integrating all three scales is recognition of the breadth of tourism functions and land development. Just as many landscape architects are now practicing, this broad scope requires a team of designers, planners, and often other specialists.

Linking with *regional plans* has many advantages. It is virtually impossible in the West to establish a tourism project without being influenced by state or federal policy on resource use. All resource management agencies have not only legal mandates but policies and practices that impinge upon tourism land use. The FS, for example, has extensive land use policies for all development on private inholdings often developed for tourism. Concessions, such as for marinas, hotels, food services, river rafting, and campgrounds, must adhere to many regulations of agencies such as the NPS, FS, BLM, Bureau of Reclamation, and US Army Corps of Engineers when building on their lands. Any tourism project within their jurisdiction or influence can be affected by regional plans of these and state resource management agencies.

Equally significant are regional plans by state departments of transportation, parks, and recreation. Although most of the responsibility for understanding these important regional policies lies with project owners, designers must be part of this loop of understanding. Linking site planning to regional plans will result in better land use compatibility, better visitor satisfaction, increased sustainability, and may even avoid a financial disaster. Awareness of regional plans is not only an opportunity for better design project work, it is a responsibility.

Although tourism promoters tend to foster tourism everywhere, some areas of the West have greater potential than others. To determine zones of potential, a lesson was derived from agriculture's experience, that the same crop is not suited to every geographical location. Believing that land analysis for factors supportive of tourism would be useful to identify zones with greatest potential, a process was experimented with in the 1960s in Michigan's Upper Peninsula.[12] Further refinement of a such a geographical analysis process in recent decades using GIS (geographic information system) was applied by the author to several areas: Washington, Oklahoma, Delaware, Illinois, and northern South Carolina.[13] The resulting zones were helpful to local areas for knowing their potential for tourism development.

Key factors used for overlay maps included: natural resources (water, wildlife, topography/soils, existing natural resource development), cultural resources (prehistory, history, economic development, existing cultural development), transportation, and cities. When these factors were mapped, converted to computer graphics, and aggregated, zones of greatest potential were delineated.[14] Such a process is available to landscape architects for application in the West, to determine areas best suited to tourism development. Local areas then can take the next step in making localized analysis to determine if environmental capacity has already been reached or if new development is desirable.

Another important linkage of all tourism site design projects is at the *destination scale*.[15] For today's tourism, a destination can be defined as a community (or several) and its attractions within and in the surrounding area. Even promoters are recognizing that travel market segments are more likely to be attracted to community destinations than to political units, such as counties or states, a practice often used in the past by governments for allotting funds for marketing. Increasing greatly in guiding the development of tourism in the West are community governments and citizen groups. It is their decision making that controls all the infrastructure so important to tourism: streets, lighting, water supply, waste disposal, police, fire control. They have the power to accept or deny new tourism developments such as sports arenas, park and recreation areas, zoos, historic sites, and shopping areas, as well as food and lodging services. Governments and agencies having jurisdiction in the surrounding areas often have policies that govern access, land use, and the establishment of attractions. Again, even though the major responsibility for understanding these destination conditions lies with the developer, the designer cannot create viable designs and plans unless they are in context.

Of course, as is being demonstrated more frequently in the West, individual site scale is very important for all tourism project design and development. The greatest recent design and planning change is the use of a team rather than a single designer approach. This is new recognition of the great complexity of tourism and tourism projects, requiring input from a variety of specialists. Where history is an element, a specialist in that event or place is needed. If water control is an element, a hydrologist should be part of the team. For special soil situations, a soil scientist is required, and if interpretation is a function, exhibit designers and technologists need to be part of the design team. In most instances, engineering and architectural services must be integrated with landscape architectural design. In addition to the client, a travel market specialist should be added to the team to represent the interests and needs of the potential visitors. The future of tourism design in the West depends upon collaboration of many specialists into an integrated team.

Of great importance at the site and community levels in recent years has been public involvement.[16] In the past, many governmental resource development agencies used public hearing for this function. Usually these were political disasters and merely token efforts by the agencies. All design and planning decisions had been made without earlier public input. Now, a much more effective but complicated and time-consuming process involves public constituencies early in the design and planning process. Even though this step delays the creation of concept plan alternatives, it usually avoids conflict later on. Many public involvement techniques have proven effective—focus groups, workshops, Nominal Group Technique, and surveys. In some instances, a standing tourism advisory council can oversee such public involvement. Of course, for today's environmental sustainability the traditional principles of landscape design must be applied to all tourism site design.[17]

Create Better Wayfinding

A major challenge in tourism for the West today is improvement in how highway visitors can find their way. Psychologists and geographers have delved into the science of cognitive mapping to gain insight into how human beings understand spatial relationships and guide themselves when they travel.[18] Wayfinding has been described as a cognitive process requiring a cognitive mapping ability to understand the travel environment, a plan-for-action ability, and a decision-making ability to transform plans into action. Although landscape architects cannot cope with all the wayfinding ills of travel today, they can collaborate with highway planners and information producers to help travelers find their way.

Pretrip information is a first step in travel guidance. Many influences can assist the would-be traveler before leaving home. Past travel experience helps in creating a cognitive map of how to get from home to a destination. Travel literature and friends and relatives also assist in creating this mental map. Some travelers will prepare detailed itineraries whereas others prefer impulse travel. Today, a great amount of information on destinations and travel is available on the Internet. Assistance is obtained also from other sources such as tour companies, travel agents, and the American Automobile Association.

Maps offer graphic delineation of routes but their preparation is very critical. Map design is frequently abused, prepared by advertising artists who focus on style rather than by cartographers who understand communication processes. Frequently landscape architects cooperate with cartographers to integrate their project design (logos and signage) with the map delineation. Too often map information does not agree with the ground truth—different from route signs or place names. The only purpose of a map is to convey information clearly. Frequently the type font is too small to be legible, an especially critical issue for travelers with some visual impairment. Map interpretation also assumes that travelers understand the graphic symbols—meaning of scale, keys to points of interest, route numbering, color codes, and shading. Some travelers do not take the time to understand the full meaning of the cartographer's rendition and rely only on cues along the way, often wasting much time and leading to difficulty of finding a destination. Companions of male drivers frequently cite the cliché that men often wander about aimlessly because they refuse to stop and ask for directions. Map-reading ability is not universal. The mental transition from a two-dimensional map on paper to the real landscape varies greatly with individuals. Greater understanding of the traveler's ability to read and use maps is essential for designers, developers, and producers of travel information. Modern geographic positioning systems (GPS) are providing important travel guidance.

For generations, *signs* have been used (and abused) to assist travelers in finding their way. Highway engineers provide signs for control (speed limits, stop signs, caution signs), for directions (exits, right/left turns, connection with routes), and jurisdictional and place names (city limits, "city hall," etc.). Generally, highway signage has improved over many decades of experimentation and use. However, with increased volumes and speeds of traffic movement and proliferation of travel objectives, the mix of public and private signs has become so numerous, conflicting, and ambiguous that rapid comprehension is impossible. Greatly needed is sign-highway design integration that follows the traveler's mental flow of sequence from place to place. Planners can do their own test driving and noting of inadequacies and even inaccuracies of signage. Landscape architects, psychologists of cognitive mapping, highway engineers, and surrounding developers need to combine their skills to provide newer and much better wayfinding for travelers in America's West.

Create New Tourism Curricula for Landscape Architects

Because tourism is such a major economic driver in the West, university curricula in landscape architecture and related planning disciplines throughout the nation should emphasize the many meanings of land planning as it relates to tourism. Even though basic courses and studios in landscape architecture should remain, needed are lectures and references regarding tourism at the higher undergraduate and graduate levels. It may be possible to offer a special option on tourism. When these students become educators or practitioners, they will be better equipped to meet the growing demand for creative professional design in tourism.

Following are topics that would qualify future landscape architects in the West and elsewhere for work on tourism projects:

- Roles and opportunities for design professionals in tourism.
- The heterogeneity of resource distribution; not all areas have the same potential.
- Techniques for public involvement.
- Tourism land use as part of urban and rural planning.
- Sources of travel market research.
- Politics and economics of tourism land use.
- Eco-ethics of tourism planning and design.
- Site design in context of community and regional planning.
- Sustainable design principles for tourism development.[19]

A significant opportunity for long-range tourism design sustainability in the West is for practicing landscape architects to become more *active in university matters*. Professors of landscape architecture often feel isolated and lacking in administrative understanding and support. Valuable to them are voices from the field, especially on environmental issues. Unless deans, vice presidents, and chancellors are fully aware of the field of landscape architecture it is easy for them to place organizational and financial support on other disciplines. Some departments are holding regular seminars, assemblies, and conferences with presentations by outside landscape architects to which administrators are invited. In great need is stronger linkage between professors, students, administrators, and practicing landscape architectural firms regarding the field of tourism.

A very productive avenue of education for tourism land planning is adult education. This is an age of career change, requiring new educational programs for existing workers. University departments of planning, landscape architecture, and architecture have opportunities for public service programs, such as short courses and additional degree programs. Existing tourist business operators in the West would benefit greatly from this input.

Needed: A New Awareness

In great need is for the developers of tourism—businesses, nonprofit organizations, public agencies—to demand the services of design and planning professionals rather than go it alone. Professional input will greatly aid planning decisions on location, site planning, and building design. The results will be more appealing to visitors, better adjusted to the local economy and society, and more environmentally sustainable for a long period.

Landscape architects have the capability of restoring and renewing landscapes so that the visitor values that made the travel explosion of the 1920s possible and so rewarding can again be won. Two factors today foster this challenge: travel market demand and resource foundations of the West. A huge travel market interested in cultural and natural resource attractions continues to grow. This market is of diverse demographics, from old to young, from wealthy to modest incomes, from domestic to international, and from white race to a variety of national and ethnic origins. The West remains a powerful American icon for all.

Many people today are interested in archaeological, historic, and legendary sites. Growing numbers are attracted to museums, interpretive centers, fine art exhibits, and performing art productions, all related to cultural events and objects. The icon of western lore continues. In addition, the volume of visitors to natural resource areas such as national parks, forests, and wildlands continues to grow. Interest in the physical environment has spawned new categories such as ecotourists, nature tourists, birders, nature photographers, and adventure recreationists.

Coupled with this market demand is the abundance and diversity of cultural and natural resources of the West. In spite of well-documented erosion of these resources, enough remain to provide a sound foundation for viable travel objectives. The number of attractions based on the special natural and cultural resource attributes has grown tremendously throughout the West in the last seven decades. However, there remain many more opportunities for creative design and development by private enterprise as well as nonprofit organizations and governmental agencies.

Needed today are more landscape architects, planners, and architects who understand these growing dynamics of tourism demand and supply. Needed are new and creative design solutions to land development that foster excitement, reflection, and enrichment from western travel experiences. It is the designer's opportunity and even responsibility to translate the natural and cultural resource base of the West into human emotions and feelings as well as physical rewards. Many years ago, landscape architect John Ormsbee Simonds stated it this way:

> The design approach then is not essentially a search for form, not primarily an application of principles. The true design approach stems from the realization that a plan has meaning only to man[kind], for whom it is planned, and only to the degree to which it brings facility, accommodation, and delight to the senses, and inspiration to his mind and to his soul. It is a creation of optimum relationships resulting in a total experience.[20]

Designers have the capability of making the linkage between residential quality of life and amenities of communities and visitor populations, a true host-guest relationship of benefit to both. Designers and planners can take the lead in the West to establish participatory tourism planning and development. Local people as well as professionals can make major input on deciding areas to develop or preserve. Needed is greater public-private integrated planning for better and not necessarily *greater* tourism development. Under these conditions, western tourism's paradise can be restored.

Endnotes

[1]ASLA Declaration on Environment and Development. *ASLA 1999 Member Handbook* (p. 41). Washington, DC: American Society of Landscape Architects.

[2]Among the many valuable resources are: Olmsted, F. L. (1990). *The Papers of Frederick Law Olmsted: The California Frontier 1863-1865, Vol. 5* V. P. Ranney (Ed.). Baltimore: Johns Hopkins Press; and Dawson, R., & Brechin, G. (1999). *Farewell, Promised Land.* Berkeley, CA: University of California Press.

[3]Dagenhardt, C. (1995). A Global View of Changes Occurring in Development, Tourism, and Landscape Architecture. In *Proceedings: The 32nd IFLA World Congress* (pp. 17-20). Bangkok: Thai Association of Landscape Architects.

[4]Romme, W. H. (1997). Creating Pseudo-Rural Landscapes in the Mountain West. In J. Nassauer (Ed.), *Placing Nature: Culture and Landscape Ecology* (pp. 139-161). Washington, DC: Island Press.

[5]Smith, R. A. (1995). Tourism Transitions and Profession Interventions. In *Proceedings: The 32nd IFLA World Congress* (pp. 34-44). Bangkok: Thai Association of Landscape Architects.

[6]Baden, J. A., & Snow, D. (Eds.). (1997). *The Next West: Public Lands, Community, and Economy in the American West* (p. 176). Washington, DC: Island Press.

[7]Howe, J., McMahon, E., & Probst, L. (1997). *Balancing Nature and Commerce in Gateway Communities* (p. 144). Washington, DC: Island Press.

[8]Komar, P. D. (1997). *The Pacific Northwest Coast* (p. 175). Durham, NC: Duke University Press.

[9]Gunn, C.A. (1972). Concentrated Dispersal—A New Approach to Coastal Development. *Landscape Architecture,* 62(2), 133-134.

[10]Carr, E. (1998). *Wilderness by Design.* Lincoln: University of Nebraska Press.

[11]Gunn, C. A. (1993). *Tourism Planning* (pp. 25-29). Washington, DC: Taylor & Francis.

[12]Landscape architect Clare A. Gunn and members of the landscape architectural firm of Johnson, Johnson, & Roy collaborated with economist Uel Blank to develop

the first regional tourism plan in the US. The process and result were published in *Guidelines for Tourism-Recreation in Michigan's Upper Peninsula* (1965). East Lansing: Michigan State University.

[13]These plans were consulting works by Clare A. Gunn: *Proposed Master Plan for Travel Marketing and Development, Oklahoma* (1987); *Tourism in Washington State* (1989); *Upcountry South Carolina Guidelines for Tourism Development* (1990); *Delaware's Natural Resource Potential for Tourism* (1991); *Illinois Zones of Tourism Potential* (1993).

[14]Gunn, C.A. (1997). *Vacationscape: Developing Tourist Areas* (p. 92). Washington, DC: Taylor & Francis.

[15]Explanations of this concept are provided in: Gunn, C.A. (1994). *Tourism Planning* (3rd. ed., chap. 7 and 8). Washington DC: Taylor & Francis.

[16]See p. 106 of *Vacationscape: Developing Tourist Areas* (1997).

[17]See pp. 106–112 of *Vacationscape: Developing Tourist Areas* (1997). Also see basic landscape design principles in: Hubbard, H. V., & Kimball, T. (1917/1935). *An Introduction to the Study of Landscape Design*. New York: Macmillan; Simonds, J. O. (1961). *Landscape Architecture*. New York: McGraw-Hill; and Motloch, J. L. (1991). *Introduction to Landscape Design*. New York: Van Nostrand Reinhold.

[18]Several sources on wayfinding functions are available, including: Passini, R. (1984). *Wayfinding in Architecture*. New York: Van Nostrand Reinhold; and Golledge, R. (Ed.). (1999). *Wayfinding Behavior: Cognitive Mapping and Other Spatial Processes*. Baltimore: The Johns Hopkins University Press.

[19]Gunn, C.A. (1995). The Tourism Challenge. Keynote address in *Proceedings: The 32nd IFLA World Congress* (pp. 1–16). Bangkok: Thai Association of Landscape Architects.

[20]Simonds, J. O. (1961). *Landscape Architecture: The Shaping of Man's Natural Environment* (p. 226). New York: McGraw-Hill.

Chapter 11

Meanings for the Future

This historic flashback of tourism development in the West, although focused on a selection of destinations, likely has application for the entire West, from the Great Plains to the Pacific Coast and Canada to Mexico. It offers one clear conclusion: unless new solutions to the pitfalls are devised and applied, and soon, both tourism and the environment are in doubt. However dire this prediction may be, it can be averted by the inventiveness and will of westerners who wish to reverse the present trends. All those involved in tourism in the West today face two scenarios.

One: *Continue the present trend.* Encourage and accept willy-nilly every new development regardless of its social, economic, and environmental impact. Promote more visitors, ignoring present congestion and environmental degradation. Retain present standoff positions between public and private interests in tourism. Isolate tourism decisions from local people who will be impacted. With notable exceptions, these trends have dominated the past history of tourism in the West.

Two: *Take action toward new goals of sustainable development.* A new era of responsible tourism development throughout the West is feasible. There is an increasing number of communities and developers who are aware of tourism's impacts on the local social, economic, and environmental status. They more frequently obtain professional assistance on location, design, and feasibility and involve local people in their decisions. Much of western paradise of the 1920s can be restored but it will require major changes in thinking, organization, planning, and action by those concerned with tourism's future in this important region.

Conclusions

To draw conclusions on the impact of the travel boom of the 1920s and beyond is a formidable challenge. Rather than a statistical approach, this volume represents a qualitative assessment of changes of tourism over seven decades in the West and their consequences for the future.

Contrary to the popular belief that promotion is the most significant need, two other factors have shown their importance. New planning and action on visitor access and resource protection now take precedence. The automobile reshaped the West and brought it within easy access for multitudes. It was the tremendous lure of the West when combined with near-universal access that set off the explosion of mass travel to the region in the 1920s. This happening was unprecedented and has never been equaled since. The event demonstrated that so often it is not the big accomplishment but rather the small one that changes the world. The simple innovation of mass-produced Model T Fords initiated an entirely new social, economic, and environmental era, not only in the West but the entire planet.

The autocampers of the 1920s saw the land in its native and raw state, now dramatically changed. Places then revealed the extensiveness of this vast frontier and results from settlement for mining, fishing, and forestry. Since then, monumental land use impositions for tourism have taken place: highways, airports, resorts, recreation areas, parks, winter sports areas, vacation homes, theme parks, commercial lodging and food services, billboards, and entertainment, just to name a few. These mass tourism developments have absorbed millions of acres of land and, in spite of some planning progress, this great growth has seldom followed sustainable policies.

The results reveal a paradox. On the one hand, much of the abundance and quality of many places, such as mountains, valleys, rivers, Pacific coast, wildlife, forests, flowers, and historic and archeological sites, have survived for decades and continue to have their appeal for visitors. On the other hand, modern travelers have accepted generations of change wrought by new tourism developments, quite in contrast to the past.

With the nation's increased awareness of environmental stresses, many questions accompany tourism's growth. Especially in the West, exponential demand on limited water supply is a critical issue today with a predictable future impact on tourism. There is ample evidence that in many resort areas sewage treatment is inadequate, posing a threat to aquifers and beach use. Other natural resources have been eroded severely. Cultural assets, such as historic mining towns, have been decimated by new casinos and other noncompatible tourist development. Negative influences stimulate a call to action by tourism leaders for a new vision for tourism in its future.

The following discussion, derived from examination and evaluation of seven decades of tourism in America's West, includes three main topics: *assets, constraints*, and *opportunities*. A major conclusion is optimism for abundant opportunities to restore the essence of paradise to western tourism.

Assets

Remaining in this region is a great abundance of water resources, inland and coastal, important for resorts, campgrounds, second homes, cruising, boating, fishing, hunting, organization camping, wind surfing, rafting, and even historic redevelopment. Spectacular is the topographic variety—mountains suited to mountain climbing, hang gliding, scenic viewing and photography, trails, and winter sports. Plains and deserts also have much merit for specialized tourism. Unusual geological formations offer an abundance of waterfalls and extraordinary geysers that entice travelers. The great variety of vegetative cover, from shrubs and wildflowers to forest monarchs, offers habitat for diverse wildlife as well as great tourist appeal.

Over these seven decades, a mammoth high-quality tourist physical plant, especially for lodging and food facilities, has emerged. New and abundant tourist attractions based on natural and cultural resources draw millions of tourists to this region. Industries, convention centers, universities, and retreats now provide for a great amount of business and educational activities for visitors.

Very powerful lures are the unusual prehistoric and historic assets that provide enriching cultural satisfactions to millions of visitors. Nowhere else are the legends, lore, and ethnic appeals as great as in the West—novels, film, entertainment, crafts, foods, customs, and arts. Scattered throughout the West is a diversity of small, medium, and large communities that offer a profusion of services and attractions. Highway, air, and cruise ship access provide tourist transportation from domestic and foreign travel market demand. These and many other basic assets are still more numerous and richer than many other destinations and continue to support the West as a compelling tourist icon. Probably the greatest asset for future tourism is the profusion of human resources—planners, designers, environmentalists, politicians, developers, and a sophisticated local citizenry.

Constraints

In spite of these assets, this examination of western tourism has revealed several key constraints that must be given remedy if tourism is to reach the splendor desired by so many interested in tourism's future, especially modern tourists. Even though not all social, environmental, and economic problems can be laid at the door of tourism, its leaders must accept their share. It must be emphasized that the following key constraints are symptomatic of tourism's present state of the art rather than inept tourism developers of the West. Fortunately, the opportunities for resolution are abundant.

Former Tourism Values and Place Distinctions Have Been Eroded

Huge population invasion and land use changes have modified the landscape of seven decades ago. Autocampers of the 1920s were able to see open space and undeveloped land abundant in wildflowers, wildlife, lakes, streams, hills, mountains, and valleys. The slow speed of early automobiles on poor roads brought them in close contact with communities and their people. Even though new generations of travelers may not realize the change, key values of the past no longer have the rich spontaneity available to the travelers of the 1920s.

Places of the West once were distinctive. The region contains great geographical diversity. Mining, forestry, and fishing once fostered communities and land uses with special place qualities. Early historic land occupation and settlement by a variety of ethnic groups left their cultural mark on the land. Diversity of immigration gave specific areas unique architecture, land use patterns, customs, and arts. Unfortunately for modern tourists, most of these special place qualities have been replaced with new look-alike development. Sameness of communities has been fostered by landscape sprawl of standard franchise food services, lodging, and housing.

Sustainable Resource Use Has Been Lacking for Western Tourism Development

The very natural and cultural resources, so abundant in the West and significant to visitors, have been oversold, overbuilt, and overpromoted, contrary to a policy of sustainability. Waters and air have been polluted. Forests have been riddled by resorts and ski hills, adding greatly to physical degradation and scenic erosion. Excessive building on slopes and fragile soils has increased erosion and stream pollution. Bulldozed site development for tourist structures has removed important landscape qualities that once gave special character to places. An overabundance of visitor tours has diminished solitude and disturbed wildlife.

Tourist business leaders generally have not incorporated resource sustainability in their policies even though resource use is their major tourism product. Business organizations seldom have resource sustainability in their objectives. Related is the lack of linkage between the protection of resource attractions and tourist business success.

Tourism System Opportunities Have Been Hampered by Piecemeal Development

Separate tourism development projects by thousands of individual public and private entities have focused primarily on only their internal planning and management. This condition is like an automobile with its thousands of parts. Unless every part is integrated into a functioning whole, the automobile will not run. Too often, western parts of tourism lack such planned and managed interrelationship for the benefit of all. Yet to be considered are the gains that can be obtained from an overall tourism system approach that takes advantage of the interdependence of main components: attractions, services, transportation, information, and promotion. For example, the attack of September 11, 2001 dramatically demonstrated the critical relationship between air travel and all other components of tourism. The preoccupation of promotion by tourism leaders has diverted attention to the need for better integration of the many parts of tourism.

Tourism Lacks Innovative Design and Coordinated Planning

A corollary of the lack of understanding tourism as a system is inability to communicate, cooperate, and even collaborate on tourism planning for best functioning. Seldom in the West have public agencies and trade tourism organizations met, discussed mutual interests, and coordinated their planning for a better future.

Because tourism is much more complicated than popularly known, it now demands greater input from planning and design professionals. As yet, the abundant professional planners, landscape architects, and tourism consultants are seldom engaged by developers in fostering better western tourism planning. Lacking have been new visions and design concepts for better tourism.

Existing federal, state, and municipal planning agencies generally have not directed their policies and practices toward tourism planning issues. Their mandates and traditional functions have directed their actions elsewhere.

Tourism Lacks Integration With Other Forms of Social and Economic Life

Existing go-it-alone decisions and policies of tourism in the West have failed to consider impacts upon residents of communities and rural areas. As a result, residential lifestyles have often been upset by too many tourists. The consequences include escalated land prices, displacement of resident shopping with touristy businesses, and transportation glut. In addition, tourism leaders have not been on the cutting edge of overall major regional issues such as water and energy crises and environmental degradation that impact their success. Tourist businesses have not yet adopted a new business ethic that relates to the several potential impacts of their decision making.

Although many other constraints were observed during this evaluation of tourism in America's West, these cited are among the most important if tourism is to gain in the future. Encouraging are the opportunities for reversing these trends.

Opportunities

In spite of the significant negative changes in tourism in the West over the last decades there remain a great many opportunities for bringing the essence of travel paradise back into America's West. The fundamental land resources remain in sufficient quantity and quality for achieving this objective.

A vision of a better tourism future calls for action on new opportunities to reverse the several constraints. The nature of tourism here as well as elsewhere has become much more complicated, exposing the need for entirely new planning and decision making.

Time has produced a new abundance and quality of human resources in the West. Over several decades many new volunteer organizations have begun to advocate resolution of environmental, political, and social issues. There is now a great force of trained and experienced professional planners, landscape architects, and consultants. Needed today is new awareness, leadership, and dedication toward fulfilling the promise of a new tourism paradise.

Following are comments on the opportunities for resolving the major constraints listed above.

Many Older Tourist Values and Place Qualities Can Be Restored

It is not too late to restore for modern travelers many of the values important to travel markets of many decades ago.

Communities of the West can reclaim much of their past distinctiveness. Of great value to tourists are historic sites such as old opera houses that are restored and include performing arts that dramatize historic themes. To foster better host-guest relations, a program that opens local homes to visitors, popular in other nations, could be installed. Such a technique would give modern travelers insight into local attitudes and beliefs, so often lacking in packaged tours.

Highway departments could expand their policies of landscaping road cuts and right-of-way with indigenous plantings. They have many opportunities for updating their scenic route policies and actions. Tourist service businesses, such as lodging and food service, could replace stereotypical landscape treatment with localized design and development. Badly eroded sites can be restored with suitable landscape materials for new parks, interpretive centers, and other nature-oriented attractions.

The great number of federal and state agencies that control millions of acres of western lands can enhance their sites that serve tourists. They can replace invasive species of plants with natives, especially in areas visited by traveling publics: campgrounds, visitor centers, museums, historic sites, and recreation areas. Existing resorts have the same opportunities on their properties by restoring wildflowers, shrubs, and trees that once were important to tourists. Soil erosion can be controlled by new ground cover plantings.

These are just a few techniques available to enhance restoration of past traveler values. Many specialists now have the training and experience to plan restoration of older scenic and cultural values so important to past travelers.

Sustainability Is a Viable Future Goal for Tourism in the West

Throughout the region today there is new recognition of the finite resource base and need for greater policies for sustainability. These policies must stem from both the private sector and public land development agencies. For the four destinations described in this book, examples of sustainable tourism planning and development are offered in Chapters 3, 5, 7, and 9. The diversity of these cases shows how sustainability can be accomplished in different locations and resource situations.

A major opportunity is for every new tourism plan to avoid *potential social costs* as a goal for sustainability. Some questions asked in the early planning stages can prevent social conflicts in the long run. Are local residents willing to share their amenities with tourists? Will local people accept the tradeoff of new cultural impacts for tourist-oriented jobs? Are local businesses willing to accept and cater to visitors who may hold contrasting religious beliefs and cultural interests? Can local promoters target their efforts toward market segments that will not conflict locally? These are some pertinent questions that, if given positive answers, can foster the goal of sustainability.

When *potential environmental costs* are identified in early planning stages, negative environmental impacts can be avoided. Will the proposed project retain basic natural assets of vegetation, such as wildflowers, flowering shrubs, and other native plants? Do the plans call for adapting all structures to the existing topography and landscape character rather than bulldozing the land flat and creating soil erosion? Have plans for ecotourism considered damage to existing fragile and rare landscape features? When these issues are clarified before building, long-term sustainability is assured.

Although tourism can improve the economy, consideration should be given to *economic costs* of development. For example, will the completion of the project and use by many visitors create so much stress on water supply, waste disposal, police, and fire protection that new public investment is required for these services? Will communities, especially small ones, be able to fund new streets and parking when hordes of new automobiles, RVs, and tour buses invade the town?

As these potential costs of new tourism development are evaluated, the important question of capacity must be asked. For many areas in the West, visitor capacity (the point at which more tourism will damage its resource base) may already have been reached. Opportunities for tourism development will be found where resources still have potential for growth.

A beginning point for a new policy for sustainability is the acceptance of a new business ethic by tourist businesses. It is in their self-interest to insist on sustainability of their resource base because it brings business. Before regulation for sustainability is imposed by government, it will be much more effective for tourist businesses to take the leadership.

A clue to today's opportunity for greater cultural tourism development is the present groundswell of new museums and interpretive centers throughout the West. Citizens of western communities have new opportunities for greater protection, restoration, and visitor interpretation of their heritage.

Fostering Tourism as a Complete System Is a Major Opportunity

One of the greatest opportunities for improving tourism in the West is new planning and development as an *overall system*. Although the free enterprise philosophy has created great improvement over many decades, needed now is an understanding of the strong interdependence of all components of tourism.

If a community makes an evaluation of the overall tourism system—attractions, services, transportation, information, promotion—it may discover that the greatest need is not for a new hotel but rather the restoration and interpretation of their many historic sites to meet travel market demand for cultural tourism. This is what is meant by taking an overall systems approach.

Because of the fragmentation of the many parts of tourism, an overall view raises the question of who should accept this responsibility. For many communities the only umbrella tourism organization is the convention and visitor bureau. But for them to assume this greater role, their narrow promotional policy will need to be expanded. This will require new membership support beyond only tourist-oriented businesses. Ideally, membership should include representatives of the historic society, arts council, park department, highway department, sports organization, and environmentalists because all of these are part of the tourism system.

At the state level, instead of only a narrow advertising function, the scope could be broadened to include concerns and actions for better functioning of the entire tourism system. It could act as a coordinator for improving communication and decisions of the several components of tourism. The opportunity is there even if a new legal mandate is required. At the regional level, the excellent coordination performed by the Western States Tourism Development Council now needs greater support. The beneficiaries would be better visitor satisfactions, better business success, and improved resource sustainability.

An important spin-off from these actions would be better public understanding that overall tourism is more than hotels, restaurants, and highways, although they are very important parts of the complete tourism system.

Better Design and Planning Principles and Practices Can Create a New West

A major opportunity for better future tourism in the West is for planners and tourism interests to work together toward a common development goal. Just as an ill person seeks professional help, so can tourism interests gain professional assistance from planning professionals for diagnosis and prescription for remedy.There are many more professional planners, landscape architects, architects, and consultants available today for help.All of the challenges described in the preceding chapters apply at the site, community, and regional scales.

Each state, for example, has the opportunity to engage in a planning project that will assess the opportunities for future development based on analysis of its geographical factors. Just as agricultural science proved that not all areas were equal regarding support factors for crop production, so can a similar technical analysis show differences in area potential for tourism.The GIS overlay process used for Oklahoma, Illinois, and Delaware, as cited in the preceding chapter, could be applied to each western state.The result would delineate those zones with greatest support for tourism.Tourism leaders in each zone, with a better understanding of potential, could then plan for their tourism's future.This process also suggests that those areas between zones should not anticipate tourism growth because they lack important support factors, such as good access, natural and cultural resources for future attractions, and community service centers.

A very important opportunity is open for better urban planning for tourism. In the past, few urban planners have included tourism in their scope of work. Certainly taxpayers need priority of emphasis, but for many communities great volumes of tourists create additional planning needs.As city planners identify needs and make plans for land use, transportation, and utilities for local residents, they must also include guidance for tourist-oriented land uses as well. After all, the streets, parks, museums, and shops are now visited by masses of tourists as well as residents. Such complete urban planning requires the input from tourism constituencies as well as from local residents.

It must be emphasized that planning precedes regulation. Federal, state, and city regulations on land use and construction are effective only when they follow sound planning. Such regulation provides legal backup for assuring that plans will be followed.The challenge today is to review existing statutes to make sure they include tourism development as well as local interests.Although the West cannot be returned to its earlier pristine condition, its tourism's future can benefit greatly by better planning between private and public sectors.

In every area of the West can be found local citizens and professional designers who are capable of breaking from the norm and visualizing a new tourism future. Such a vision should include new ideas for protecting and enhancing the natural beauty and amenities that once prevailed. Open spaces, beach fronts, and enticing landscapes can provide enjoyment and enrichment at the same time that development is properly designed and planned. New tourist facilities need to be located near other intensive development, such as within or near community services, leaving the hinterland in its natural appeal. Local tourism leaders can now hold public forums to tap innovative ideas for design and planning that are especially well adapted to the local environment.

New Policies Can Integrate Tourism Into Community Life

Finally, there is no greater opportunity for a better tourism future in the West than integrating it into community life. For this to take place, new local policy is needed.

In the past, most residents of cities, large and small, have viewed tourism narrowly and as benefiting only a few. And often they consider it to be the responsibility of only hotels and the convention and visitor bureau.

Needed is a new policy thrust of education and understanding tourism in its entirety. As has been emphasized throughout this book, tourism is a huge agglomeration of parts, public and private. A great opportunity is for the tourism agency to hold educational seminars, events, and meetings of enlightenment on tourism in its full dimensions, not merely promotion.

When the image of tourism is narrow and seemingly affecting only a few, city council members have difficulty in justifying some budget items, such as new street improvements, museums, and parks. Stronger local tourism policies can reduce many of the current conflicts with the huge federal and state land owners in the West.

Opportunities are abundant throughout the West for new organizational structures and leadership that can develop the new local governmental policies best adapted to future tourism. Tourism can be guided in better directions and yet performed in concert with local citizens and tourism constituencies.

A Final Conclusion

Rather than requiring new money, virtually all of these opportunities can be realized with *new planning, design, organization, conviction, and aggressive leadership*. Fortunately, the physical and human resources required for this grand turnaround are now in place in that outstanding tourist region called America's West.

Permissions, Drawing Credits

All references to other works are cited in the Endnotes at the end of each chapter. The instances of quotes are within the general acceptance of "fair use" and will not affect the marketability of the original sources. Many statements are from governmental or non-profit sources that are in the public domain.

Permissions

All black and white photos of the Gunn autocamping trip of 1929 were taken by Fred M. Gunn, father of the author. Color photos with no source cited were taken by the author. Most of the photos of case examples were supplied gratis by the owners or designers with no special permission required. The following have provided permission for use in this work.

Page 14: 1926 road map of the US. By permission of Douglas R. McManis, American Geographical Society, New York, NY.

Page 20: Service Station of the 1920s. By permission of David LeBeau, Chevron Services Company, San Ramon, CA.

Page 78: Harvey Cars, Grand Canyon NP, 1921. By permission of Kimberly Kliewer, Library Specialist, Special Collections and Archives, Cline Library, Northern Arizona University, Flagstaff, AZ.

Page 87: Landscape restoration, sustainable design. By permission of Randy Prentice, Randy Prentice Photography, Tucson, AZ.

Page 120: Lake Tahoe transit systems. By permission of Robert McCormick, Tahoe Tourist Promotions, Kings Beach, CA.

Page 124: Feather River National Scenic Byway, CA. By permission of Suzi Brakken, Plumas County Visitors Bureau, Quincy, CA. Photo by Scott Lawson.

Page 125: Benziger Family Winery, CA. By permission of Michael Barbitta, Benziger Family Winery, Glen Ellen, CA.

Page 151: Salishan Lodge, OR, sustainable design. By permission of O. George Forster, Westin Salishan Lodge & Golf Course, Gleneden Beach, OR.

Page 195: Solar powered toilet facility. By permission of Theodore J. Wirth, Wirth Design, Billings, MT.

Credits, Author's Drawings

Page 5: Mendocino, CA. Adapted from Morgan, J. (1982). The Road to Mendocino. *Travel & Leisure* 12(5), 85.

Pages 45, 95, 135, 171: Typical Camp Site, Gunn Autocamping Tour West, 1929. Sketch by author.

Page 52: Route of Gunn Autocamping Tour West, 1929. Map by author, adapted from trip log prepared by Lila B. Gunn.

Page 63: Grand Canyon Railroad. Adapted from Thomas, S. H. (1978), *The Southwestern Indian Detours* (p. 6). Phoenix, AZ: Hunter.

Page 68: Comparison of Beale's Road, Route 66, I-40. Adapted from Wagner, J. J. (1975). *Early Arizona, Prehistory to Civil War.* Tucson, AZ: University of Arizona Press; Browman, E. G., & Smith, J. (1979), *Beale's Road Through Arizona.* Flagstaff, AZ: Flagstaff Corral of Westerner's International; and Wallace, N. G. (1955), Arizona 66, the Scenic Wonderland Highway. *Arizona Highways*, 31(5), 12.

Page 103: Benbow Inn, Garberville, CA. Adapted from author's photograph of 1998.

Page 143: Columbia River, OR. Adapted from USDA, Forest Service (1992), Celebrating the Oregon Trail. In *Gorge Vistas* (p. 10). Hood River, OR: FS

Page 179: Headquarters, Yellowstone National Park. Adapted from Fishbein, S. L. (1989). Greater Yellowstone. In *Yellowstone Country* (pp. 164-165), Washington, DC: The National Geographic Society.

Page 201: LaPosada Inn, Winslow, AZ. Adapted from the author's photograph of 1998.

Page 217: Carson Mansion, Eureka, CA. Adapted from the author's photograph of 1998. and Rasp, R.A. (1991). *A Complete Guidebook of the Redwoods* (p. 21). Redcrest, GA: FVN Corp.

Index